CATERPILLAR SEAS

CATERPILLAR
SEAS

a true story

ROBERT FRIDJHON

Published by Zebra Press
an imprint of Random House Struik (Pty) Ltd
Reg. No. 1966/003153/07
80 McKenzie Street, Cape Town, 8001
PO Box 1144, Cape Town, 8000 South Africa

www.zebrapress.co.za

First published 2011

1 3 5 7 9 10 8 6 4 2

Publication © Zebra Press 2011
Text © Robert Fridjhon 2011

Cover photographs: 'Cruising into a Storm' © iStockphoto/Faruk Ulay;
'Prisoner' © iStockphoto/Lou Oates
Author photograph: Misha Miles Photography

PUBLISHER: Marlene Fryer
MANAGING EDITOR: Robert Plummer
EDITOR: Lynda Gilfillan
COVER AND TEXT DESIGNER: Monique Oberholzer
TYPESETTER: Monique van den Berg
PRODUCTION MANAGER: Valerie Kömmer

Set in 10.5 pt on 15 pt Minion

Printed and bound by Paarl Media, Jan van Riebeeck Drive,
Paarl, South Africa

ISBN 978 1 77022 184 0 (print)
ISBN 978 1 77022 185 7 (ePub)
ISBN 978 1 77022 186 4 (PDF)

www.imagesofafrica.co.za

IMAGES OF AFRICA
PHOTO LIBRARY

Over 50 000 unique African images available to purchase
from our image bank at www.imagesofafrica.co.za

To my father

For many years I've wanted to write about these events that happened to me in my youth, but I've held back because of the implications for those involved, including the danger to myself from certain people. But time – nearly four decades of it – has, I guess, finally mitigated the possible consequences and I've decided to tell my story. I have changed names to protect people's identities, and there is one event – the crime I witnessed in Los Angeles – that I have altered substantially. I have also condensed certain parts and omitted others to keep the pace of the tale. But I have, as much as memory will allow, kept to the truth of what happened. What follows in these pages is an accurate representation of what I did and what happened to me.

Pacific Ocean – 1973

The crash slams through the timbers of the yacht, hammering me awake. I hurl myself off the bunk, mind reeling like the boat.

Have we hit something? Or has something hit us? A ship? Oh, no, please don't let it be that. The rasping and crunching on the port side of *Coracle* sounds like a big steel hull scraping past.

We've been run over, I'm sure. There are no reefs anywhere near, and the crash felt really hard. I smack my hip against the chart table in my panic to get on deck. Is there some way I can fend *Coracle* off before the mast is ripped out? Is the boat holed? Are we sinking? What if the ship's propeller is close to the surface – close enough to rip my yacht and me to smithereens?

I lunge onto the deck and peer into the night.

Nothing. There is no vessel, no looming hulk sliding by, only a rolling ebony ocean with brief white flashes of breaking seas. I stare into the dark, lit only by the stars twinkling in the uninterrupted void above.

Uninterrupted? Strange, I can see the sky as though I am standing on a desert floor; nothing blocks my view, apart from the mizzenmast. The universe is completely open above me and I am staring at the broad expanse of stars.

There is no mainmast. This revelation hits as my night vision adjusts: a weird limb-like object is sticking up at an angle over the deck, see-sawing with the movement of the yacht. It is clothed in billowing white material that is slowly inflating and deflating with ghostly opalescence in the wind.

It is the mast of my vessel. The crash was my mainmast going over the side. It is now lying across the gunwale, with the top underwater and a mess of sails and rigging spread all around it. Shit.

But a ship hasn't run us down and we're not sinking, and my heartbeat slows with relief. But that relief is skewed by another thought: I still have about three thousand miles to go to cross this ocean – without a mainmast. I don't have enough diesel to motor even for a day and I'm thousands of miles from my destination, hundreds of miles from any islands.

These concerns are not that relevant at the moment, though. I have other, more pressing, troubles. The mast is bucking and heaving over the deck with the movement of the sea, grinding across the gunwale and destroying what is left of the yacht.

I clamber over the coachroof and grab the spar near where it lies over the edge of the boat. I pull on it, trying to heave it back on board, but it is a pathetic attempt, like that of a child trying to move a ten-ton log – a log that is sawing its way through the boat with horrible grating sounds. I need to stop this destruction, and fast, but how? I can't get it back onto *Coracle*. It's way too heavy.

I'll have to push it over. Get rid of it. If I can't get the mast back on the yacht I'll shove it overboard, so at least it won't be destroying my boat any more.

I get my shoulder under it and heave. The mast swings and grates to the rhythm of the ocean, ignoring my puny efforts and digging a winch painfully into my shoulder, threatening to crush me onto the deck as it see-saws. I heave and push from different angles, trying to get it to slip off the gunwale and into the water. The mast is stuck somehow. My fear and frustration lend strength, but it makes no difference; something is holding it fast.

Breath rasping in time with the cracking and splintering of the timbers, I crawl under the draped sail, trying to see what's keeping the spar from slipping away. The darkness makes this impossible, and for a moment I think of running back to switch on the deck lights. Idiot. The lights are attached to the spreaders on the mast, now underwater.

I dash below and grab my only flashlight, with its flagging battery. By this dim yellow light I can see a wire rigging stay wound around a twisted stanchion. It's the aft lower shroud, and it's stopping the mast from going overboard. The wire is attached to a steel plate further aft along the deck, but I figure if I can just get it over the bent upright, the mast should be free to slide. So I grab the wire and tug upwards. Nothing. It's like a steel bar. There is no way I am going to be able to lift it over.

I experience a sudden surge of anger. A hopeless fury at the heavy treacherous mast, at the crappy sails draped everywhere, and at this stupid, bucking, fucking ocean that has trapped me like this, surrounding me with an immensity of water. I want to vent my anger on something, anything – strike out at the nearest object, which of course will be either steel or wood, so instead I take a few deep shaky breaths of the oxygen-rich ocean air while I figure out what to do. My anger soon turns into despair. How could the mast have fallen? Why now, when it's not even that windy?

I slip back out of the wreckage and down the companionway and grab the pliers from the chart-table drawer. Back on deck, I struggle to remove the pin that secures the shroud. The darkness, plus the tension of the wire, hinders me, but at last the pin comes out, the stay breaking loose with a heavy clunk. I feel the sail slide over my head, moving outboard with the rig. I slip out from under the cloth and, with the help of the swell, I push the spar towards the sea that seems to be trying so hard to claim it – and also me.

Finally the end goes, not with the dangerous leap I'd feared, but instead with a slow, sliding plop. At last I no longer have to listen to the sawing and crunching sound of the mast cutting my boat in half.

A harsh impact shudders through the deck and into my legs, into my already shattered nerves. Oh fuck. The mast is now acting as a battering ram, propelled by the waves into the side of the yacht. This is worse, much worse. The mast is about to bash a hole in the boat, at around sea level. Another bang spikes me with a mixture of anger and panic. Mostly panic.

I dash aft and grab a rope out of a locker, and then run back to where the pole is slamming into the hull. I stare uncertainly into the black sea, into the mess of sails and rigging around the long white pile driver. There's no choice and no time so I jump, aiming for what looks like a clear patch of water near the foot of the spar.

Although warm, the unfamiliarity and blackness of the water comes as a bit of a shock and I surface splashing and gasping, and momentarily disoriented. The mast foot bangs into *Coracle*'s planking inches away from my ear, so to avoid being pulverised I thrust myself away.

I tie the rope quickly to the spar and swim to the stern, where I haul myself back on board using the self-steering gear. Then I thread the line through a fairlead and heave, dragging the tangled mess back so that it lies parallel to the boat. I can breathe easier now. *Coracle* is rolling in the waves, still bumping occasionally into the spar, but her hull is no longer about to be breached by a 300-pound battering ram.

It will still do damage, though, so I have to get the rig away from *Coracle*. First I must free all the wires and ropes. Dawn is beginning to lighten the sky – but not my heart – as I begin to release the rigging wires from the chain plates.

One piece of wire that I don't have to undo is the backstay. It is already loose, parted from the top of the mast, where I notice a shackle has come undone. This is why the mast fell down – a stupid, lousy shackle. I think back to the storm that hit five days out of Hawaii. Why didn't the mast come down then? The storm created huge strain on the rig, yet it held up perfectly. How come it has failed now, in relatively calm weather?

It must've been the doldrums, I realise. Weeks of rolling about in a windless sea, the continual slatting back and forth of the sails probably making the shackle pin turn. It must've begun working free then, and finally come apart altogether. Because the mast is – or was – deck-stepped, there was nothing to prevent it falling.

What a fiasco. What a huge crappy mess. And all because of a loose shackle. The only consolation is that the rig didn't tear up the deck as it came down. And the damage isn't too bad: only to the gunwale and a couple of stanchions. Even the mast itself is still in one piece. Sparse comfort there, though.

The other shackles are proving, conversely, extremely tight, and my hands are bleeding by the time I finish struggling with them. But at last all the ropes and stays are freed and overboard, hanging into the depths along with the sails. I loosen the rope holding the base of the mast to the boat, and then jump overboard again. I push the pole away from the side of the boat with my feet, and as it moves off I re-board the yacht.

Coracle drifts away, blown by the wind until she fetches up against the line tethering her to her cast-off rig – useless flotsam behind my equally useless boat. The mast is now acting as a sea anchor, pinning the yacht to the empty waste of ocean.

She wallows helplessly in the waves rolling past, endless undulating ridges of water heaving towards distant lands – lands that I myself might now never reach. Envying them their mobility, I am filled with a crushing sense of despondency. After the long frustration of waiting in the doldrums for wind, just when I'm making good speed again and when it looked as though I might be escaping from this vast watery prison, this happens. Now I'm truly stuck here. The boat has no means of propulsion, the nearest land is nearly a thousand miles away, and I am in a virtually untraversed tract of ocean with no means of calling for help. My future looks shittily bleak and empty.

My stomach is empty too. The exertion of the last few hours has made me hungry. The sun has climbed higher now, high enough to exert its tropical heat. And I haven't had breakfast. But the thought of eating raises another issue.

How much food do I have on board? Not a lot after my three-week sojourn in the doldrums belt, I suspect. I'd better go and check, see how long I have to live until my supplies run out. At least I'll be doing something, instead of sitting here and staring at the waves. I go down below.

* * *

Well that's it, less even than I thought. Nine cans of tinned meats, eight of spaghetti, three of baked beans, five of assorted vegetables, plus three bottles of beetroot, a packet and a half of sugar and one jar of coffee. Also, I have three boxes of cereal, half a can of powdered milk, and about three pounds of rice. Slightly less than four boxes of crackers and half a tub of peanut butter make up the rest of the supplies – enough for about three to four weeks, if I eat carefully.

Coracle could drift around out here for months without being found. There's been no sign of civilisation for more than five weeks now, and I seriously doubt whether any ships pass through this desolate expanse of water.

After eating some crackers – peanut butter spread ultra-thin – I force myself into some sort of action. I tidy the mess caused by the dismasting, and attempt to straighten the bent stanchions so as to have some sort of safety line around the boat again.

Later I sit staring out gloomily over the darkening expanse of water. I wish now that I spent the last of my money on diesel to fill the tanks, but then reflect that it wouldn't have helped anyway. This is just too far away from any land. In the doldrums I sat for days on end on the stationary boat waiting for wind. But this is much worse. At least then I could figure that wind would eventually come and that I'd be mobile again. Now I'm waiting for nothing at all.

I watch until the sun disappears over the vacant horizon, dragging with it the last light of the day and also what seems to be the last of my fortitude.

* * *

Dawn eventually arrives, sparing me from the torment of night. Though tired and drained, I hardly slept at all. *Coracle* has a strange motion now with the mast gone. She rocks and bobs annoyingly – annoying maybe because I know none of this motion includes any forward. The dark hours tortured me with the knowledge that I am no longer going anywhere, have nothing to look forward to, no anticipation of reaching land or seeing people again in any conceivable future. The one time I fell asleep – for maybe half an hour – I woke as usual to check my course, and then remembered that that was no longer necessary. No joy in that discovery.

I sit in the cockpit sipping coffee, staring out over the barren grey sea again. The dismal sunless morning does nothing for my spirits. With no ships around, I have a near zero chance of being found. How long would it take for the ocean currents to push me to the nearest island? Too long, I suspect, with my limited supplies. I'll have to try to construct some sort of jury rig, maybe set the spinnaker pole upright and hang a makeshift sail from it, even though I know the pole is really too short to do much. But I'll have to do something, although I feel reluctant to start, not convinced at all that I'll be able to rig anything that will give *Coracle* propulsion again. My misery has put me into some sort of deep funk and I need to shake off this inertia somehow, to rid myself of this clinging despondency that seems to be strangling my instinct for survival.

My food shortage is a major concern, but my loneliness outweighs even the fact that I could be facing death by starvation. I've been yearning so long for this voyage to be over, to reach civilisation and be a part of humanity again. But this is obviously not going to happen now, not for a long time – maybe never.

Another wave of desolation sweeps over me, an aching sense of abandonment. Why has this happened to me? What have I done to deserve it? But then, I think, maybe I *do* deserve all this. If I'd never become involved with the Russians, never allowed myself to be dragged to that awful meeting, I wouldn't be in this predicament. It's hard to believe that it was only ten months ago that I finished studying and left South Africa, master of my own fate at last and brimming with anticipation of fun and adventure. Adventure – a stupid idea, an immature notion that made me leap without much thought at Mihai's offer. Why didn't I consider all the consequences of that decision? I wish – not for the first time – that I'd never met Mihai. That I'd never hitch-hiked on that particular stretch of Californian highway, and that he'd never picked me up. And that my subsequent decisions had somehow been different.

But I mustn't allow myself to sink into that particular morass. All these weeks at sea, I've managed not to think about those past events with the Russians, to keep my mind away from any morbid reminiscing – a kind of mental rubbernecking that might leave me depressed. I should be doing something, figuring a way out. But it all seems too much now. Inertia is worming into the core of my being; my misery is like a dark well, bottomless and filled with thick ooze that is sucking the life force out of me.

I can't believe that one moment I was sailing to freedom, happy after the doldrums and being pushed again by wind, seeing an end to my loneliness as my beautiful yacht ate up the miles and delivered me from this desolate ocean. And then the next thing I'm trapped here, my boat floating helplessly, towing its broken limb – useless now, a vessel of doom.

1

California – six months earlier

A high-pitched whine burrows through the silence, tunnelling into my daydreams and disturbing the perfect peace of the deserted countryside.

It is the sound of a car, and I squint against the late afternoon glare towards Los Angeles, about eighty miles to the west. The empty highway snakes away from me, the tarmac winding through the undulating terrain and breaking into shimmering fragments at its vanishing point near the distant horizon. The source of the noise is hidden, obscured by a low hill about a mile away.

I'm mildly irritated at the intrusion, enjoying my solitude at this empty intersection with its lack of human contamination. Traffic, for instance. Although, since I'm hitch-hiking, this kind of intrusion should, in fact, be welcome.

The isolation gives me a grand sense of my own autonomy, and I'm happy just to stand here and absorb it. The beautiful open vista fills me with a promise of my future. Waiting for a ride, I have the sense that this junction offers me paths, not just towards various destinations, but also to destinies – destinies I have the liberty to choose. I am administrator of my own fate now; decisions are my own and the world is at my feet. I'm twenty-one years old, independent and carefree, with forty dollars in my pocket. I can do anything and go where I please.

I see it now, a distant speck that shimmers and oscillates and then resolves itself suddenly into a motor car, winking its windscreen at me just once before disappearing behind another low hill. The sound becomes muffled and then loud again as the vehicle reappears on the other side, closer now and white – a Volkswagen panel van. The pitch of the engine lowers and the volume rises as it nears and slows, and then the van turns onto the ramp that leads to where I am waiting.

As the vehicle approaches I stick my thumb out and it pulls dustily – and noisily – to a stop just ahead of me. I swing my heavy backpack onto one shoulder and run to the waiting van, its engine still clattering.

'Hello,' I say to the single occupant, a rather strange-looking individual about thirty years old and oddly disproportionate, with a short, thick torso and long, thin arms and legs, plus a round face with innocent blue eyes. A Humpty Dumpty man.

'I'm going to San Francisco,' I tell him.

'Well, howdy. Hop in,' he answers. 'I'm only heading as far as Hollywood, though you're sure welcome to ride with me as far as I'm going. I can take you to the turn-off about thirty miles further down.' He has a strange accent, not American, and his words are somehow determinedly colloquial. 'More cars out that way, y'know, so I figure you should be able to get a ride pretty easy over there.'

'Thanks very much. Should I put my bag in the back?' I ask with careful courtesy, displaying awareness of the man's beneficence.

'Yeah, sure. Chuck it in the back and jump in,' he answers, so I pull the handle and slide the door back, hoisting my backpack onto the empty floor. Rattle and slam as I drag it shut, and then I climb into the passenger seat. We drive off. I'm on my way again.

'Name's Mihai Kranova,' he announces, changing gears with a yank on the lever and then offering me his hand. His self-assured manner and strong grip seem a little at odds with his appearance.

'Rob,' I answer, shaking his hand as I struggle with my seat belt. 'Rob Fridjhon.'

'So you're headed for Frisco then?'

'Um, yeah, well, perhaps.' No destination is fixed for me; I'm a wandering spirit, free to go anywhere.

'Where're you from?'

'South Africa.' I'm aware of the adverse opinions about my apartheid country, but I've found that most of the people I've met in my travels don't really care. 'I'm from Cape Town.'

'Hey, far out, man. South Africa? Must be pretty wild there. Like as in wild animals and things?'

'Yes, well, actually it's not that much different to America. Except that we don't have TV there.' It's 1973, and my country has yet to be introduced to television. Which *is* pretty wild, I suppose.

He grins. 'So, what brings you out this way?' Same questions that nearly every other driver has asked since I started hitch-hiking across this vast country.

'I um … I'm going to San Francisco to join the Transpac Race,' I tell him, avoiding a more lengthy explanation of my travels.

'Cool, man. I've heard about that. That's the yacht race from San Francisco to Hawaii, right? They have it every two years?'

'Yes, that's right.' I'm a little surprised at his knowledge. Yacht racing is not exactly a spectator event, and unless you had a definite interest in the sport you'd be unlikely to know about the race. I've always loved sailing and have been involved with it most of my life, starting as a kid on racing dinghies and then later moving on to larger ocean-going yachts. I left South Africa some seven months ago, following a dream of sailing across the Atlantic. I signed on as crew on the *Stormvogel*, landing up in the Caribbean, where I spent the season working on charter yachts up and down the islands. Now, after sailing to the US East Coast, I'm headed for the 1974 Trans-Pacific Yacht Race – the Transpac – one of the premier yachting events of the world, and one I've always wanted to participate in.

'So you've hitch-hiked right across America for this race?' he asks. 'Do you have a boat to sail on?'

'No, not yet,' I tell him, and then add a tad sheepishly, 'but I recently found out I got the date wrong. It's next year, so I've got a year to wait. I guess I've got a little time to find a boat.'

Mihai laughs. 'You hitch-hiked out in the wrong year?' He changes gears jerkily as the van struggles up an incline.

'Yes, unfortunately,' I admit. 'So, where are you from?' I ask, steering him away from my blunder.

'From Romania,' he says. 'From a town called Braşov.'

'Isn't that a communist country? How'd you get out? I mean, don't you have to defect or something?'

He laughs. 'Yeah. I escaped.'

'Really?' My curiosity is aroused. 'How'd you do that?'

Mihai tells me his tale. We roll past empty fields, distant farmhouses and occasional clumps of cows, or horses, or whatever is being farmed out here, and he tells me of his childhood in Romania and of his father, an outspoken lawyer who rebelled against a system that held people in the crushing grip of the secret police. He tells me too about labour camps and general shortages. He tells me of a crashing on the door late one night when he was eight years old, about heavy boots and coarse shouts, his mother terrified and tearful in her nightclothes, his father hustled away with his arms rudely cuffed behind him.

Mihai watched from a window with his younger sister as his father was bundled into the back of a black ZiL automobile. That was the last time he ever saw him.

Over the next four years he developed his own hatred of the

system that had deprived him of his father. He denounced the government to his schoolmates, and then he too was taken from his home by a group of men one cold dark night. His wailing mother clutched his sister as she watched her twelve-year-old son being thrown into the back of a black automobile just like the one that had taken her husband four years earlier.

Mihai spent five years in a youth detention camp. He shows me scars on his arms where he was beaten and tortured, and he hints at horrors that have scarred him emotionally for life. Finally, at the age of seventeen, he was released, returning to a mother whose spirit was completely broken. She lived out her life of drudgery with the same apathetic hopelessness that showed in the faces of all the people queuing for staples such as milk and bread in the dreary government stores.

He was determined to escape, to find a better life, and for the next two years he schemed and plotted ways of fleeing Romania and the communists. Eventually, in the middle of winter, he said goodbye to his mother and sister and made his way across the country to the border with Yugoslavia. There, in sub-zero temperatures, he managed to evade the border guards and cross to freedom. He was just nineteen.

Mihai was granted asylum in West Germany, and after about eight years of petitioning he was allowed to come to America. He tells me that his hatred of communists is now equalled only by his love for his new country.

I am suitably awed by his story.

We reach the turn-off for Hollywood and Mihai pulls over onto the shoulder to let me out. For a few minutes more we continue to chat, and then I grab my bag and begin to leave.

'Listen, Rob,' Mihai cocks his head. 'Why don't you come on down to Hollywood and stay the night with me and my wife, Mary? It's Friday night, time for a bit of partying, maybe.'

I hesitate, holding on to the door handle, and consider my options.

On the one hand there's the road north, its very emptiness inviting me onwards, with San Francisco beckoning – for so long now my journey's end. But on the other hand there is Hollywood, a magical place of movie stars and famous people. And since the Transpac Race doesn't require my immediate attention I see no reason, apart from a rather pressing need to make some money, why I should hurry to Frisco. Also, the thought of a home-cooked meal and a shower suddenly transcends my desire for the freedom of the road.

'Sure, Mihai, if it's no inconvenience and if your wife doesn't mind, I'd love to,' I say to my new friend, removing my hand from the door handle.

And so we continue down the road towards Hollywood, leading me to events that will change my life for ever.

* * *

Mihai lives above the shop that he owns, and Mary greets us at the door to their apartment. Not conventionally pretty, she is attractive in a robust sort of way, with a sturdy, all-American pioneer-stock quality about her.

'Hi, Rob, pleased to meet you.' She shakes my hand as Mihai introduces me. 'Welcome to our home, and please make yourself comfortable. Help yourself to whatever you want, and don't be shy.' She gestures at the apartment, welcoming me into their household and seeming to accept my presence with complete equanimity.

I am immediately at ease with her, though a little surprised at her lack of regard for my slightly vagrant appearance. I've been on the road for nearly six weeks now, including a two-week stay at the Grand Canyon where I lost nearly all my money by leaving it in my clothes at a local laundromat while I camped at the bottom. I'm grubby, hair down to my shoulders, sporting a scraggly beard, and wearing clothes that haven't seen an iron for weeks.

But she doesn't seem to care, and shows me to a room in the large apartment where I unpack my meagre belongings. The bed looks inviting after all my camping along the road, and I see with some delight that I have my own television set. I plan some late-night viewing.

After luxuriating in a long hot shower, I rejoin my hosts in the living room, where I find that Mary has prepared dinner. I tuck in.

'Hey, Rob, you up to hitting a party later?' Mihai asks. 'Some friends of ours are having a bit of a shindig in Beverly Hills tonight.' His effort to sound American is kind of endearing. A forkful of food hovers near his mouth, and I suspend my own fork's yo-yo activity.

'A party? Yeah sure, Mihai. I'd love to.' A party in Beverly Hills? Would a vulture turn down an invite to a bushkill?

So after dinner we get ourselves ready and then Mihai introduces me to his other car, a Citroën-Maserati, a rare and beautiful masterpiece and also one of the most expensive vehicles in the world, so he tells me. I am properly impressed, and when he turns on the ignition the car raises itself a few inches on its hydraulic suspension. Cool.

We motor away from the strip and are soon rolling along Rodeo Drive in Beverly Hills, the names of the home owners spilling from Mihai like a roll call of the rich and famous. Then he pulls up outside a house and he and Mary study the double-storey pillared building for a while, the engine purring almost inaudibly. There are no other cars outside, and it doesn't look like there's any sort of party going on here, so I wait patiently to hear why we've stopped.

'This used to be our home,' Mihai eventually says with a hint of nostalgic regret. 'Mary and I lived here for three years just after we came to California.'

I'm impressed. 'You serious, Mihai? How on earth did you afford to live here?' I seriously revise my opinion of my host's status.

He tells me he worked for a company in Switzerland while he was waiting to be accepted into the United States. The company, MED, employed him while still in its infancy, and then had grown rapidly into an extremely successful gold-brokering business in Zurich. After Mihai moved to America, he'd carried on working for MED, amassing considerable wealth which enabled him to rent the house in Beverly Hills, and buy his Citroën-Maserati as well as a Cadillac convertible for Mary. His income came from lucrative deals involving the paper transfers of large quantities of gold stocks, and with the sudden increase in the price of gold he made money hand over fist. But then a sudden sharp fall in the gold price caused a downturn in his fortune, forcing him to vacate the home, sell the Cadillac, and move to downtown Hollywood. Although he still makes an occasional deal through MED, he tells me, most of his livelihood now comes from his shop.

He relates all this in a somewhat casual manner, but I realise his present existence, though in the centre of Hollywood, is a far cry from what it must have been in Beverly Hills, out among the stars. Yet he doesn't dwell on this lost wealth, his demeanour more like someone who regards it as a mere temporary setback in his quest for riches. His soft appearance is deceptive, concealing a much stronger and rather more intriguing core.

* * *

We arrive at the party, which is in a rambling ranch-style house with cars crowding the area, parked in every available space along the surrounding pavement. The party is at the back, around a large kidney-shaped pool. I'm introduced to three or four people, but I circulate alone, drinking vodka that Mihai has pressed upon me, and enjoying the feel of a party in Beverly Hills. People dance near the pool and drift in and out of the house. There are maybe a couple of hundred partygoers, I guess, a pretty large affair. Nearly everybody here is older than me, and way better dressed, and I feel a bit out of place. But I still enjoy myself.

Around one o'clock, Mary suggests we leave. I'm feeling the effects of all the vodka I've drunk, and I suspect Mihai is too. We depart in our motoring masterpiece and Mihai takes a different route than the one we took to get to the party, which was presumably a detour to show me his former house. We turn into a road that runs between high walls and only slightly higher palm trees, where massive iron gates block the entrances to houses. Mihai slows, allowing the car to come to a crawl to negotiate a wickedly steep speed bump. The front wheels go over and the car drops.

And stops. A sickening crunch tells us that the low-slung vehicle has caught itself on the top of the hump. Its cool trick of raising itself on its suspension wasn't enough for it to clear the bump.

'Sheeit!' Mihai's exclamation is full of indignant disgust. 'What a stupid fucking road bump. How come they've made it so high?'

We climb out and consider our predicament. Even with our weight out of it, the car is jammed. All three of us try pushing and lifting the vehicle, trying to ease the car off the bump. But to no avail; it's stuck fast. After a while, Mihai takes his jack out of the trunk and raises the front of the Maserati. We dig around on the kerb for sand and stones, which we tuck under the front wheels, one side at a time. Eventually, we are able to ease the car over the hump. Both of us then lie on our sides trying to see if there is any damage underneath, but fortunately everything seems to be okay.

We drive on, sweaty and dirty, having entirely lost our high spirits.

'What a dumb place to put a bump like that,' I say as we drive towards Hollywood, mostly to fill the silence.

'Yeah, fuck. I feel like going back and telling the owners of those houses they should do something about it. Flatten it or something. How can they put such a stupidly high bump there?' Mihai is angry, seething in fact.

We're driving past a large empty lot, and through the darkness I can see the shapes of vehicles and earth-moving equipment on what seems to be a building site.

'There's a steamroller over there,' I say from my seat in the back of the vehicle. 'Why don't we see if we can start it, do the job ourselves?'

Mihai snorts and looks out towards the dimly perceivable machinery. He hits the brakes.

'Hey, you're right. I wonder if we can get that thing going?'

'Maybe we should go take a look,' I say with vodka bravado, Absolut foolishness.

'No way, you two,' Mary says, her usual serenity replaced by concern. 'I don't think this is a good idea.'

Mihai stares towards the building site. 'Maybe they've left the key somewhere,' he says, ignoring his wife. 'Like under the sun visor or something.'

'C'mon, Mihai.' Mary shakes her head. 'This is just another of your lame-brain ideas.'

'Hey now,' he smirks, a quick mood change for my Romanian friend. 'This here's our chance to do something for somebody else. Like good Samaritans, y'know? That bump's for sure going to make some other guy damage his car.'

He exits the vehicle and I follow.

'Mary,' he says, 'follow us with the car.'

She looks unhappy but slides dutifully over into the driver's seat, muttering. We saunter through the dark over the uneven ground towards the steamroller. From up close it's a Goliath, much larger than I thought. It's the biggest steamroller I've ever seen.

With some trepidation, but also with a small thrill of anticipation, I swing myself up onto it. Mihai follows. The cab is really high and it seems to give us a view over half of Beverly Hills, but not too much of what's directly ahead of us. The tremendously long hood and enormous front wheel block our view of anything in front of the vehicle. We begin searching in the dark, feeling among the array of knobs and shifts sticking out of the floor as we look for ledges and cubbyholes where a key might be secreted. I run my hand along the inside rim of the steel roof. Nothing.

My search is thorough, although possibly lacking complete commitment. I wonder whether Mihai feels the same as I do: that we are probably not going to find a key and that possibly it is for the best. He is bent forward, feeling near the stack just outside the cab. We've just about exhausted the possibilities for a hiding place and it's time to admit defeat. I pull my small Swiss Army Knife from my pocket as Mihai returns to the cab.

'Nothing, Rob. No key.'

'Maybe this'll work,' I say with no real conviction. I open the blade and slide it into the ignition slot. I give it a twist and the diesel roars into mind-shattering life.

'Holy sheeit!' I make out Mihai's words mostly by lip-reading. The massive motor drowns out virtually all possibility of hearing anything. He has a hugely triumphant grin wreathed about his face.

'How do we make it move?' I yell the question at him, not a hundred per cent certain of my own triumph. We grab levers and pull and push, and suddenly the behemoth lurches forward. I can't tell which lever has done the trick, one of Mihai's or one of mine.

Our glee at our forward progress lasts approximately two seconds. We both realise that we are now heading towards a half-completed building with no idea how to turn or stop the thing. Frantically, we begin grabbing and pulling on knobs and shifts. Mihai yanks a long lever and, after a slight pause, the massive front wheel begins to turn, steering us away from the building. We exchange looks of combined satisfaction and relief.

I hang on to the front of the cab as the vehicle slowly completes a half-circle, which will take us back towards the road where Mary is waiting in the car. The darkness slides by, shattered by the pounding of massive pistons. A crunch and a slight lurch warn me that we have ridden over something that was invisible in the darkness, and I jump to the back of the cab and peer down. Dimly, I can make out a wheelbarrow – Picasso-like, totally flattened.

I turn back to see Mihai making frantic shooing motions out of the cab with one hand while he clings to the steering stick with the other. He's waving Mary and the Maserati away, worried no doubt that our tenuous control of our new vehicle might cause us to flatten his lovely car too – with his wife inside.

The Maserati shoots off as we near the road, and Mihai jerks the steering lever over to turn our lumbering joyride onto the pavement, towards the road with the speed bump. Unfortunately, he hasn't quite got used to the delayed reaction of the steering and we roll right over the kerb on the other side of the road. A garbage can goes the way of the wheelbarrow, the contents no longer in need of trash compacting. Another small lurch and we regain the road, Mihai yanking and heaving the stick as if he's trying to pull it out of the floor. He laughs and shrieks demonically, the steamroller straightening itself as it clanks and grinds down the tarmac.

The noise is tremendous, the huge diesel sounding as though most of the combustion is external. The machine is full of clattering and banging sounds, and the massive weight of the front wheel grinds and shudders over the road. Our earth-mover is probably causing people to think that the tectonic plates of the San Andreas Fault are catching up with themselves. I look behind us. Lights are being turned on in nearly every house that we pass. I get the sensation that we're steaming through the suburban night on a big, noisy yellow boat, creating a long electric wake.

I tap Mihai on the arm and indicate the awakening neighbourhood, and he reacts by grabbing a ratcheted lever on the front of the cab. He pushes it forward and we accelerate, the diesel – impossibly – becoming even louder. I keep an eye out for the flashing lights of a cop vehicle.

As if by telepathic instinct, Mihai grabs my shoulder and pulls me close. 'We see cops coming we switch off and run, okay?' I nod emphatically. We carry on in a silence created by the wall of sound around us. Half of Beverly Hills must have woken up by now.

We reach the road containing the speed bump and, with slightly shaky expertise, Mihai guides our steamroller into it. There is a lurch as we pass over the bump and I grab the stick that I've now ascertained is the clutch, pulling it back. The machine stops, and we fiddle for a while with some likely-looking knobs until we suddenly begin backing up. We hit the hump again.

We engage forward gear once again, flattening the hump even more. After stopping the vehicle Mihai makes a throat-slitting gesture. I reach down, turn the Swiss Army Knife, and the diesel dies, its pounding roar ceasing and leaving a resounding silence in its wake. We turn and stare back at the road.

The streetlights show a flattened hump. Maybe not absolutely completely flat, but it will never again trap another unwary low-slung motor vehicle. Then, as we turn to each other with self-satisfied congratulatory grins, we become aware of another sound – the whoop of sirens.

Our grins congeal in cold panic.

'Shit, Rob. Let's get out of here.' Mihai clambers off the vehicle and I follow him, equally urgently. We run back to the road we turned in from, in the hope of finding Mary.

The Maserati isn't anywhere in sight, but a cop car is. I can see the lights of the vehicle, blue and red flashing on its roof, speeding towards us less than a quarter of a mile down the road.

'Oh shit, run!' I pull at his arm, back towards the road we've just come from. 'Quick, Mihai. Back this way.' There aren't too many other options. He turns and follows me as I sprint back past the steamroller, looking for somewhere to hide.

But there is nowhere to conceal ourselves, no cover at all, any access from the road cut off by the high security walls and steel gates. The road is short, though, a mere two hundred yards to a T-junction, and we may be able to find a hiding place in the next street. I run to the intersection, spurred on by the fast-approaching engine and siren.

I glance back to see if Mihai can join me behind the hedged corner before the cops see us.

But when I see him I immediately lose hope for this. He is way behind, flailing down the middle of the road like a big spider with half its limbs missing. His arms and legs are jerking about, his head is weaving and his belly is heaving – but there's not a lot of actual movement forward.

He makes a weak gesture towards me. 'You run, Rob. I'm ...' The rest of what he has to say is lost as the police car comes squealing round the corner, headlights silhouetting the Romanian as it draws up alongside the steamroller. Panic fires a last shot of adrenalin into Mihai's limbs and his arms pump a bit harder, knees jerking like a puppet on amphetamine. He lunges forward to where I'm waiting.

Shit, too late, I think. They must have seen him. But then I figure maybe the police saw only one of us, since I'm mostly hidden behind the hedge.

'Quick, get down there,' I hiss as the car begins to move forward again. I shove him towards the bottom of the hedge. 'Hide. I'll run and draw them away.'

He ducks into the dark gap, inhaling air with strangled gasps as I take off towards the next corner. The cop car is accelerating, chasing after me, and I wonder how I'm going to escape. A gravelly cliff to the right, maybe twenty to twenty-five feet high, extends all the way along the street, and on the left walls and hedges are half as high. Nowhere to duck to at all. Damn. A car will quickly overtake me.

The vehicle swings around the corner, headlights lighting up the road as well as a single big tree growing right next to the cliff. I swerve for the tree.

The vehicle screeches to a halt behind me and I hear footsteps chasing. I hit the trunk running, push against the bark with one foot, and leap for the lowest branch. My hand makes contact with wood, and I grab, hitching my body up with a desperate twitch so that I can hold on with my other hand. I pull myself up as two cops arrive below me. One jumps, but I'm too high already.

'Get back down here,' he yells at me. 'You're under arrest. Come back down immediately.'

I ignore these instructions and scramble higher, to the level of the cliff top, and stare through the dark. A house looms, set back from the cliff edge. There is also a long branch, slightly higher up, that extends over the top of the cliff, and I ignore the shouting from below and clamber along it until I'm over the edge. Hanging from my hands, I swing down and then drop, landing on top of the cliff. I peer down and see the cops running back to their car. They jump in and roar off, lights flashing and sirens blaring, hurrying no doubt to intercept me along the top somewhere.

So I clamber back over the edge, feeling along the cliff for toe-holds. With a tenuous grip on the face I lower myself until I am able to jump the last few feet. Mihai emerges from the shadows as I approach the place I left him.

'Hey, Rob, you got away.' He's relieved, and has regained his breath somewhat. 'Good. C'mon, let's get the hell out of here.'

We trot back along the road in the opposite direction to the one the cops took, past the road with the steamroller. At the next inter-section Mihai plucks at my sleeve.

'Up here,' he puffs, pulling me towards a road that runs parallel to the one where our recent acquisition is parked. 'Let's see if we can find Mary. We've got to get ourselves away from this area.'

I agree wholeheartedly with that sentiment, but I doubt she has stuck around. I imagine that she's hightailed it for the security of her apartment in Hollywood, leaving behind her lame-brained husband and his idiot new friend. We're going to have to find our own way out of this area, I suspect – if we can evade the posse of cops looking for us. We emerge onto the road where we drove the steamroller and turn left, away from the scene of the crime. A car is parked against the kerb about fifty yards further down. A Citroën-Maserati.

'There she is,' Mihai pants, as though it was entirely to be expected that his wife would be there. Mary's pale face is discernible inside the dark interior. What a girl. My first impression of her was correct. This was the sort of woman who stood staunchly behind her husband and loaded his rifles as he blasted away at the Apaches.

We pile into the car and Mihai yells, 'Go! Go!' Unnecessarily, as Mary is already pulling away before we've even closed the doors. My friend lets out a whoop and a gasp signalling his triumph, and maybe also his relief.

'God, Mihai,' Mary says as we accelerate away. 'I thought you were both going to be caught.'

'Nope,' he wheezes. 'We got clean away.'

'You're an idiot, though.'

'Yeah well, we got the bump. We flattened it all right. The only thing that fucker'll bump now is a shopping cart.' His laughter is like the clatter of a cheap alarm clock, and his weird accent makes his statement all the funnier to me.

2

The next day my mood has taken a marked turn for the worse. I get up and splash water on my face, and then I sit and wait for my hosts to surface. When Mihai eventually appears he looks as bad as I feel. We perform a small bonding ritual, reliving our previous night's escapade and comparing our headaches, trying to decide whether breakfast would be a waste of time – it might cause us to throw up, but it might also help to absorb the remaining alcohol and so reduce our hangovers. Eventually we settle on coffee.

'Listen, Rob, I want to thank you for last night,' Mihai says as we carry our cups to the table. 'If it wasn't for you we wouldn't have gotten away.'

'No problem, Mihai.' I smile at him. 'It was fun.'

'So where'd you learn to climb like that? You shot up that tree like one of those things you have in Africa. A baboon or something.'

'On boats,' I say with a shrug. 'I'm used to heights because of being up in the rigging.' This isn't altogether true. These days, you don't actually spend that much time climbing masts, and if you do have to go aloft it's usually in a bo'sun's chair, winched up with a halyard. But it's better than saying my tree-climbing abilities were inspired by pure fear.

'So you've done a lot of sailing then?'

'Pretty much, I suppose. Most of my life.'

'And you want to sail the Pacific now? On the Transpac Race?'

'Well, yes. I don't know if I'm going to wait a year for the next Transpac, though. Maybe I'll just look for a yacht heading west.'

'How? Just ask for a ride?'

'Well, actually, it's called crewing. I get a job as a crew member. Help with the sailing and do watches and stuff.'

'Could you captain the yacht yourself? Y'know, do the navigation and everything?'

'Um, yes, sure, I think so. I've never actually navigated myself but I've learnt from some of the skippers I've sailed with.'

'I've always wanted to sail a boat, y'know. Cruise around the world or something. Mary and I talked about it.' He looks down reflectively.

I wait for him to finish his thought, expecting him to expand on this topic. Then he quickly lifts his head.

'Look, Rob, if you don't have to be in San Francisco immediately, why don't you hang around for a few days?' He surprises me with the sudden change of subject. 'See some of the sights of Hollywood with us. You can stay here.'

'I don't know, Mihai, it's maybe better I move on. You and Mary have been too kind already.'

'Bullshit,' he says. 'After the way you saved my ass last night, Mary and I would love it if you stuck around. In fact, I insist.'

His offer is tempting. I like Mihai, and would enjoy a few days off the road, seeing Hollywood. Well, okay, I think, another couple of days. I'll enjoy the company of my new friends for two more days, and then I'll be on my way again.

'Okay, sure, Mihai,' I tell him. 'Yes, thanks, I'd like that.'

* * *

The next day my hosts suggest we go out along the strip to see the action. After weeks on the road this is a welcome diversion. It's all so totally different from rigidly puritanical South Africa, where being 'way out' means having your hair over your ears and homosexuality is about as acceptable as being a rabbi in Nazi Germany. The apartment where Mihai and Mary live is in the centre of Hollywood, right on Sunset Boulevard. Embedded in the pavements outside the restaurants are the handprints of stars, and the pavements themselves bustle with people from all walks of life: would-be movie stars, hustlers, drag queens, producers meeting scriptwriters for lunch, and even ordinary souls like myself – though probably not quite as agog with curiosity as I am. Mary and Mihai enjoy my naivety and we have fun.

That evening, Mary cooks dinner for the three of us and we sit in companionable silence, watching news on TV. Evel Knievel has just attempted to jump the Snake River Canyon on his motorbike and we watch a replay. After the tremendous build-up to the event I am disappointed by the pathetic little jump, the motorbike dropping into the depths as Evel parachutes off the back of it. The bike didn't even reach a quarter of the way across, though I suppose taking off on a jet-propelled motorbike across a mile-wide chasm could be sort of daunting, even if you are wearing a parachute.

The rest of the news is mostly about Watergate, and the chances of Nixon being impeached or resigning. The country seems to be divided equally over his culpability in the whole affair. Even Vietnam has slid into obscurity, both the war and anti-war sentiment overshadowed by the population's split over the president's involvement in the bugging.

'You think he'll quit?' I ask.

'He should, after all the things he did,' Mary answers. 'Tapping phones and stuff. It's criminal, don't you think?'

'Well, I don't know,' I say. 'Doesn't necessarily make him a bad president. I mean, as long as he does the right things for his country.'

'You figure it's okay being a criminal?' Mihai asks.

'Depends. On the type of crime, I guess.'

'What d'you mean?' He has a curious glint in his eyes. 'What type of crime?'

'Well, like some white-collar stuff. Where nobody really gets hurt. Things like insurance fraud, for instance. The loss of profit is so small when spread among all the shareholders that it wouldn't really matter very much to anyone.' I suspect I sound a bit naive, but I've been drawn into this discussion and feel I have to defend my answer.

'You ever thought about being a criminal, Rob?'

'Not really, but maybe, if the circumstances dictated it. Like if I thought the insurance company had cheated me, I suppose, or if I really needed the money for an operation or something.'

Mihai nods thoughtfully and glances at Mary. He tilts his head slightly and raises an eyebrow, and she answers with the faintest of shrugs. A longish silence ensues, and I figure the subject is closed. I watch TV again, but then Mihai makes a little throat-clearing noise.

'Rob, we've uh … we've got something we want to talk to you about. Something Mary and I were discussing last night, actually.'

His demeanour has turned serious, and I sense that this must be something important to him and Mary. He sits and continues to think about what he's going to say. Mary waits as well, her wide shoulders set with tension now.

'You know my situation at the moment – financially, I mean,' he says at last, waving one hand about briefly. 'Mary and I are …' He casts about for words. 'Well, as I told you, we don't have the kind of cash we used to have.'

I nod, not understanding, but in puzzled empathy.

'There's something we want to ask you.' He seems tense, anxious maybe. 'Something we were discussing last night. After that thing with the steamroller we feel we've pretty much got to know you. We trust you, you know, and I think we're pretty much alike, if you know what I mean.' He tosses me a half-smile, more of a grimace really.

I wait, not really seeing where this is going.

'It's a little um … weird to approach you with this now, so soon in our friendship,' he continues after another longish moment. 'But we both feel that it's okay to ask you, you know? So I'm just going to come out with it.'

Oh shit. He's going to touch me for a loan. Or ask me to pay for my stay here. I feel my smile slide downwards. Damn. Considering my appearance and obvious financial status, this shows some serious desperation on his part. His circumstances must be far worse than I thought.

'Listen, Mihai, I don't have very much,' I say hastily, thinking of the forty dollars I've got rolled up in my pocket. It's all the money I have, all that stands between me and destitution. 'I've got a little cash I could spare, I guess, but …'

'Oh shucks, no! No no no. I'm not asking you for money, Rob.' His explosive chuckle and denial make me feel both relief and embarrassment. Not so much relief that he's not asking me for money, but relief that I'm not mistaken in my impression of my hosts.

'You're our guest here, and that's the last thing on my mind.' There is a glimmer of amusement in his eyes now, and Mary is smiling as well, though a trifle nervously.

'I've been thinking about a plan to *make* money,' he continues, his amusement fading. 'A *lot* of money.' I get a hint of what may be behind all this.

'I've been thinking about a plan to insure Mary and me for a large sum – say, a million dollars each.' He looks at me intently, sternly almost, like he's admonishing me for something I haven't yet done. I say nothing, waiting, anticipating.

'Because of my credit rating when we had money, and, y'know, because we were pretty rich then and still appear rich, we can insure ourselves for a large sum of cash. The insurance company doesn't have to know what our situation is now, and I think we can still get ourselves insured for a million bucks each.'

A million bucks? I know nothing of the requirements to be able to get that kind of insurance, and I know no one who would be insured for that kind of money. In fact, apart from a couple of yacht owners in the Caribbean, I'm not even sure if I've met anyone with that much boodle.

'After we get the insurance on us I was gonna buy an aeroplane and learn to fly.' He waits a bit to nail my attention, and then says, 'And then I was gonna crash it.'

He focuses intently upon me as I widen my eyes obligingly. This has him hitching his shoulders with satisfaction.

'A fake crash, of course,' he adds, casting a faint smirk towards his wife, including her in this scheme of his – a family complicity.

He switches back to me, serious again. 'My idea was to file a flight plan to fly over the Rocky Mountains.' He pauses once more for effect. 'But I wasn't going to reach the other side. I was gonna fly some-where else. Land in the desert and paint new numbers on the plane. Then fly maybe to Canada.' He looks at me with another expectant pause. I am forced to give him a nod.

'Mary would stay here, and after a while she'd collect the insur-ance on me. And then, say after about a year or so, she'd join me wherever I am. We were going to make a million dollars out of the insurance company.' He leans back in his chair now, waiting for my reaction. I think for a moment.

'But they'll look for the plane. When they don't find any wreck-age they'll be suspicious,' I say.

Mihai nods his head slowly. 'Yeah, but the Rockies are big moun-tains. It's possible that the plane could be lost out there somewhere in that wilderness.' Then he leans forward again and holds up a finger. 'But you're right. That's the weakest part of the plan. That's the major flaw.'

I hesitate, a question on my lips. Why have you told me about this? What part do you think I have in this scheme? Mihai reads my face.

'I've let you in on our plan because Mary and I were talking last night. And now I've come up with another idea.' He has that air of contained excitement again, about to impart something momentous.

'What if we buy a sailing boat instead?' He flashes a sort of triumphant, expectant look. 'What if we buy a yacht, say, to go around the world, but the yacht disappears. They can never find a yacht if it's on the bottom of the ocean. Instead of the plane, we use a yacht.' He half smiles, a smug expression, looking wholly pleased with his idea.

'But what about collecting the insurance?' I ask. 'If you're both on the yacht, then who's going to collect the money?'

Mihai winds his smile up fully. I think I detect something like relief in it. I've passed the first test; I haven't reacted adversely to what he's just told me – I haven't said he's crazy and made as if to leave.

'That's where you fit in,' he says, cocking his head at me. 'What would you say to coming in with us? We need someone who can sail the boat. Either Mary or me has to stay to collect the money, and we need someone who knows how to sail.'

Although I am half expecting this, I'm still rocked by his proposal. I don't know what to say.

'Shit, Mihai, I don't know. I mean, I'm not so sure about this. I need, um, to think about it.'

He narrows his eyes slightly and says, 'Sure, Rob. Go ahead.' Mary is waiting as well, waiting for my answer.

So I do think, or at least pretend to think. Or think about other things while I'm pretending to think. I thought Mihai was a person of substance; an honest, hard-working citizen in his adoptive country. And Mary ...? My hosts have totally surprised me.

'Rob, listen,' he says, suddenly holding up a hand. 'Sleep on it. You don't have to answer now. Just think about it tonight and give us your answer tomorrow. Okay?'

* * *

And so, later that night I lie awake, unable to sleep and dwelling on this unexpected proposal as I toss and turn. I've never been involved in any criminal activities before, never been in trouble with the police or even seriously thought about crime. Mihai's offer is intriguing, though. Should I do it? Could I do it? Is it something that I *want* to do? Like any average middle-class kid, I've never really had to question my morals that closely. I've always thought of myself as a basically honest person, never stolen anything from anybody in my life, and always believed in a simple principle: You can do whatever you like in this life as long as you don't harm anybody else.

But that's what I am wondering about now. How much harm is this crime actually going to do? How much will it affect anybody personally? Not much, I think. Insurance companies are huge amorphous bodies without individual personalities, just thousands of shareholders. And nothing really affects those shareholders except the annual dividends, which are usually pretty good since insurance companies make a fortune through their economic principles.

And these are really the only principles that they do have. I don't believe that insurance companies actually have any moral principles. Not that this is anything to do with the personalities within the company; it's merely corporate policy that has developed from dealing with people like … well, like Mihai and me, I suppose. So, if we're successful with this scheme, who exactly are we hurting? Nobody really, I think, or it's at least a hurt that is diluted among so many thousands that it'll be negligible to any one individual. So, how bad is it to fleece an insurance company? How much of a conflict is it with my principle of not hurting anybody? Not that much, it seems, although some niggling part of me wonders if I'm not just trying to rationalise what I'm now beginning to contemplate with more than a little edge of excitement.

I have no actual thoughts of jail, and not much trouble with the illegality of what we're considering. I've always believed my abstention from crime to be a result of my personal morality, rather than the mere observance of what is legal and what is not.

My mind suddenly jumps back to a conversation I had with a girl called Joanne, a girl I became involved with in the Caribbean. We were sitting on the foredeck of the yacht *Sealestial*, crewing together and heading for America on a beautiful calm night, a universe of stars filling the heavens above and the bow wave crunching and hissing beneath us as the vessel sliced through the sea. As we talked, she nestled in my arms and asked me what I intended to do with the rest of my life after we got to the States.

'I don't know yet,' I shrugged. And then added, mostly kidding, 'But here's my plan: I think before I get to the age of thirty I'll be a millionaire.' Then I paused, and added with a smile, 'Or maybe just in jail.'

'And how are you thinking of doing that?' she asked, referring, I thought, to the first part of my statement; her slightly nervous laugh I took to be reaction to the second part. Or maybe it was something else – I had used the moment of distraction to move my hand up onto her breast.

'Mm … pull a scam on an insurance company, maybe. They cheat and lie, so I guess I've got no scruples about robbing them.' I said this without any real intent or thought then, but my words seem almost prophetic as I recall them now.

I think back to that occasion, and also to Joanne's sweet face as she firmly removed my hand. If only she could see me now – about to prove that my words were not merely jest, empty bravado, which they were at the time. I wish she were here.

I'm starting to feel an edgy sense of anticipation, a tantalising glimpse of a new adventure. Why not? After all, isn't this why I set out from South Africa? Excitement? Opportunity? Adventure?

I begin to see this as a natural part of my quest. I feel like one of those fairytale characters who sets out from home to make his fortune in the world, and then meets a genie along the way who offers the chance. Even though crime was not what I had in mind when I began my odyssey, this opportunity has a daring allure – and it comes with a boat. I lie awake and think and dream. It seems that I've met my genie, an ex-communist genie.

3

Mihai offers me a slow loopy grin when I give him my answer, and then holds his hand out. I shake it, our grip remaining firm as we test the strength of my decision.

'Good, Rob,' he says. 'I'm glad.'

Mary goes to make more coffee, and Mihai and I begin to plan in detail. The first thing is my identity. Unlike Mihai and Mary, I am not prepared to disappear from the face of the earth. Mihai has no family to worry about, having lost contact with his mother and sister. Mary's grandmother cared for her after her parents were killed in a car crash when she was eighteen, and this grandmother has since died. She has no living relatives, so there is no one to mourn her loss.

But I have parents, kind and loving parents who gave me a good start in life, and I have no intention of leaving them bereft at the thought of my death. I intend to return to South Africa and live there, so we cannot have investigators coming around and asking questions later. The choice is clear. I have to have an alias.

After some thought we decide that I'll be Robert Greene from the

UK. The Americans nearly always mistake my accent for English, so I'll say that I come from Portsmouth on the Solent, a prime yachting area in the south of England. In fact, I've never been there; I haven't been to England at all. We'll say that I'm here on holiday, and that Mihai has offered me a job as his yacht captain. We intend to convey the idea that Mihai and Mary have decided to pack up here and go sailing, that meeting me has firmed a long-held desire of his to embark on a world cruise with his wife. From now on I will be introduced as Rob Greene, the future captain of Mihai's yacht.

Of course, there are complications. We're still left with the fact that somebody has to remain behind to collect the insurance. The logical choice is Mary. Mihai and I would sail away for a 'shakedown cruise', testing the boat, and then disappear. Mary would collect the money. However, there is a drawback to this. Mihai is unsure whether Mary will be able to handle the interrogation by insurance investigators, and possibly the police. It would be better to have him face the questions and collect the money. A sneaky thought enters my head that maybe he doesn't quite trust her.

We toss ideas around, and then I have another plan. What if we bought the yacht in Hawaii? We could make preparations to bring it back to the US mainland to ready it for the round-the-world cruise, and then just before we sailed from Hawaii, we would make it known that Mihai had an urgent message from his shop that he was needed there immediately. He'd fly back, and we'd put out the story that Mary and I were going to sail to America without him. But in fact, we would sail the other way, towards Australia. In due course, we'd be posted as missing, and much later, after collecting the insurance payout, Mihai would join us in Australia. I explain that, apart from providing a reason why Mary and I would be sailing without Mihai, this plan has another advantage. We'd be sailing 180 degrees from the direction we were supposed to be going, so any air or sea search would probably be in the wrong area.

Mihai likes the plan. It solves the problem of why he is not on the boat with us. I wonder briefly if the idea of not having to sail all the way across the Pacific might not also hold some appeal for him, but then I remind myself that this is a man who crossed heavily patrolled forests in the middle of winter to escape to freedom. He is no stranger to hardship, no shirker of danger.

The day slides by as we plan in more detail. I suggest that we might fake a gas explosion on the boat. Most yachts use propane to cook with, and this is an ever-present risk. Propane is derived from methane gas, which is colourless and odourless, and though the gas used for cooking has a definite smell, it doesn't linger.

What makes gas so dangerous on a yacht is the fact that it is heavier than air. A slow gas leak sinks to the watertight and airtight bilge where it collects, filling the boat until a carelessly lit flame sparks it off – and then the vessel blows up like an expensive bomb. Before heading west, we could singe the life rings and toss them into the water along with other identifiable debris a couple of hundred miles towards the US coastline, leading everyone to believe that we've had a gas explosion on board.

We decide to make sure that the yacht we use has a gas cooker.

I tell Mihai that we need a boat around forty feet in length, costing in the region of thirty-five thousand dollars – the price of a large house.

'Mm. Well, Rob,' he says, looking thoughtful. 'I've got some money saved, but not enough to buy the yacht *and* pay for the insurance premiums. And I also have to keep up a pretence of still being wealthy, you know?' He strokes his chin. 'We have to get some more cash together.'

I think of my forty dollars. Not much help there, I guess.

'I might have a job for you, Rob,' he says, squinting one eye at me. 'A way we can make some moolah quickly. It's pretty easy and pays well – really well, in fact. I do it already. It's one way I've been able to keep the car and this apartment.'

'What is it?' I ask.

'I have a friend, a Russian called Dmitrievich Polotov, somebody I do business with sometimes. He runs an organisation that sends religious pamphlets and stuff to Russia. They get donations and contributions from all around the world to do it.' Mihai flashes a grin at me. 'We call him the Priest, although he isn't actually one.'

I smile back, a little uncertainly.

'But the Soviets don't allow that sort of thing,' he continues, 'so the only way he can get the letters through the postal system is to address each envelope by hand, like a personal letter. He's made lots of money from doing this.'

I wait, puzzled, not seeing where I'm going to fit in, unless I become a courier, sneaking bags of religious mail across the snowy wastes of Siberia on a husky-drawn sled. Mihai's next words dispel that enticing little dream.

'All you'll have to do is write the addresses on the envelopes,' he says. 'I'll teach you how to write in Russian.'

'Okay,' I say, still not seeing where the money-making prospects in this are. It sounds pretty boring. 'How much does he pay?'

'Eighty dollars for five hundred envelopes. I can sometimes do fifteen hundred in a day.'

I do a quick mental computation.

'Wow. That's like two hundred and forty dollars a day.' I've revised my opinion of this scheme. 'Yes, sure. I'll do it.'

'Great.' Mihai smiles. 'Why don't we go and meet him? We can go there now. I'll phone him.'

* * *

We go in the Maserati, Mary sitting in the back as though in deference to my new status: Mihai's new partner in crime – plus future co-envelope-addresser.

The Priest lives a few miles from Sunset Strip, in a solid brick mansion surrounded by high walls. We have to press a buzzer at the wrought-iron gate, which slides back to allow us passage up a circular drive.

Dmitrievich meets us at the door. He's about sixty-five years old, and large. Not just large physically; he takes up space, filling his surroundings with his personality. He gives us a wide smile, revealing rows of yellowed teeth with gaps between them, like corn on an unhealthy cob. He throws his arms out as if to embrace us, and then yells in heavily accented English.

'Hello, hello, hello. Come in, my friends, come in, come in.' He ushers us towards the door with expansive sweeps of his arms. Mihai introduces me and the Russian squeezes my hand hard and then pats it on the back as though consoling it for the undue pressure he has just exerted on it.

'Hello and welcome, welcome to my home,' he says to me. 'Come in, come and sit down.' He shows us into a large and beautifully furnished room. Two men are lounging together talking, a third is standing apart, near the window.

'This is Rob. He is from South Africa.' Dmitrievich claps me around the shoulder with a proprietary gesture as he introduces me. 'These are my friends, George and Alex,' he says, indicating the two men talking. 'And that is Vlazo.' He motions towards the short man by the window.

I shake hands and acknowledge their greetings. George is foreign – Eastern European like Mihai and the Priest – but Alex is American. I turn to the man at the window, ready to shake his hand as well.

He sort of draws his head back and pulls his chin down, staring along his nose at me as if looking down at me, even though I top him by at least six inches. 'Yes, 'ello,' he says abruptly with a hard dark stare, and with no sign of wanting to shake my hand. He moves away immediately and pours himself another drink, with his back to me.

George and Alex begin questioning me about South Africa while

Mihai draws Dmitrievich to a corner of the room, speaking to him in a strange language – Russian, I guess. My friend flicks his eyes my way and I assume he's asking if I can help address envelopes. The Priest immediately nods his head.

'Da. Yes. Sure, of course.' He turns to me and opens his arms wide, palms up. 'Why not? Sure you can come to my little organisation. You write hard and you make good money, yes?'

'Yes,' I answer. With that over, Dmitrievich switches to other matters. George and Alex join in and chat and laugh, but not Vlazo, who just stares.

Our host seems to swell with bonhomie but I sense another aspect to him, a certain cold control behind his apparent geniality. He dominates his surroundings. His expansive joviality is just a cover, I suspect. He is not a man to be taken lightly.

* * *

'Interesting guys,' I say to my friends. We're on our way home again. 'They seem pretty nice.'

Mary makes a face. 'Except Vlazo. I really don't like him.'

I feel the same, but I don't want to cast any aspersions on my new friends' friends.

'He does seem a bit … standoffish,' I say.

'He's more than that. He's horrible. He scares me.'

'He's a fuckhead,' Mihai interjects. 'I don't like him either, but Dmitrievich finds him useful. Fortunately he has nothing to do with the letter-writing stuff.'

'Speaking about that, when will we start?' I ask.

'Pretty much straight away. We just need to find you somewhere to live first, and I think I have an idea about that.'

It turns out he has a Romanian friend, Mikhael, or Mike as he is more often called. Mike lives in El Monte, the Mexican area of Los Angeles, where he shares a house with an American guy called Pete.

Back at the apartment, Mihai phones him, and they chat in Romanian for a while.

Listening to the foreign language rolling from Mihai's lips, I suddenly get the feeling that I'm being pulled onto some strange roller-coaster ride, a roller-coaster made in Siberia out of suspect parts. I'm being drawn into something thrilling and scary and unknown, leading me towards new experiences and an uncertain fate. But I'm going along for the ride. I feel totally alive, the kind of life-affirming kick I'd set out to find when I left South Africa.

'Okay, that's settled then.' Mihai puts the phone down and turns to me. 'You can move in with Mike and Pete. They have a spare room and the rent's cheap. We'll go over there tomorrow.'

* * *

Mike is a short fat guy, not given to speaking much. In fact, for the first couple of days I worry that he hates me. I think maybe it has something to do with the fact that I come from South Africa, or maybe he simply resents my intrusion into his life. Later I find out it is just his way. He mopes around with an air of quiet displeasure, a surly antagonism, which suddenly dispels, like a swirl in a fog, to reveal a strange dry humour or even a shy friendly gesture. But only after he has known someone for at least a month or two.

Since he is Romanian, I suppose his story is similar to Mihai's. But he never speaks of his past. He never speaks of anything, really, except occasionally about his occupation – making hollow-cast bronze mouldings of statues and artworks that people bring to him from time to time. At the back of the house are two kilns, one for burning out the hollow wax copy he makes of the original, and the second to melt the bronze to its required temperature before pouring it into the mould after the wax has been burnt out.

Pete is easier to get along with, more laid-back and interested only in his motorbikes and women. And also occasionally in the chickens he keeps at the back, supposedly in a coop, though they prefer to roam free, sometimes joining us while we watch TV in the living room. What he does for a living is a mystery, but I suspect it's not much. In any case, he's away for a lot of the time, staying with a girlfriend.

El Monte, I discover, is not really considered a 'nice' neighbourhood to live in. In fact, when I tell LA residents where I live, they often express amazement that I haven't been knifed to death by some greasy kid for whatever paltry few dollars I might be carrying with me. In actual fact, the neighbourhood is peaceful and the people are friendly.

Both Pete and Mike know me by my alias, Rob Greene, and I carefully avoid using any of the words and expressions that might give away my South African origins, such as saying 'ja' and calling traffic lights 'robots'. I affect a British accent too, saying 'bloody' instead of 'bladdy'.

* * *

For my new occupation, Mihai shows me how to write Moscow in Russian – Москва – not quite joining the letters. I also learn to write CCCP instead of USSR – heavy job-training.

We develop a technique, he and I. Mihai writes the name of the person and the street address on the envelope, and I add the name of the town or city, and CCCP. Our handwriting is not that similar, but Mihai assures me it doesn't matter. The Priest is not really religious, he tells me, and doesn't actually care if most of the letters are intercepted. But his organisation has to show something for the contributions he gets from around the world, so he needs the hand-addressed letters. Together we complete over three thousand envelopes a day, which earns us around five hundred dollars. After about two weeks, however, we both begin to have trouble with our fingers swelling up, and we're forced to slow down somewhat. But we still manage to average nearly four hundred dollars a day between the two of us.

This is more money than I've ever made in my life, but I retain only enough to pay my keep and for the occasional night out with my new housemates. The rest I give to Mihai to be used for our scheme.

My partner in crime has contacted an insurance company and applied for a policy for him and Mary, to insure each of them for one million dollars.

Our next step is to find a yacht, and to this end we begin visiting yacht brokers in the area, mainly in Marina del Rey – the largest yacht marina in the world – and Newport Beach. We're looking specifically for a suitable boat located in Hawaii, so that we have the excuse to sail it back to California.

* * *

We climb out of the Citroën-Maserati, having just arrived back at Mihai's apartment block after looking at pictures of boats in various yacht brokers' offices at Newport Beach. My partner has been rather quiet on the way back, subdued and a little perturbed, perhaps, by our lack of success in finding a boat.

'Don't worry, Mihai,' I say to him as we head for the stairway. 'We'll find something soon. The right boat will come along. We'll find something for sure.' Each vessel we've looked at so far has had something wrong with it – price, location, lack of gear, whatever.

'Um yeah, great, Rob.' Mihai answers my enthusiasm with somewhat less than total commitment. Another long silence ensues, at odds with his normal volubility.

'What's wrong. Mihai?' I eventually ask. 'Is there a problem?'

'No, not really. It's just ...' He shrugs, making a small dismissive motion with his hand as he unlocks the front door. I wait for him to say what's on his mind, but it's obviously something he's not all that keen to confront me with. Finally, he turns to me with an embarrassed grimace as we enter the empty apartment. Mary is downstairs, in the shop.

'Look, Rob, there's another thing I have to speak to you about.' I'm not sure, but it seems to me there's a blush on his cheeks. I cock my head a little and raise my eyebrows, inviting him to continue, but not without a little trepidation.

'I've been thinking,' he says. 'If you and Mary disappear together, some people might get the wrong idea. And to tell the truth, I don't really like the thought of you and Mary being uh … alone together for so long, you know?' His voice firms up. 'It's not that I don't trust you or Mary or anything, but, well … I mean, you're both human, after all.'

His gaze is fixed firmly upon my face, but his Adam's apple jumps, signalling his distress. I'm embarrassed as well, and not merely as a reflection of Mihai's discomfort. I've also thought about this aspect, of sailing alone with Mary for such a long period, and I've wondered what Mihai's feelings about this were. And also about the other problem: if Mary and I were to disappear on the yacht without him, it's possible that insurance investigators might later suspect that we'd eloped, that we were possibly having an affair and used the boat to give Mihai the slip. This might give them cause to investigate further.

I've come up with a solution, but have been unsure whether to broach it. Joanne, the girl I sailed with from the Caribbean to America, said she'd like to rejoin me if I found a boat heading west. She has a wild streak in her, a desire for adventure equal to my own, and I think she would be a perfect choice to sail with us. I ignore a small silly voice inside me whispering that this perfect choice could also perhaps be my desire to see her again.

I've wondered in fact whether I should mention Joanne to Mihai, but felt that he might object to another person joining our scheme. We'd have to split the money further and also, more importantly, we'd have another, unknown person party to our plans. But I decide to go ahead and tell him about her, explaining that I know her to be a reliable person who'd probably be okay with our nefarious scheme.

Mihai is thoughtful. 'Are you sure you can trust her?'

'Yes. Definitely. We even spoke about getting involved in some sort of scheme together.' A slight deviation from the truth, perhaps. 'She's a different sort of person, really together. You'll see when you meet her.'

'Do you know where she is now?' He has accepted my plan, and I feel a rush of pleasure at the possibility of seeing Joanne again.

'Yes, I have her phone number with me.' I pull my wallet out, and with a small flourish I produce a card where I wrote her New Jersey home number.

'Give her a call, then.' Mihai gestures towards his phone, and then looks at his watch. 'It's nine o'clock over on the East Coast now. It's not too late to phone her.'

A coil of anticipation burns in my belly, and I pick up the phone.

'Listen, Rob.' He grabs my shoulder. 'Don't say anything on the phone about what we're doing. I think it's possible that the FBI still keeps a tap on it. They may still be watching me.'

I nod briefly, but my mind is more occupied with the prospect of speaking to Joanne. Mihai has mentioned to me before that the FBI might still be monitoring him – Red paranoia, apparently – but I put it all down to melodrama. Why would they continue to be interested in him ten years after he was admitted to the country? I dial Joanne's number.

'Hello?' I recognise her voice immediately.

'Joanne? It's me, Rob.' I'm unable to be cool, to mask my excitement. I'm hardly even aware that Mihai has left the room.

'Rob! Where are you? How are you? You shit! Why haven't you called?' Her voice fills me with delight. I've thought of her often while hitch-hiking across America, even though I haven't contacted her.

'Hey, I'm sorry I haven't phoned. I've been on the road and …
and, well, phones are difficult. But anyway, how are you?'

I listen to her answer and think how much I've missed her.

We knew each other for only two months, but I came to like her
very much. Our parting was difficult, but she had to go back home
to finish her schooling, and I had, so I thought, a Transpac Race to take
part in. So we each went our own way with a promise to keep in touch.

We talk some more, and then I pop the question.

'Joanne, you remember what we spoke about? You and me sailing
together? And me doing something that would make a lot of money?'

'Yes, of course' – no hesitation – 'I remember that.'

'Well, I have a boat, and an … ah, interesting scheme. Do you still
want to join me?'

'What's the scheme?' she asks. 'Is it legal?' She's quick, is Joanne.

'Let's just say that there's a lot of money involved, over one million dollars, and a lot of sailing. I can't say any more over the phone.'
I'm only half-mindful of Mihai's warning. 'Are you interested?'

'Well, as long as it has nothing to do with drugs. And if it's on
a boat,' she says with thoughtful precision. Then she hesitantly asks,
'But when were you thinking of doing this?'

'Well, probably not for another two months at least. It'll take that
long to get everything sorted, buy the yacht and get it ready. But I'd
really like for you to join us.'

'Oh, that's great, Rob! I have about another two months to complete school here.' I can hear real pleasure in her voice now. 'If you
can wait, I'd love to come.'

We talk some more, both of us elated at the idea of seeing each
other again. I promise to call her more often and put the phone down,
a wide grin stretched across my face.

My new adventure has just become even more appealing.

* * *

A day later, Mihai phones.

'Hey, Rob, what's up? How're you doing?' he greets me, his colloquialisms still strange to me in his funny accent.

'Good, Mihai. What's up yourself?'

'I had a call yesterday,' he says, enigmatically. I can tell he has some important news.

'Oh, yeah? From who?'

'The insurance company.'

'So?'

'So they wanted to ask me some questions.' There's another long pause, and just as I'm about to prod him, he continues. 'They wanted to know why Mary's maiden-name initials are MED, the same as the company I work for in Zurich.'

Now I pause. 'So, why are they the same?'

'Because her maiden name was Mary Elizabeth Denton,' he says, like a schoolteacher to an obtuse pupil. 'But it's just a coincidence.'

'So … oh!' I see the problem. 'Shit, they're suspicious.'

'Exactly,' he says. 'They've been investigating me.'

Oh crap, this could be a problem. 'D'you think you'll still get the insurance then?'

'I dunno, we'll see,' he says slowly. 'It really is just a coincidence, y'know, so it shouldn't be a problem. MED is a legitimate company in Switzerland. But they're just brokers, in an office in Zurich. There is no big warehouse full of gold or anything. So I guess they got suspicious when they were trying to verify my income, like they believe I made the company up or something. But of course it's true, MED really does exist.'

'Well, it should be okay, then.'

'Yes, but the fact that they are digging through my background isn't so good,' he says.

I agree with that, and I hope it's not going to spoil our plan.

4

In the offices of Calley Yachts, a brokerage in Marina del Rey, we find a suitable vessel. She is a beautiful thirty-eight-foot ketch in Hawaii called *Recluse*. I pore over the specifications with Mihai, and I'm immediately taken with her. *Recluse* is a long-distance cruiser, fast, comfortable, seaworthy and elegant. And she possesses all the requisite features for our plan and for an extended voyage – a self-steering system, long-range fuel tanks, a rig that is easily handled, and a gas cooker.

But these are not the only reasons for my delight. I am in love with the boat itself, for the grace of her lines and the beauty of her deportment. The pictures show her to be the perfect embodiment of the vessel I have always dreamt of owning. Mihai and I have decided that the spoils from our scheme will be split, with three-quarters of the money going to him and Mary, while I'll get the yacht and whatever is left after all the costs have been deducted. Joanne's share would come from mine, at my discretion. I agreed to the arrangement without argument, my mind focused more on the adventurous aspects of our undertaking and the boat. In fact, I'd probably have accepted the yacht alone as my share.

Driving back from the marina, anticipation tautens my emotions. I'm excited; our scheme is coming together, finally.

'Well, Mihai,' I say, 'we can fly across and take a look at the boat, and if it's okay we can give them a deposit. We should have the insurance cover soon, I hope, so then we can get going with our plan.'

'Hmm,' is all he says.

'I have such a good feeling about *Recluse*,' I continue, regardless. 'I feel for sure that this is the right yacht for us.' Right yacht for me maybe, but this is a notion that doesn't quite surface as a coherent thought. *Recluse* is perfect for our plan, and, anyway, she's definitely the right sort of vessel to sail across the Pacific.

'Um, yeah, great, Rob,' Mihai says. 'But we might have to wait a while before we actually buy the yacht.'

'Why? Because of the insurance?'

'Well, yes, that. But also because it's a bit more than I expected to pay, y'know? I don't have as much as I thought, and I need to keep some for other expenses, like paying the premiums for the insurance when it comes through. We're making good money with the envelopes, so in two to three months we should have enough.'

'Okay,' I say after a while. 'We'll just have to carry on making the cash for *Recluse*, I guess – if she hasn't been sold by then.'

We drive on in silence, each with our separate thoughts. There's not much I can say or do about this, but I'm more than a little disappointed. I thought he had the money. But I have to admit the yacht is priced slightly higher than I'd expect for a boat of that size. Still, I really like *Recluse*, and the idea of owning a yacht like that is something of a dream.

After some minutes, Mihai says, suddenly, 'Actually, Rob, I do have an idea how we can get the money now to go ahead and buy the boat.'

'What's that?' I ask. 'I mean, what are you thinking of doing?'

'Getting rid of this car.'

'Selling your Maserati?' I'm impressed. I know how much he loves his car. 'What do think you can get for it?'

'No, not selling it. I'm thinking of getting rid of it permanently. Pushing it over a cliff in the San Fernando Valley where it won't be found for months, or maybe even years. It's insured for thirty-five thousand dollars, more than I could get if I sold it.'

I stare at him, my brain going into overdrive. I shake my head.

'No, that's crazy, Mihai.' I shake my head again. 'We're about to claim a million dollars' life insurance, and also whatever we insure the boat for. It would be just crazy to claim for your car as well. They're bound to become suspicious.'

We argue, Mihai trying to convince me that we could get away with it, and me becoming nervous at a certain lack of control I am beginning to feel. Although I have convinced myself that knocking off an insurance company is not that morally disturbing to me, this seems to be going altogether too far – as though too much crime might cause me to become a habitual criminal or something. One transgression I can justify to myself as not actually making me a real thief, but any more than that and I'll have embarked on a life of crime. Alarm bells are ringing, and my agitation is causing me to step back from our scheme as if I've suddenly found myself at the edge of a precipice. Maybe Mihai senses this, because he suddenly stops.

'Okay, okay,' he says, holding his hands up in capitulation. 'I won't do it. If that's the way you feel about it, we'll just have to find another way to get the cash. Carry on addressing envelopes, as you said. I just thought that this would be a way to be able to buy the boat now. But I guess we'll just have to wait.' His surrender is a ruse, I'm aware. He knows how much I want *Recluse*.

* * *

A few days pass, and Mihai comes to see me. I've been addressing envelopes and my fingers are hurting, and I'm glad for the break. We sit sunning ourselves on the front porch with beers in our hands, watching the chickens strutting about as if they owned us, instead of the other way around. Behind the house we can hear the sounds of Mike firing up his kiln. Mihai looks thoughtful.

'Rob, what did you say on the phone when you called that girl on the East Coast?' he asks, his mien switching unexpectedly.

I'm wondering what has prompted this line of questioning as I think back to the conversation I had with Joanne. I shrug.

'I told her I was going on a sailing trip and did she want to come along.'

'What did you say about our scheme? Did you say anything at all about what we are doing?'

I concentrate on recalling what I told Joanne, still puzzled as to why he is asking me. 'I just told her that we were doing something with a boat,' I answer carefully. 'I didn't say what it was. Why are you asking me this?'

He tells me that a stranger, wearing a suit, highly polished shoes and sunglasses, walked up to him on Sunset Boulevard outside his shop that morning. Without once looking directly at Mihai, the man said out of the side of his mouth, 'Don't do it. We know what you're up to. Don't do it.' And then the stranger walked away.

Mihai adds, 'I think he was FBI.'

'Do you think he knows about us, what we're doing?' I groan inwardly, hating the feeling of being unable to retract such a stupid question.

Mihai narrows his baby-blue eyes at me. 'He knows *something*. I don't know what you said, but I told you that my phone might be tapped.'

'Listen, I never said anything about what we're doing.' I try not to sound defensive, merely analytical. 'I did mention that we were going to make a lot of money, but nothing about how.'

Mihai nods slowly, his eyes still fixed on me, but not, strangely enough, all that accusingly.

'Do you really think he was FBI?' I ask, seeking a way out. 'You don't think it was maybe somebody playing a joke?' I curse myself for not taking Mihai's warning more seriously.

'Listen, Rob, you'll have to be a lot more careful in future,' he says, not bothering to answer my question. 'I don't know if this is connected to our plan or not, but you must watch yourself. Don't say anything to anyone again.'

I agree, though I'm a little surprised that he is not angrier about my slip or more concerned about the FBI possibly knowing what we are up to. He seems almost too casual about the incident, and makes no mention of aborting our operation. I guess that, like me, he has committed himself to the plan and is determined to go through with it.

* * *

A week later, Mihai appears unexpectedly at the house. He's driving his company panel van, the Volkswagen that he was driving when I first met him. I'm addressing envelopes.

'Hey, Mihai. What's up?' I ask as I let him in.

'Got any cold ones?' Mihai has a fondness for beer, and I'm tempted to tell him that it is contributing to his growing gut. He sidles into the kitchen, with me tagging along behind. I take a look in our rusty refrigerator and grab two Coors. I hand him one, and he takes it with his left hand. I notice that he has a bandage around his right thumb.

He takes a long pull at the bottle, belches softly and then says gently, 'The car's gone.'

'Gone where?'

'Over a cliff. Two hundred feet down the side of the San Fernando Valley. I pushed it off.' He has a nervous, triumphant grin.

When I speak again it seems as though minutes have passed, not just seconds.

'You're kidding, right?' My face feels hot. I can't believe what I'm hearing.

'Nope.' His grin fades when he sees my expression. 'I pushed it over a cliff early this morning.'

'Shit!' My voice is getting tight. 'What the fuck, Mihai?'

'Hold it, hold it,' he says, pushing his palms towards me. 'Listen to me. Listen to what happened before you lose your cool.'

I control myself with an effort, various thoughts competing for attention – all of them bad.

'Yesterday I had an accident.' He holds up his bandaged thumb, talking fast. 'I hit the back of another car on the freeway. Not that hard, but hard enough to catch my thumb on the ashtray.' He turns his hand as if to show me the wound under the bandage.

'I had to go to the hospital. I cut it quite badly and the doctors put ten stitches in. I was gonna drive home afterwards but they told me I couldn't drive my car because of the anaesthetic and the shock, so I phoned Mary to come and pick me up.' He pauses, attempting another weak smile. 'Later it hit me: this is the perfect opportunity. The Maserati is in the hospital parking lot, and I'm at home with an injured thumb and a perfect alibi. So I got Mary to drive me back, then I jumped into the car and drove it out to the valley, and then I pushed it over a cliff. Mary followed me out in the van and took me back home. Nobody saw us.' His smile widens tentatively as he expects, or hopes, to share his triumph with me.

'Fuck you, Mihai.' His smile freezes. 'You know what I felt about another claim on the insurance. How can you do this without telling me?'

'Hey! Hold it. Hold on now, Rob. How could I tell you?' His shoulders are raised so high that they press against his fat cheeks. 'It all just happened. I had to take advantage of an opportunity and

I didn't have time to come and ask you. I just hadda do it. I took the chance when it came.'

'Yeah, well, we talked about this.' I fling my hands up. 'What's going on? What're you up to? I told you it would be stupid to try and claim on your car as well. How could you just go ahead and do this?'

Mihai glances towards the back where Mike is working.

'Shh. Speak quietly,' he hisses.

'Listen, Mihai, I really don't like this.' I hold my voice down with some difficulty. 'I don't like what you've done and I don't like the way you're just doing things without telling me. We're supposed to be partners, remember?' I have a bad feeling of being sucked into something that is definitely not within my control.

He shakes his head. 'Rob, I swear, this just happened. I didn't plan on doing it. The opportunity just came up. I know what we agreed, but I thought that if we could get this money now we can go ahead with our plan. We can buy that yacht you want. We don't have to wait any longer; we can sign the deal for the boat.'

He has struck me at my weakest point. I have thought often of *Recluse*, unable to allay my disappointment at not being able to buy her. But this argument – our first serious one – has sparked a doubt, a feeling that I can't altogether trust my partner. Still, I believe that he is telling the truth about what happened. That he took advantage of an opportunity that happened too quickly for him to consult me. I am still committed to our plan, so I decide that I must overcome the disquiet I feel. I should maybe accept what he has done as a fait accompli. I don't like it, but it's been done, and it might even get me the boat I want so much.

Yes, maybe he's right, maybe the insurance company will simply pay out for the car and we can go ahead with our scheme. Buy *Recluse*. The thought begins to grow in my mind like an unplanned child; unwanted but nevertheless loved.

* * *

'We have it, Rob.' Mihai is excited, more upbeat than I've heard him for a while. We've not communicated much since he told me about the car, and when we have we've been a little distant with each other. But not even the telephone can hide his enthusiasm now. 'We have the insurance now. The policies arrived this morning. I'm worth a million dollars, and so is Mary.'

'Hey, that's good.' I experience a strange reaction – both excitement and alarm. I'm excited that this essential element in our plan has actually worked, that the insurance company has bought into our ploy, but I also have a feeling of having passed from make-believe into sudden, scary reality. Planning the operation had an element of bravado about it. But now there's no going back, no abandoning our plan as simply talk. Mihai's news opens up a variety of possibilities to me, the chance of owning my own yacht, sailing off into the Pacific – going to jail.

But I decide that I am more excited than daunted. Everything is coming together at last; there's a million dollars waiting, some of it, plus a yacht, for me.

'That's great Mihai, really great.'

* * *

He is giving me a ride to LAX international airport in Los Angeles. We're late, Mihai having arrived to pick me up at ten in the morning. My flight leaves at eleven, and we have some distance to go along the massive complex of LA freeways. Mihai received a $34 500 insurance cheque a few days ago for the loss of his car, and I am off to see whether *Recluse* is as good as the promise of her photo. At last we have the money to buy the boat.

Though I have travelled more than a third of the way around the world by boat and motor vehicle, this is the first time I have flown. I conceal my excitement from Mihai, and instead deport myself like the sophisticated world traveller that I figure he should perceive me to be.

But my carefully cultivated insouciance is soon shattered as we run into a traffic jam. I begin to sweat, both of us cursing as we crawl slowly past the wreckage of an accident. By the time we approach the huge spider-shaped terminal of LAX international it is almost eleven and I am a heap of discomposed nerves.

Without any hope, I run into the terminal building only to discover that a bomb threat has delayed all flights. I secretly thank whichever fruitcake or terrorist phoned in the message.

Thirty minutes later I'm in the air, whizzing through the stratosphere at a speed that covers as much distance in one hour as the average sailing boat travels in four or five days. I'm off to see my new boat. Jetting over the Pacific, an international man of crime. This is exhilarating stuff.

* * *

Steven Henshaw from Calley Yachts meets me at Honolulu airport. He's dressed casually in shorts and a plain sports shirt, a pleasant contrast to the loud Hawaiian garb worn by most of the tourists. He's in his mid-thirties and reminds me of Paul McCartney, probably because of his mop-like haircut.

We climb into Steven's rented car, leaving the airport and its exotic staff, the women with flowers in their hair and soft-voiced 'alohas' handing tourists leis, and grass-skirted men playing ukulele welcomes. It's a sort of conveyor-belt tourism: whip them in full of enthusiasm and excited bonhomie, and then whip them out full of sunburn and wilted as their leis.

We travel along a road with lofty green peaks on the left visible over the tops of the skyscrapers of Honolulu. On the right lies the inky blue Pacific, fronted by white beaches and coral reef. Despite its small size, Oahu is an island of magnificence. The cars and buildings are all modern American, but against such a lush and tropical background they seem especially vivid and interesting.

Recluse is in a marina called the Ala Wai Yacht Harbor. It's on the south side of the island, next to the famous Waikiki Beach, a few miles from the centre of Honolulu. My first sight of the boat confirms everything that the photographs have inspired in me.

She is lovely.

She sits tethered like a thoroughbred racehorse; her every line, tall elegant limbs and taut sinews evince her longing to be at sea. She is beamy, with rakish lines, a glossy white hull covering her strong wooden bones. A thing of beauty fulfilling every dream I have ever cherished in a yacht.

Steven has the keys from the owner, Jim Johnson, who lives in Los Angeles. We step on board and go below, and I explore the vessel with a proprietary yearning.

Steven starts the engine, a three-cylinder Bukh diesel, smelly and massively proportioned, belying the small horsepower it delivers. The engine, I know, has one important redeeming feature, though. It is an extremely reliable type of motor.

'Would you like to take her out?' Steven asks. I'm unsure whether he's nervous to take control of the vessel himself or whether he has perceived my longing. Or maybe he is simply a clever salesman, hooking a customer by creating an early sense of ownership.

'Yes. Sure.' I nod quickly, keen but nervous. I've never actually driven a boat from its mooring before.

I back her out carefully, the engine throbbing to my commands, and the graceful bow swings away from the dock. We move slowly between the other yachts, and as we reach the channel that leads to the sea I ease the throttle open.

She picks up speed happily and I begin to relax, past the tight corners and protruding yachts that pose a threat to my beautiful new lady. And then suddenly and without warning she turns and heads for the rocks lining the sea wall.

'Shit!' I spin the wheel frantically and watch as she responds with agonising slowness. Her bow creeps back, turning away from the rocks, and my heart starts to slide back into my chest, and then with amazing rapidity she whips around and heads towards the other sea wall. Oh fuck.

Steven is staring with stupefaction at my crazy navigation, and briefly I panic, not knowing whether I should try to bring her back on course with the wheel again or try to stop her suicidal rush towards the black rocks with the engine. Instinct tells me that the helm will not be sufficient, and I wrench the throttle and gear control back into astern, reversing the engine at maximum power.

Black smoke billows out from under the stern, and the throbbing of the wildly revving motor is joined by a juddering as the propeller throws a boiling wash out along the starboard side of the boat.

She slides to a halt, her bow no more than five feet from the rocks, and then begins to move astern. I ease the throttle back with a shaky hand and let her reverse slowly away from the evil-looking rocks.

'What's happening?' Alarm has raised the broker's voice several octaves. The anxiety on his face reflects my own feelings of mystified shock.

'I don't know.' My own voice betrays me with a slight squeak. 'I think something's wrong with the steering.'

Recluse has come to a halt in mid-channel, and with the engine in neutral I climb out of the cockpit and move aft, looking back to see if a rope, or something else – a submarine, maybe – has attached itself to us. I quickly realise the cause of our near-shipwreck.

'It's the self-steering,' I say to Steven, who has joined me. 'Look.'

I point to the blade of the rudder hanging from the stern. It is an auxiliary rudder, controlled by the wind vane that allows the boat to be steered by the wind. The big blade is moving idly, swinging freely.

'It needs to be locked, otherwise the tab on the back of it will make it swing around and steer the boat,' I explain, reaching down and inserting the pin that locks it into a central position.

'Well, phew, that was close,' Steven says, looking somewhat happier now that we know the problem has a simple solution.

'Yes. You're right.' I'm also relieved. 'I nearly wrote the boat off on the rocks before we even bought her. That would have been a fine mess.'

'Hmm, well fortunately she's well insured. She's actually insured for more than the owner is asking for her. But of course I wouldn't have got my commission,' he adds with a grin.

We carry on out with no further mishaps, and once clear of the breakwater Steven and I pull the sails up. I steer her through various points of sailing, testing her upwind capabilities, sheeting her hard into the wind so that she leaps over the waves with water streaming over her leeward scuppers. I hoist various sails, and try the self-steering apparatus, tacking and gybing with Waikiki Beach and Diamond Head providing a picturesque backdrop. Eventually, we return her to her berth.

* * *

Steven ties off the bow line and walks back towards me.

'Well, what do you think?' he asks. It's a superfluous question; I have been singing the vessel's praises ever since we turned to come back in.

'She's perfect. We're going to buy her, for sure,' I say, conviction lending me an authority that transcends my true status. 'As soon as we get back I'll tell Mihai he should make an offer.'

Steven drives me back to the airport, where I have a couple of hours to kill before my flight at eight thirty that night. At the check-in counter I hand over my ticket, made out to Robert Greene.

'Could I see your identification, please?' the attendant asks politely.

My mind goes blank, and then heaves itself back into action like a cornered rat. I have no identification verifying my existence as Robert Greene. My passport says Robert Fridjhon, and we have not tried to establish a false written identity for me. We hadn't anticipated that the airlines would check identification on a domestic flight, so we decided not to use my real name to avoid leaving any trails.

'I ... I think I've left it in my other bag.' My lameness shouts guilt, and the gesture I make towards the door leading out of the concourse seems ridiculous even to me.

'Well, we need to see it,' she says firmly. 'We cannot issue you with a boarding pass without it.'

'Hang on, please,' I say, hoping that the cold draining sensation on my face is not a visible whitening. 'I'll go and get it. It's with a friend.'

I turn and walk away, leaving my ticket open in front of her, and exit the airport building with no plan except that I must escape before I am thrown into the airport jail, or wherever they place felons such as me. There is a bus returning to Honolulu, and I board it, thinking furiously and clutching the only bag I've brought, a small holdall that Mihai lent me, containing my toothbrush and one change of clothing.

There's no way I can ask Steven for help, and I know nobody else on the island. I check my wallet to see how much money I have, and discover $145. This I know is approximately the cost of a ticket back to Los Angeles.

I get off the bus in Honolulu and walk around aimlessly while I try to figure out what to do. Hopefully I can buy another ticket tomorrow in my own name – assuming I have enough money – and then check in again when the woman who dealt with me isn't there.

I can't pay for a room for the night in case it doesn't leave me with enough to buy the ticket. Expecting a meal on the plane, I haven't eaten, and I dare not spend any money on food. Somewhere near one o'clock in the morning, my stomach growling, I spy a dark patch of land, bush-covered and deserted, and decide to sneak under the foliage, hoping I can rest without being disturbed for vagrancy. I'm sleepy now, tired by the excitement of the day and worry over my predicament.

So I crawl in, pushing through the dark leaves and branches until I am far enough in not to be observed in the daylight. I find a space clear of twigs and stones, and set up the holdall as a pillow. The night is warm, so I won't need a cover.

Suddenly I spy a shoe, its toe pointing upwards. As my eyes adjust to the dark I make out that it is attached to a trousered leg.

Oh no. There's a dead body here with me.

A sinking feeling, part revulsion, part fear, and also part frustration at the disturbance to my rest, settles over me and I crawl slowly forward to investigate.

I am nearly upon the leg, my gaze riveted on the shoe, when suddenly something, a primal instinct maybe, causes me to look up.

About three feet from my face is another face, eyes glowing in the dark and fixed intently upon me. And then I catch sight of something else: a knife, its blade reflecting the starlight, clutched in a hand that is poised to attack.

'Oh fuck. Oh shit. I'm sorry. It's … it's okay. Listen, I'm sorry, I thought you were dead,' I stammer. Slowly, I start retreating, trying not to provoke an attack with any sudden moves. My heart is hammering. 'I'll go find somewhere else to sleep. It's okay, I'm going now. I'm … I'm just leaving – okay?'

There is no answer from the figure, but his eyes never leave mine. Mine never leave the knife.

'I was just looking for somewhere to sleep,' I croak. 'But you can have this bush. Really. I'll go find another one.'

There is still no answer, and I suddenly realise that he might be just as frightened as I am. I continue to crawl backwards through the bush, never taking my eyes off the man. Fear could be the strongest motive for him to attack me, so I'm being ultra-careful. He has still not uttered a sound, but I keep talking all the while, making sure that he understands that I am leaving.

Then I grab my holdall and hightail it out of there.

Later, clammy with sweat, hungry and nervous, I crawl behind a wall and try to sleep next to some empty drums. The perception I have of myself as a worldly member of the crime fraternity is at an all-time low.

5

Mihai doesn't seem to share my enthusiasm. I've been back in Los Angeles for two days now, having bought another ticket in Hawaii and eluded the posse pursuing me, and this is my first meeting with him since my return. I thought he'd be keen to hear the verdict on *Recluse* but he's been strangely reticent, eventually agreeing to meet me after claiming various business commitments.

'She's beautiful, Mihai,' I tell him. 'Perfect for our plan.'

'Sure, Rob, I understand you like the boat. But I think we need to go a bit carefully here. Let me think about it for a few days.'

'What's there to think about?' A shadow flits over my excitement.

'A few things,' he says airily, 'some things I have to consider.'

'What's to consider, Mihai? It's definitely the right boat. It's exactly what we were looking for.'

'Yeah, you may be right,' he says. 'But let's not rush into it. We have time.'

'But what if somebody else buys it?' I can hear the exasperation in my voice. Or is it desperation? We're so close now, and *Recluse* will surely be sold soon. I really want this boat, and don't see why we should wait any longer. We have the money now, from his car insurance.

'Then we'll find another one,' Mihai says.

'But why'd I go over there to see it? What was the point?'

'Look, if it's sold, Rob, we'll just find ourselves another one,' he reiterates. 'There're other boats just as good.'

'Yes, but in Hawaii? Like *Recluse*, with all the things we need? I've seen and tested her now, and it'd be such a waste of time and money if we didn't buy her. Especially when we know this is the right boat.'

'Look, I don't actually have the money at the moment. If you can tell that guy, what's his name – Henshaw? Just tell him that your boss is too busy right now to make a decision. Just hold him off for a while.'

'What d'you mean, you don't have the money?' I'm shocked. 'What about the money from the car? And from the envelopes? Where's all that cash?'

We've been addressing envelopes for over three months now, and although the demand for envelopes has dropped off over the past couple of weeks, I figure that between us Mihai and I should have made over ten grand. Mihai's kept nearly all of it, and he indicated to me before I went to Hawaii that we definitely had enough for the boat. What's happened to the money? Why, once again, is the cash mysteriously not where it's supposed to be?

'I have the bucks, but not right now.'

'What do you mean, "not now"?' I press him. 'Where's it gone?'

'Something came up,' he says vaguely. 'I do have the money, but it's just not available right now. Don't worry about it.'

'Don't worry about it?' I'm incredulous. 'How can I not worry about it? I'm involved here as well, you know. You told me you have the money and now all of a sudden you don't. What's going on? First you push your car over a cliff without telling me, and now this. What else are you involved in? What's going on?' My voice has gone brittle as my anger starts to take hold.

'Look, Rob, it's nothing to get upset about.' Mihai has a hard glint in his eyes – and again I realise that his soft exterior is deceptive. 'I'll get the money, but not immediately. Just be patient, okay?'

'No, it's not okay, Mihai. Where is the money?'

'The money is safe, but right at the moment it's locked up in another deal that I have going with the Priest. Just give me a couple of weeks.'

'What sort of deal?'

'A really lucrative one. I can't tell you more at the moment.'

'I'm beginning to totally lose my trust in you, Mihai.' I pin him with my gaze. 'You're not being straight with me. You're doing things behind my back, and I don't like it at all.'

'Just wait, Rob,' he tells me again. 'I'll have the money soon and then we can go ahead. Just be patient. Keep your cool.'

But I am furious, my anger exacerbated by my sense of having no control over things. I'm frustrated that we may lose the boat and there is nothing I can do about it. And I'm not even sure whether Mihai has spent the money or is telling me the truth about it being tied up in something else. What else is he involved in? I can feel distrust poisoning my mind, and serious flaws developing in our nice foolproof little plan, cracks like those that appear on an ice-covered pond just before you fall through.

'Listen, Mihai,' I keep my voice carefully controlled. 'If you don't tell me what's going on, I'm out of it. The whole plan. I'm walking away from it.' I'm not sure if I really mean this, because I still feel committed to our scheme, but I need to know what's happening.

My partner stares at me for a long, solid moment. Then he looks away thoughtfully.

'Okay, Rob,' he says at last. 'I'm going to let you in on what I'm doing. But you have to keep your trap shut. All right?'

A prickle of concern digs into me. I get the feeling that whatever it is that Mihai's involved in, I'm not going to like it. But it's too late now.

'Don't mention anything to Pete and Mike, or anybody else. You understand?'

The concern digs deeper. 'I'm not going to tell anyone.'

He narrows his gaze. 'D'you know what PCP is? Angel dust?'

'Yes.' I've heard Pete and Mike talk about it a couple of times, a kind of drug. 'It makes you high.'

'That's right. It's the "peace pill" – phencyclidine. We manufacture it,' he says, rather proudly. 'We've got a guy who knows how to make it. Alex. You met him, he's our chemist. He's one of the few people in the world who knows the formula. It's not easy to make.'

'Who's "we"?' But this is the wrong question. It's not what I want to know. 'I mean, what the fuck are you doing involved with phency... with drugs, Mihai? Are you crazy?'

'No. No, I'm not.' He carries on rapidly. 'The Priest owns this operation. He's real clever, knows exactly what he's doing. He's been making the dust for some time now, and he's made lots of money. The stuff sells for a fortune.'

'I thought you said he became rich with the religious stuff?' I'm battling to come to grips with this new revelation. I feel a slow, draining sensation inside myself, a loss of everything gathered from these past three months.

'Well yeah, sure, he made some money from that as well, but not nearly as much as from the PCP. There are some problems with that religious operation anyway, which is why we haven't had much work to do there the last two weeks. But this thing with the angel dust is much better. We'll make much more out of it.'

'So, what do you have to do with it?'

'I've invested a lot of money in it,' he says. 'I'm partners with him now.'

'For fuck's sake, Mihai.' My voice sounds strangely hoarse. 'This is really stupid. Getting involved in drugs. That's crazy.'

'Uh-uh. No, it's not. We're going to make so much cash from this I'd be crazy *not* to be involved.'

I hesitate as if for a landmark moment. 'Yeah, well, I don't want to be.' I've made a decision.

'You don't understand. I'm not asking you to be involved.' His tone changes, becomes colder and more distant. 'This is my deal. The boat thing is something else, something apart from this operation.'

'No, Mihai, *you* don't understand. I mean, it's everything I don't want to be involved in. Not our insurance scam or this drug thing.' I also feel cold and distant, or maybe just a desire to be distant.

Now it's Mihai's turn to stare. 'But we'll have the money, Rob. When we get paid for the drugs we can go ahead and buy the boat. We have the policies now, and soon we'll have everything we need to go ahead with our plan.'

'No, Mihai, I just want out.'

'Rob, if it's about the money we can discuss your share. You can have a third plus the boat.'

'No, I don't care about that. It's not about the money.'

'But after everything we've put into this, everything we spoke about, sailing around the world on your own boat. Are you just going to walk away from it all?'

'Yes. Too much has gone wrong, the FBI, the car. I want out of the whole thing.'

He has a similar look to the way I feel now – sad. 'If that's the way you feel, I guess.' He shrugs and looks away, out the window. 'Shit, Rob ...'

'I'm sorry, Mihai.'

6

My ex-partner tries to change my mind over the next few days, but I'm adamant. I no longer want anything to do with this. It's over for me. Finished. I just want to carry on with my life as before, regain the freedom I had before I met him. I want to leave, forget about drugs and everything else, get out of LA and head on up to San Francisco, as per my original plan. But I have a problem. I'm almost flat broke – all the money I earned addressing envelopes was put towards our scheme. Or invested in drugs, as I'm now aware. Mihai doesn't have the money to pay me back what I earned, and I don't have any cash coming in any more, since the envelope work has now dried up.

Mihai phones me one morning.

'Hey, Rob, watcha doing?' We try to maintain a friendly civility, though his continued efforts at re-recruiting me have put a bit of a strain on our friendship.

'Not much,' I say. 'Hanging out.' And wondering what he's going to come up with now. Also wondering whether it's worth just writing off the money he said he'd give back to me when they got paid for the drugs, and just go with the few dollars I have left. But it'd be a lot easier if he repaid the money, which is why I'm not hitting the road again just yet.

'Listen, Rob, I gotta go meet someone. It's the guy we sold the PCP to. I think we might be able to get the money now. We're supposed to be meeting the guy who owes it to us, and I might be able to pay back what I owe you now.'

'Oh yes?' That'll be good.

'Yeah, but listen, I want you to come with us. Come see I haven't been bullshitting you about where the money is.'

'Why me, Mihai? It's got nothing to do with me.' Apart from the fact that some of it is my money, of course. 'I mean, I believe you, so why do you want me to go?' I'm trying to get out of it, but politely. I need the cash.

'You remember George and Vlazo? At Dmitrievich's house?'

'Yes, sure, I remember them.'

'George is the guy who normally deals with our buyer, but he's in Europe right now trying to sort out the religious operation. So Vlazo has to go. The Priest asked me to go along to keep an eye on him.'

'So?' I don't like the sound of where this is heading.

'So I need you to come with me. I don't trust Vlazo, and I need someone for support. Someone I can rely on. Vlazo's a fuckhead.'

Crap. This I really don't want to do. I don't trust Vlazo either and I don't like him. But, more to the point, I don't like drugs. And why should I get involved in this?

'I know nothing about this, Mihai, and I really don't want to know, either.'

'Please, Rob. I'm asking you because I don't have anybody else I can trust. I'm a bit nervous about Vlazo because he goes off half-cocked all the time, and also we don't really get on. I just need someone with me, on my side, you know?'

'Yes, but I don't want to get involved. This has nothing to do with me.'

'Well, actually it does. I'm doing this so I can pay you back, Rob. So I can get the money for you that I said I would give to you. Some of it is your money.'

This is a blatant attempt at obfuscation, as well as persuasion. Maybe some of it *is* my money, but it wasn't supposed to be in drugs.

'I still don't want to go along, Mihai.'

'Please, Rob. I'm asking just this one last thing from you. With our scheme gone, I'm left hanging, still with insurance policies to pay, y'know? I'm not blaming you for abandoning our plan; that's your choice. I'm just asking for your help to get our money back.'

Another bit of Mihai manipulation. He could probably just cancel the two policies. But I do feel a bit bad about quitting the plan. I feel maybe I owe him something.

'Listen, Rob,' he says. 'I'm asking one last favour. I'm not trying to get you involved in anything. I just need moral support. For the sake of our friendship, please, come with me.'

Shit. Okay, I think to myself, if I do this, maybe I can get the money I'm owed from the envelopes, settle any indebtedness to Mihai, and then leave. After all, it's only a meeting about money, not a drug deal.

'All right,' I say to my friend. 'I'll go with you.'

* * *

We drive to an area of Los Angeles that I've never been to. It's out towards the mountains near the San Fernando Valley, a partially dis-used industrial site. Some low-cost housing borders the area and the streets are untidy, with scraps of refuse lying everywhere. There are no people about because it is Sunday. Mihai parks the van in a deserted street. A single car is parked in front of us, a lone token of humanity in a place of grim weekday toil. It's the kind of place that always makes me feel slightly depressed, possibly because of some vague fear that someday I might have to knuckle down and work in a place like this.

The building we're parked next to is single-storeyed, with crumbling brickwork and small windows high up in the walls. There are no indications of what takes place inside.

Mihai checks his watch, but makes no move to get out of the van. I assume we're early. About five minutes later a car pulls up behind us. We exit the van as Vlazo climbs out of the car.

'What's 'e doing here?' are his first words, as he points a finger at me. It's a rude greeting, but I'm not about to tell him so.

'He's come with me,' Mihai says. 'He's okay, we're doing some other stuff together and also he works for Dmitrievich. I trust him.'

Vlazo stares at me and I stare back.

'Let's go in,' Mihai says, maybe to distract Vlazo. We head towards the building.

'Where's the nigger?' Vlazo asks as we enter.

'Bainesfield? He'll be here,' Mihai replies.

I assume Bainesfield is the man we're about to meet.

Inside, there's a small untidy office with one occupant, one of the men I met a while back at the Priest's house. Alex, if I remember correctly. Mihai reintroduces us and I shake the man's hand.

Vlazo asks him the same question about 'the nigger'. I decide that I really do dislike this man.

'He'll be here soon. Maybe he's a little late, but he'll be here. Don't worry. He'll come. Why don't you make yourself comfortable?' Alex seems a bit nervous, chattering to cover his unease. He motions towards two chairs that don't look too comfortable to me. Vlazo ignores him, and in fact all of us, as Mihai and Alex begin to talk about unrelated topics. Through a window on the inside wall I can see into what must be the laboratory. A long bench against the wall contains beakers, test tubes, pipettes and rubber hoses. Strange-coloured liquids are contained in glass vats along a shelf. In the centre of the room is a contraption on a table: two large glass containers connected with pipes, Bunsen burners, what looks like a burette, and some copper cylinders. This, I suppose, is where the angel dust is made.

A car pulls up outside, and a moment later a tall black man enters the office. He has an Afro hairstyle and a thin goatee, and snappy shoes peer from under his wide bell-bottoms. I'm intrigued by the Afro; in South Africa, the black guys wear their hair short.

'Hey, Bainesfield, how're you doing?' Alex greets the newcomer. 'This is Vlazo and Rob. You know Mihai.' The new man and Mihai nod at each other. I wonder whether Bainesfield is his first or last name.

I shake hands with the drug dealer. Vlazo doesn't shake hands, or smile, or even nod. Maybe it's his racism, but it's hard to tell since he seems to dislike everybody. Mihai walks to the other side of the desk and seats himself, and Bainesfield sits in the only other chair.

Vlazo moves forward and hefts a hip onto the corner of the desk, so that he now looks down at the black man. Alex and I stand near the door, as there is nowhere else to sit. There is an uncomfortable silence as we wait for someone to speak.

'So, what's up, man?' Bainesfield asks eventually, addressing Mihai.

'Well, we've come to talk about what you owe us,' my friend replies.

'George says …'

'We 'ere for the money. It is time for you to give us the money,' Vlazo interrupts suddenly in a hard, flat voice. 'You pay us what you owe us. Now.'

Mihai shoots him a look to shut him up and opens his mouth again, but Bainesfield beats him to it, his face hardening as he answers Vlazo.

'Hey, I explained all this, I don't have the money. Not yet. I tol' George this already, man. I'll pay you when I get the cash.'

'You tell us this weeks before. We give you the drugs and you sell a long time ago. Now we want the money,' Vlazo insists.

'No, man, I haven't sold the stuff. There's lots of cops on the streets at the moment, and my boys are laying low. Sales are quiet and we're waiting for the heat to settle again.'

'Yeah, but we need to have some cash,' Mihai chips in. 'A payment, at least.'

'I don't have any cash just now, Mihai my man. I gotta pay my boys. I got expenses, you know. I'll pay you soon as things loosen up.'

'Fuck your expenses,' Vlazo says. I feel Alex twitch next to me. 'We got expenses too. We need our money.'

'Hey, you not listening to me, man.' The black man stares up at the little Russian. 'I done tol' you, I ain't got the money at the moment. You jus' have to wait, man.'

'You not listening to me, man, I done tol' you too.' Vlazo's parody sounds weird in his Russian accent. 'We want our money now. We tired of this fucking waiting.'

'Well, I just ain't got it.' Bainesfield is unconcerned, dismissive almost. 'So you'll have to wait some fucking more now, won't you?'

Vlazo shifts himself away from the desk. He faces the Afro-man, arms hanging loose, but his hands turned out slightly in a way that carries threat. 'You get the money, my friend' – low and venomous now – 'we give you the drugs, you sell them and now we want our money. We not waiting no more.' He has somehow made himself squarer, more stocky. His head is settled back on his shoulders and his chin thrust upwards. I feel uneasy.

'Hey, I deal with George, man,' Bainesfield replies, aggressive now in turn. 'We got a deal, him and me, so you can jes' fuck off.'

'George knows we're here,' Mihai interjects quickly, trying to calm things down. 'We just want to know when you can pay us.'

The two antagonists concentrate fully on each other, ignoring Mihai.

'I tell you now.' Vlazo leans forward. 'You don't pay us the money, you in big shit, you ass'ole.'

'From you, little man?' Bainesfield is not at all cowed by the Russian. 'What're you going to do? Sue me?'

'I'll fucking shoot you!' Vlazo shouts now. 'I put a bullet in your 'ead, ass'ole. You want know what I do? I kill you, motherfucker!'

'Hey, cool it, guys.' Mihai holds out his hands. 'Just keep cool. Let's talk about this calmly. No need to get excited.'

By now I'm feeling really nervous.

'You fucking short-shit prick, don' you come threaten me like that, man,' Bainesfield says, again ignoring Mihai. 'You keep your fucking mouth shut you can't put some respeck in it.' He gives a short laugh. 'You too fucking small man, tha's your problem. Makes you too excitable.'

'You wan' see me excited?' Vlazo's voice is ominously low. 'You don't give us the money now I show 'ow excited I am, you mother-fucking ass'ole.'

Bainesfield grins. I have to admire his cool. The black man has adopted an almost languid pose.

'Calm down, honkey, I get the money later. If you lucky,' he says. 'But I don't take no shit from you, you hear?'

'Me a monkey? *You* the monkey,' Vlazo rants. I'd be amused by his mishearing of honkey – but for the fact that he now has a gun in his hand. I didn't see him pull the lethal automatic that he's now waving in front of Bainesfield. 'What about I give you some shit now, nigger?'

My gut hollows at the sight of the weapon, but Bainesfield remains calm. His face stretches and his smile disappears, but he remains cool.

'You got a gun? You think it scares me, man?' He gets out of the chair. 'George won't like this, you know, you being stupid, waving that thing around.' The drug dealer stands squarely in front of Vlazo. 'So you put it away now, little man.'

'Yeah, Vlazo,' Mihai urges. 'Get rid of the gun.'

Alex is silent next to me, but I can sense his fear. I'm beginning to hope that Vlazo might obey, that he'll come to his senses at the lack of support from his colleagues. I'm not too reassured, though, by the way Bainesfield is facing up to him.

Vlazo pulls the trigger. The bang isn't that loud. Bainesfield staggers back and his expression crumbles. He has a strange, sad look on his face. Vlazo fires again, and the dealer collapses. He lies on his back with his arms spread wide and one leg twisted underneath him. Blood begins to spread around the front of his shirt.

'Oh fuck. Fuck fuck fuck. Oh shit.' Alex's face has sagged, gone grey. He is leaning into the corner, away from the spreadeagled body and Vlazo, who is standing with the weapon still trained on the bleeding man.

'Jesus fucking Christ, man, why'd you go and do that, Vlazo?' It's Mihai, his voice a high squeak, close to breaking.

'Fucking nigger.' Vlazo is staring at Bainesfield. 'Calls me the monkey. What's 'e think I do? Nothing? Dumb fucking nigger ass'ole.'

'Shit, Vlazo.' The Romanian seems to be regaining composure. 'Are you fucking crazy? What do you think you've gone and done? You've fucking killed him.'

I think he's right. I think Bainesfield is looking pretty dead. It's the first time I've ever seen a dead person, but I'm pretty sure that's what he is now. He's stopped moving and his eyes are semi-open and vacant, and his face has a peculiar slackness to it. His right hand, which was twitching and scratching at the floor a moment ago, has flopped still, and he isn't breathing any more. I feel weirdly removed from the scene, from the actuality of what has just happened.

'He call me monkey and little man,' Vlazo hisses, holding the gun aloft. He has begun pacing now, walking back and forth. 'I show him little man, fucking nigger bastard. I show him good. Fucking bastard.'

'You didn't have to shoot him,' Alex hisses.

'You think I do nothing? Fucking nigger. Fucking bastard. No pay us and call me that too, so I shoot the fucker.' It crosses my mind that he might just begin shooting the rest of us as well. The Russian seems to be in a little cocoon of his own insanity.

'Yeah, well, how's he going to pay us now, Vlazo?' Mihai asks. 'How're we going to get the money from him now?'

'Fuck the money, 'e was no going to pay us anyhow.'

'Shit, Vlazo, you can't just shoot a guy for that. Jesus Christ.'

'What about 'im?' Vlazo says suddenly, gesturing towards me with the weapon. 'What we do with 'im?'

'He's okay; he won't say anything,' Mihai says hurriedly.

Vlazo moves closer to me. He lifts the gun and aims it at my nose so that I can see down the barrel.

''Ow I know you don't go to the police, 'ey?' he says to me. 'Maybe I shoot you too. Maybe I make so you can't say nothing, eh?'

I shake my head and cast about for some sort of reply, anything at all, when Mihai steps between us. He pushes Vlazo's arm down. I relax a bit, though I still have to keep a tight hold on my sphincter.

'Leave him,' my saviour says. 'He's my friend. He works for us, for Dmitrievich.'

Vlazo pins me with a murderous glare for a long, horrible moment. Time seems suspended as my future is decided by this loony thug. I try to hold his gaze to conceal my trembling, and Mihai also stares hard at him. Eventually, the little Russian shrugs.

'You keep your mouth shut or I kill you too.'

I nod.

'What are we going to do now?' Alex says with a perceptible tremble in his voice.

'Get rid of 'im.' Vlazo motions towards Bainesfield.

He sends Alex out to check that no one is around, that no one has heard the shots, and then he and Mihai lug the dead man out into the street. I stand and watch as they load Bainesfield into the trunk of a dark-blue Pontiac Thunderbird. Bainesfield's vehicle.

Vlazo drives the dead man's car away, and Mihai follows in his own. I wait behind with Alex, feeling a numbed sensation of ghastly regret: at the death of a human being, at what I've been forced to witness, and mostly that I allowed Mihai to talk me into coming with him. I also feel a hollow sense of relief that the little Russian has gone – for the moment, at least.

7

For two days I'm in a dull torpor, hanging around the house depressed and unable to plan anything, waiting to be arrested.

I'm in the kitchen, staring at a pile of unwashed dishes, unwilling to tackle even this relatively small task. Pete's been away for the past two days, and Mike never bothers with the washing up.

Last night I hardly slept at all, tormented again by images of Bainesfield dying, and anguished over what to do. Should I go to the police? Is that the right course? But if I do I'll have to tell them about Mihai's involvement, and my own. I was there at a murder scene, as a kind of accessory, so how guilty am I in the legal sense? What'll happen to me? And to Mihai? Plus, I'd probably have to reveal our involvement in the insurance scam. I'm in a total funk.

The horror of Bainesfield's death keeps coming back to me, his expression when he collapsed and the way his hand kept twitching, as though calling for help. Was he aware he'd been shot? Was he aware he was dying?

I'm sick every time I think about it. The most disturbing thing about his death was its triviality. The lack of reason. One moment he was a human being with thoughts and emotions, plans and memories, and then, without any real transition, he was just dead meat, tissue waiting to decompose. There was no significance to his dying, no sense of drama. A simple bang, and his future ended. The banality of it all horrifies me.

I consider leaving, going away immediately and getting back on the road, hitch-hiking the fuck away from this place. But I've got no money and there are a few things I have to do first. I can't just leave without telling Mihai, though I feel a deep anger at what he's got me into.

And I must also contact Joanne. There's no way I can allow her to come out here now; it's too dangerous and I don't know what I'd be getting her into. But I'm loath to take this step. I desperately want to see her again, to feel the comfort of a normal, sane companion and take refuge in her warmth. I know that if I make the call I'm unlikely ever to see her again, but I have to break this connection. It'd be morally wrong to bring Joanne out now. I go to the phone and dial her number.

'Hello, Joanne. It's me.'

'Hi, Rob.' The sound of her voice fills me with tricky emotions, and I'm silent a while before she asks, 'How's it going? How are you? You sound … different.'

I can't help the flatness in my voice. 'I'm fine, Joanne. And you?'

'Good. And how's everything else there? What's happening?'

'That's what I'm phoning about, Joanne. It's all off. We're not going sailing any more.'

'Oh.' There is a pause. 'Why not, Rob?'

'Um, things have changed around here. Stuff's happened. The plan I was telling you about isn't going to happen.'

'So … what are you going to do now?' She sounds a little flat now herself.

'I don't know,' I say. This is where it's difficult. I know how much she was looking forward to coming out here, us being together. 'I might still go to San Francisco. Try to get on a boat there, but I'm not sure.'

'I see.' She sounds distant. 'What about us? D'you still want me to come out?'

'Well, it depends on what happens in San Francisco.' I dodge her question. 'I'll have to call you from there. If I find a boat for us, maybe you can still come out and join me.'

'D'you want me to?'

'Well … yes, of course, but I don't want to get your hopes up, Joanne. It depends on what I find there.'

Fifteen minutes later I put the phone down. My heart feels leaden. She sounded disappointed and hurt, but not as much as I'm feeling right now. The fact that the call was necessary is no consolation to me.

I make another call. This time to Steven at Calley Yachts.

'Um, Steven,' I say, after the usual pleasantries. 'Listen, the reason I phoned is because Mr Kranova isn't going to buy *Recluse* any more. He's given up the idea of sailing around the world. I'm sorry I kept you hanging on so long.'

There is a brief silence. When Steven speaks again he is as friendly as ever.

'That's okay, Rob. Don't worry about it,' he says. 'So, what are you gonna do now? I mean, what are *your* plans?'

I wish I knew. 'I'll probably look for a job, I guess. A boat heading down to the Pacific Islands, maybe.'

There is another pause. Through the wires connecting us, I sense the yacht broker thinking. I wait, knowing intuitively that he's about to make some sort of suggestion. Eventually, he speaks again, spacing the words out carefully.

'Would you be interested in working for us?' he asks. 'Doing some delivery work?'

This I never expected. My first reaction is one of excitement and relief at the thought of being able to escape to sea. But then I remember a hitch, a problem concerning who – or rather what – I am: Robert Fridjhon, South African, a crook-to-be, or very nearly one. Steven knows me as Robert Greene from England, and there is no way I can suddenly inform him that I was recently intent on stealing a million dollars and disappearing on the yacht he was going to sell to us. So that means I can't do yacht deliveries unless it's around the coast here, and not offshore where I'd have to show my passport. But I desperately want to go to sea, to be out in that clean, pure environment and away from my present sordid surroundings.

'Whereabouts is the delivery work?' I ask, trying to inject some enthusiasm into my voice at the same time I'm wondering how to stall him, to find a way to go, any way.

'It's from Hawaii to here,' he says. 'A forty-two-foot yawl. It's a good boat. Fast and seaworthy.'

From Hawaii? My spirits rise again at a sudden thought. I won't need my passport for this, I figure. I'll be sailing from an American port to an American port. I won't have to declare the yacht as coming from a foreign country, so I won't have to show my passport to immigration.

'Yeah sure, great, Steven,' I say, my eagerness genuine this time. 'When do you want it here?'

'Well, soon. The new owner wants to sail back as well. He hasn't sailed before, and he wants the experience. I think he's hoping that the captain will teach him to sail on the way back.'

'Yes, sure, I'll teach him,' I say. 'So, when do I go to Hawaii?'

'You can arrange that with the new owner. His name is Jack Nichols, and I'll give him your number. He'll want to talk to you.'

After I hang up I return to the stack of unwashed dishes, my spirits lifted, and raring to be on the open ocean again. Away from

Los Angeles, away from murderous Russian drug dealers, and away from the possibility of being visited by suspicious policemen. I tackle the dishes with renewed vigour, and for the first time in two days I can see the bottom of the sink where they've been lying.

* * *

The flight to Hawaii does not hold the same excitement as before. I am now a seasoned air traveller, and, also, the object of the trip does not hold the same allure as when I was about to view the boat that I had begun to consider as my own. Now the flight has a different appeal, winging me out over the Pacific Ocean where I'd so like to be, and away from Los Angeles.

The boat, *Windsong*, is in the same marina as *Recluse*. It's a pretty yawl, speedy-looking and heavily varnished, though the varnish is patchy and in need of redoing. She is not as beautiful as *Recluse* but she's a nice enough boat, and I feel a twinge of envy and regret when I spy the shape of *Recluse*'s bow through the rigging of the other craft in the marina.

I call out and a man emerges from below. He is in his mid- to late thirties, tall, with sharp features and an outdoor tan. I introduce myself and he invites me aboard. Jack Nichols and I have had one fairly brief telephonic conversation, and I recognise his slow Texan drawl. As I climb up he tells me that he only just arrived that morning.

I see immediately that the condition of the yacht is not as good as Steven has led me to believe. She is dirty and neglected, and the air inside her cabin is musty, with a bilgy smell of old diesel oil, mould and rancid sea water. It's obvious that she has not been looked after while sitting in Hawaii. In fact, as I soon discover, *Windsong* is far from ready to go to sea. The engine smokes, the compass is cracked, both primary winches are rusted inside and immovable, and one of the cockpit locker lids has come away from its hinges. Some of her gear is missing, and we find that many items, such as bilge pumps, don't work.

When I dutifully, if rather reluctantly, inform my proud new boss that *Windsong* is not quite as shipshape and seaworthy as she should be, he accepts it with equanimity, having already discovered that Hawaii itself holds much attraction. The place is full of women – beautiful Hawaiian maidens, exotic Japanese ladies and mainland-America girls – all hanging around the marina in sexy T-shirts and cut-off jeans, or bikini tops and sarongs. Jack figures that the plethora of women more than makes up for any delay in going to sea. And I'm happy about anything that delays my return to LA.

So we settle into a routine that is somewhat less than onerous. Jack goes off every day to tour the island or to pick up women on the beach, while I fix the boat. I repair pumps, free off the winches and re-coat the varnish. Jack is enthusiastic about the changes to his boat and buys additional items, such as a self-steering system that I install for him. This extends the re-fit period, but neither of us is particularly concerned. There are many attractions that make our stay here in Hawaii pleasurable.

At night we hit the Waikiki strip, behind Waikiki Beach, which is filled with bars, clubs and, of course, women. Jack occasionally insists I drop the work and go exploring Oahu with him. Living together and working together, I soon come to regard Jack as my friend, even though there is a fifteen-year age difference between us. Life here is fun, and slowly – with many interruptions – we prepare *Windsong* for the passage back to Los Angeles.

* * *

About a month has passed since we first arrived in Honolulu. The work is near completion, and it is time to start stocking the vessel with food and supplies. I approach Jack at the stern of *Windsong*, where he is busy with the new flag he has purchased – the ensign for his yacht – and show him a sheet of paper.

'Jack, I've made a list of staples and dry foods we need, the quantities and type of stuff,' I say. 'If we go to that big supermarket we can figure out what else we need to buy.'

Jack holds the flag without answering. He's been trying to tie it to the flagpole, and I can see that he is struggling with the knots. He glances at the list, and then pulls on the flag halyard. There is a strange, evasive air about him.

'Rob, I've been thinking,' he says after a while, as the flag falls off the pole. 'I don't really see the point of me going back to LA.'

I nod slowly, although he isn't actually looking at me. I feel like the flag – let down. But this not entirely unexpected; I've begun to suspect from Jack's attitude that something like this might happen.

'I mean, why should I leave all this?' He gestures towards three girls walking past, their cute derrières swinging in their bikinis. Tossing another glance at me, he says, 'Hell, Rob, I can leave from here whenever I'm ready to go cruising, and this is a far better place to be than crappy old Marina del Rey, don't you think?'

'Yes, sure, Jack. I understand. I'd do the same, I guess,' I say as I watch his awkward attempt at retying the flag. 'More fun out here, that's for sure.'

I would probably feel the same in his shoes. However, it does put me out of a job, which means that I'll have to return to the mainland, and without the money I was to be paid for sailing *Windsong* back.

'I'm sorry about the delivery,' he says, tugging the knot closed, 'but, oh well, *c'est la vie*. I'm sure you can another one.' Then he pulls the halyard and the ensign falls off once again. He rips irritably at the flag as though it is being difficult on purpose.

'That's okay. Something'll come up, I guess.' I contemplate the next step in my life. A return to crime-ridden Los Angeles, I suppose. I'll have to phone Steven at Calley Yachts and inform him of this development. He may have something for me to do here before I fly back. Anything just to keep me here in Hawaii.

'You're welcome to stay on board *Windsong* for a few more days until you go back or whatever.' Jack tosses the flag onto the deck and faces me squarely – relieved, I guess, at my easy compliance. 'I'll pay you for the work you've done.'

'Thanks, Jack.' I'm careful not show him my disappointment.

* * *

Later that day, I go to the marina office and make the call to Calley Yachts.

'Steven, hi. Listen, Jack Nichols has decided to stay in Hawaii. He doesn't want the boat back in LA any more, so I may as well come back. Is there anything you want me to do here before I fly back?'

There is a silence on the other end.

'Yeah, Rob. I think there is.' Something lifts in me – a tiny hope, perhaps. Maybe I won't have to go back immediately. 'You remember that boat you and your friend were going to buy? *Recluse*? Well, the owner is thinking of bringing her back to LA. He can't sell it there, and we've told him there's a much better chance of selling it here. Maybe you can sail her back to Los Angeles.'

'Really? You serious, Steven?' I say, my tiny hope transformed into major excitement.

'Yeah, we've been talking about it. I mentioned you bringing it back to the States, but thought it might be a while before you got here. This could now suit us all very well.'

I'll say this could suit us all very well. Me especially. This is good; I'll stay here for a couple more weeks getting *Recluse* ready, pick up some crew, and then sail her back. She's a much better boat than *Windsong* and, much as I like Jack, my decisions will now be my own.

'When will you know?' I'm eager now.

'I'll phone the owner immediately. If you're available to bring the boat back now I'm sure he'll want you to. Call me back later and I'll let you know.'

Every time I've walked past *Recluse* I've viewed her with regret. Now at least I'll be sailing on her. I decide to tell Mihai.

'Hey, Mihai, what's up?' I say when he picks up the phone.

'Rob, shit, I've been hoping you'd call. Are you still sailing that boat back for the brokers?'

'Yes. Well, another one. Believe it or not I'm sailing *Recluse* back.' I'm aware of the urgent way he asked the question, so I ask, 'Why, Mihai? What's going on?'

'Just call me back.'

He gives me a safe number and when I phone him back, this is what he tells me: 'There's some bad shit going on back here. Alex has been killed.'

'What?' I feel a weird sense of disconnection.

'Alex was killed here the other day. He was shot.'

Alex? Killed? Oh shit. I'm almost afraid to ask the next question.

'How? I mean, do you think that it had something to do with Vlazo? With what happened to … you know?'

'I dunno.' He sounds tense, deeply rattled. 'Yeah, I think so. Maybe. He was gunned down at his house as he was getting into his car. Maybe it was something else, but it's a bit too much of a coincidence.'

'Shit, Mihai—'

'Listen, Rob, don't come back here,' Mihai interrupts. 'If you can, you must stay out there, or get on a boat going somewhere else. I think it's become very dangerous for you here.'

'What about you? What are you going to do?'

'I'll be okay. I don't think Vlazo would bump me off,' he says. 'I'm too close to Dmitrievich and Vlazo knows I wouldn't say anything. But he could think you're a risk. I'm not sure whether he'd have you killed or not, but just don't come back here. It's definitely not a good idea to come back.'

After I put the phone down I walk slowly towards *Recluse*. I stand and gaze at her beautiful lines and contemplate the voyage to America. I think about returning to my rather precarious life in Los Angeles and the possibility of being arrested, or worse. I think about Vlazo, and the total lack of remorse I saw in him after he shot Bainesfield. Then another thought hits me.

I can steal her.

Sure. Why not? I can steal *Recluse* and sail away. Nobody, apart from Mihai and Mary, knows who I am. And there's no way they'd rat on me. Also, I know too much about Mihai. A bubble of excitement rises in me and I look at *Recluse* with a new vision. She could be my ticket out of this mess. I could take her and sail away, for ever.

The bubble suddenly deflates when I realise what I am contemplating. Steal a yacht? I've never stolen anything from anyone before. This is different from the crime that Mihai and I were contemplating. This is stealing from an individual, not divesting some large amorphous group of insurance investors of a tiny percentage of their earnings. I feel more than a niggling shame at what I am now considering.

But then I remember what Steven told me when I almost ran *Recluse* onto the rocks. The boat's insured for more than the owner, Jim Johnson, is asking for her. And he hasn't managed to sell her here in Hawaii. If I steal her, he'll get more than his asking price and he'll also be rid of the burden of trying to sell her. And I'll get the yacht and a ticket away from America and Vlazo. Mr Johnson wants to sell her anyway and can't, so I will in fact be helping him, sort of.

Some other part of me recognises that this is bullshit – that all I'm now doing is trying to justify and rationalise this new crime; I'll still be a common thief. But I consider the facts: if I go back to America I could be killed, or arrested. These are real threats, and the comparative injury to *Recluse*'s owner is not that significant. I walk away with my mind in turmoil.

* * *

The next morning I am back at *Recluse*. I spent the night unable to sleep, flip-flopping between excitement and conscience. Will Jim Johnson agree to let me sail his boat back? Should I or shouldn't I steal it? Crime seems to be controlling me, rather than the other way around. All I've wanted since the murder is to get back to the life I had before I met Mihai. But the reality is that I have no money, no prospects in Hawaii, and no other means of escape except to sail back to Los Angeles – back into the Russian's den, as it were.

As I stare at *Recluse*, a resolution begins to form in my mind. If I can, if the delivery job comes through, she'll be mine. I'm going to take this boat. I feel a warm kernel of pleasurable excitement growing at the thought of sailing westward on *Recluse* into the pure blue of the Pacific Ocean.

I walk slowly back towards Jack's boat. As a scruffy twenty-one-year-old I don't look much like a yacht owner, but if I can somehow forge the papers that give me title to the yacht I might be able to get away with it. If I can sail far enough away before coming into contact with civilisation again, there should be no questions about my owner-ship as long as I'm in possession of some sort of paper to this effect. The sea is a vast hiding place, and there are too many ports to search them all. And besides, if I plan it right, there is a good possibility that the authorities will think the boat was lost at sea. I'll set off for the mainland as if I'm delivering the yacht, and hope they think I never made it.

The only problem with my plan is crew. If the owner of *Recluse* agrees to the delivery, I'll have to persuade him that I should sail the yacht back single-handed.

* * *

Later, sitting in a bar with Jack, excitement fills my chest like a pres-surised tank that I can barely contain. Steven has confirmed that Jim Johnson would like me to sail *Recluse* back to America, and so it looks like the fates are conspiring in my favour. I still have more hurdles to overcome, but I might actually be given the opportunity to escape on *Recluse*.

Jack clasps me on the shoulder and shouts for more beers. I try to match his cheer, but my thoughts are elsewhere. I'm dreaming of islands covered in palms, aquamarine water surrounded by coral reef. I am sitting on a golden sandy beach, watching *Recluse* as she pulls gently against her anchor chain, her hull gleaming white and her sails folded neatly along her spars. She is waiting for me, waiting for us to resume our travels together as we explore the world, heading for more distant lands and exotic ports ...

'... you think?' Jack's voice intrudes into my dreams.

'Uh, sorry, Jack. What'd you say?' With an effort, I tear my mind away.

'I said: if you don't find any crew here, will they fly crew out from the mainland?' I've told him about delivering *Recluse*. I've even begun to lay the groundwork for my plan by mentioning the lack of available crew here. The hurricane season is approaching, and most of the 'yachties' have disappeared.

'I don't know, Jack, but I've been thinking about sailing back without crew.'

Jack looks at me doubtfully.

'*Recluse* has a good self-steering system,' I explain, 'and she's a staysail ketch. She has an easy rig to manage. I can sail her solo, I'm sure.'

He raises an eyebrow, and I suspect he is wondering about my age and my capabilities.

* * *

The next day I speak to Jim Johnson on the telephone. When I mention sailing solo he hesitates only briefly before replying. 'Rob, I had a long chat to Steven Henshaw and he told me he's very impressed with you. If you honestly feel confident that you can sail back alone and that that's what you want to do, then I trust you. You do whatever you feel best.'

I feel a strong twinge of guilt at the deception I am about to commit, at the betrayal of the trust this person is offering without even having met me. Speaking to him on the phone has made me feel worse about what I am planning to do. I console myself with the thought that he will be compensated fully for the loss of his boat. I close my mind to the thought of any trauma he might suffer as a consequence of believing that it was at his instigation that I'd sailed to my supposed death. It is a small price to pay for my union with *Recluse*, and for not having to go back to Los Angeles.

I tell Jack the news, and his only comment is that I am wasting an opportunity to get some of the women around here to sail back with me.

* * *

And so I move onto *Recluse*. Although she is basically in good shape, it turns out that there are many items that need attention. I get to work immediately, but take a break every now and then to use the surfboard bungeed to the rigging to ride the waves off the Ala Wai Yacht Harbor.

The self-steering gear, probably the most important piece of equipment I will need, has frozen up at the wind-vane mechanism. The cogs won't budge and I have to loosen them slowly with a mixture of diesel and oil. Two of the halyards are frayed dangerously where they pass through the blocks at the top of the mast, so I splice new ones and pull them through. I change the oil and the filters on the engine, and then empty and flush the water tanks. I am, in fact, preparing for a much longer voyage than the 2 500 miles back to America, and I want to fix as much as I can before setting sail. The more seaworthy the boat is, the better my chances of crossing the Pacific without any problems.

I am also trying to work out how to arrange the paperwork that will identify me as the owner of the vessel. *Recluse* has no papers on board, as Jim and Steven have obviously figured I won't need them to sail back to America. In fact, I have no idea at all what ships' papers look like. I have received a letter from the owner, signed on a Calley Yachts letterhead, authorising me to take delivery of the yacht, and I am to present this to the Ala Wai harbour master and customs at Honolulu to get permission to leave.

The formalities of arriving and departing in a foreign port consist basically of getting a clearance paper at the departure port, which allows entry to the next foreign port. You're then issued an entrance paper at that port, and when you leave you hand that in and are given the next clearance. As long as you hold one of those documents, keeping the chain of paper formalities unbroken, there are no questions asked when you arrive at the next country.

My immediate problem is to get hold of a clearance paper. I don't have an entrance form for Honolulu, I don't have the boat's papers, and I can't let anybody know that I'll be sailing to Australia. There's bound to be an investigation of my departure, even if it is thought that I have been lost at sea. I have to find some way of obtaining a clearance paper without informing the authorities of the direction I'll be headed.

So I come up with a plan.

I'll assemble papers that will show I have recently finished constructing a brand-new thirty-three-foot vessel. I will call the vessel *Coracle*. This is the name of a dinghy that my parents owned when I was about seven years old. She was the first boat I sailed on. *Coracle* also has the same number of letters as *Recluse*, a fact that will come in handy later.

I will present these papers to customs in Honolulu, requesting a clearance for this vessel to sail to Australia. Because the yacht will supposedly be new and built by myself, I'll have no registration papers for it, thereby averting the need to show proof of title or an entrance certificate from when the yacht entered Hawaiian waters.

The risk is that the customs officers might come down to the vessel to inspect it, as they would normally do in a smaller harbour. If they do, they will see immediately that it is not thirty-three feet long, or new, and is in fact named *Recluse* – and I'll be busted. I'll have to rely on the fact that Honolulu is a busy port and the Ala Wai marina is some distance away, so it's unlikely that they will pay the yacht a visit.

A week later I'll present myself again at customs, after making sure that there are different officers on duty, and give them the letter from Jim Johnson allowing me to take *Recluse* out and requesting permission to leave Oahu for America.

In this way I should obtain a clearance form for a thirty-three-foot yacht headed for Australia, which by careful manipulation in a typewriter I can change to read thirty-eight-foot yacht. As long as no one tries to verify the paperwork I supply for my 'newly built' boat, and if customs don't check whether I actually leave when I say I will, I should have the requisite papers.

There are many boats sailing in and out of Hawaii, and who is going to connect a thirty-three-foot yacht called *Coracle*, headed for Australia, with a thirty-eight-foot yacht called *Recluse*, which cleared one week later for America? My plan seems foolproof.

8

One big problem that I have is money – or the lack of it. I have a little cash from Calley Yachts for expenses and a small amount in savings, but I have to prepare the yacht for a long voyage, so the money is running out fast.

Jim Johnson has sent me a cheque for $150 to buy the supplies that I need for the trip, but the problem is that I can't cash it. I need to show some sort of identification, and the only identification I have is for Robert Fridjhon. I can't leave a record of that at the bank, so the cheque is useless to me. But I need the money.

In Honolulu I find an obscure marine shop, where I buy the charts I'll need to cross the Pacific. I also find sight-reduction tables that cover the lower latitudes of my route for the sextant navigation I will have to do.

Then I go to the yacht chandler at the Ala Wai marina and buy the charts I'd need if I were really sailing back to America. I'm minimising the risk that a later investigation into my activities here might reveal my destination by finding out what charts I bought. This cuts into my budget another $110, but charts and reduction tables are an expensive necessity.

I also have another concern. My parents are aware that I'm in America, but they have no idea of where I am or what I'm doing. I am about to set off across the Pacific single-handed, and it is coming into hurricane season. If I don't make it they'll be faced forever with not knowing what became of me, and my disappearance will be an eternal anguish for them.

Thinking of this, I consider confiding in Jack. He and I are good friends now, and he has hinted at certain nefarious deeds he committed as a GI in Germany. Most of this is probably macho bravado to impress me, but these confidences – and our friendship – make me feel that I can trust him. Another reason I feel inclined to let him know of my plans is that I feel guilty at the thought of how my supposed death might upset him. I won't say anything about Vlazo or Mihai, or exactly why I have decided to steal the yacht. If I tell him what I am going to do, I can make an arrangement with him that if he doesn't hear from me within a certain period, he should tell my parents. He should send them a letter I will write, telling them about everything, so that they will know what happened to me.

There is something else as well. Maybe I can ask Jack to cash the cheque for me, and if he's asked about it later he can say it was to reimburse him for my air ticket from LA.

I have kept my alias for so long now that I almost think of myself as Rob Greene. The thought of letting go of this secret creates a sudden strong desire to do exactly that. The absolute restraints that I have imposed upon myself not to reveal my identity are breaking down. I try to control this urge, to proceed with caution and think it through, but the more I think about it the more compelled I feel to do it. Jack would not betray me, and I would feel better if he knew what really happened to me. But, most of all, if I don't make it, I want my parents to know what happened.

* * *

The next day I meet Jack for a beer at a bar called Fred's, which has become our favourite hangout. It is close to the marina, one street up from the Waikiki strip, and is used mostly by the marina crowd and local surfers. Tourists are discouraged from entering because of its dingy appearance and its lack of a Hawaiian-sounding name such as 'Aloha Bar'. This suits us fine.

Jack has been going on about sailing, describing what he's gleaned recently from reading and a couple of offshore trips. Yachting is all about experience and knowledge. Actual physical skill – though necessary in yacht racing, for example – is not as important as knowledge. Every yachtie tries to out-knowledge other yachties, or out-experience them – sailing on bigger boats, bigger distances, or bigger seas. Jack has taken to this competitive aspect of sailing with remarkable rapidity. And although sailing is probably the thing I love most in life, I'm finding his pontification irritating. So to change the subject, I decide to take advantage of a moment when his attention is diverted by ordering more drinks, and tell him about my plan.

'Jack, listen. I've got something I have to tell you.' My portentous statement has no effect on him. He is busy clicking his fingers at a waitress. Feeling that he should be agog at my impending bombshell, I control the urge to repeat the announcement that I have an announcement to make.

'I'm not Robert Greene,' I say to him.

'You're what?' he says with a small grin as if this is some sort of joke. 'What do you mean, you're not Robert Greene?'

'Jack, I'm not who I say I am. I've been lying to everyone.' I feel a strange rush as I say this, a burning of bridges. 'My name is Robert Fridjhon and I'm South African.'

Jack gives me a puzzled stare.

'It's a long story.' I relate some of the details of Mihai's plan, leaving out incriminating facts like his name and any reference to his car and the San Fernando Valley, and particularly to a murder in a drug laboratory. Jack nods and smiles when I tell him that I was involved in a plot to rip off an insurance company. I've thought carefully about what I'll say to Jack, not wanting to reveal too much of Mihai's scheme, but allowing him enough to understand why I assumed an alias, and how I've become stuck with it.

'So you had to give up the whole idea?' he replies. 'What a pity. It sounds like it was a good plan. The insurance companies are just a bunch of fucking fat cats.'

Though this is not quite the way I'd put it, he is echoing some of my own sentiments. Encouraged, I continue. 'Yes, well, I'm doing something else now. But I want you to promise that you won't say anything to anyone. You have to keep quiet about all of this.' It's a bit late for such an entreaty, I realise.

Jack leans forward and shakes his head. 'You can trust me, Rob,' he says in a low, earnest voice. 'This is between you and me. You're my buddy, I won't tell a soul.'

I hold his gaze a moment longer, for effect.

'I'm going to steal *Recluse*.'

Jack's expression is gratifyingly astonished. 'You serious?'

I nod.

'How?' he asks.

'I'm just going to sail her west, to Australia. I've been planning this for a while now. Nobody knows who I am, apart from my friend in Los Angeles and his wife – and now you. The authorities will think I've been lost at sea, and even if they're suspicious they'll never find me.'

Jack's reaction is as I hoped. He is immediately encouraging.

'Fucking A-one, Rob. Go for it!' He grins at me with an air of connivance. 'Take the boat, sail away with it. Hell, the owner gets his money and the only people who lose out are the fucking insurers. Do it, man, I wish to fuck I could go with you.'

There's admiration in his voice. I knew I was right to tell him. How could I allow a friend like this to think that I'd died?

We discuss my plans, and I tell him that I'll contact him when I reach the other side of the Pacific. We agree we'll stay in contact, and maybe when he's ready to sail he'll find me, and then we can cruise together on our yachts. Jack assures me that any help I might need from him will be immediately forthcoming.

I also ask him to inform my parents of my fate if he doesn't hear from me. I tell him I'll write a letter giving them the details of my plan and also his name if they want to know more. And I'll ask them not to institute an official inquiry.

* * *

Jack agrees to cash the cheque, so I have another $150 to buy supplies. There may even be a small amount left over for when I reach the other side of the Pacific.

Strangely, I feel more guilt about taking this money from *Recluse*'s owner than I do about stealing his boat. Knowing that I'm not going to use the money for its intended purpose makes me feel like a petty thief. However, not only do I desperately need the cash, but it would also look suspicious if I didn't take it. I even wonder briefly if it would be possible to return the money anonymously to him at some future date.

I begin to assemble some papers that I hope to present to customs as proof that I have just built a brand-new yacht. Jack has lent me his typewriter and allows me to see the bill of sale that he has for his boat. I copy it, creating a fictitious seller called Peter Holden from Los Angeles, who supposedly sold me an unfinished boat a year ago. The boat I put down as a thirty-three-foot ketch built of wood, named *Coracle*.

Jack also gives me the receipts that he has for the new self-steering system, as well as two new winches and a few other items he has purchased for *Windsong*. I put them into a file, along with a radio licence and some documents I have found aboard *Recluse* – paperwork that makes no mention of *Recluse* and pads the flimsy file of documents I have prepared. This will, I hope, give more credence to my newly built yacht ownership.

On board *Recluse*, I have repaired or replaced all the items that might affect the seaworthiness of the vessel. I've pulled out all the sails, spreading them over a large grassy patch in front of the marina office. Two small tears I repair with a sail repair kit I purchased at the yacht chandler near the marina.

I've also hauled myself up the mast and minutely inspected all the fittings and hardware, and checked for frayed areas. I've run my eye over all the running rigging – the halyards that pull sails up, and the sheets that pull them in. I've re-sealed the main hatch and made sure the boat is watertight. The engine, always an area of concern, I have taken particular care with, changing the oil, all the filters, and any leaky seals. Even though the boat doesn't carry enough diesel fuel to motor any great distance, I'll need the engine to keep the battery charged and also to motor into port.

I have bought as many spares as my meagre finances will allow: a V-belt and oil for the engine, a spare sailcloth, some extra line, and various other things I might need. I have no dinghy or life raft, but these I will have to do without. The surfboard will have to be my means of going ashore when I reach port. My intention is to get to Australia and find a job straight away, working until I have enough money to cruise again, sailing until I find myself somewhere I can work some more to replenish my finances once again, and so on. In this way I can keep cruising until there is no more world left for me to see.

9

I am ready to take the step I fear most: presenting my pitiful pile of papers to US customs for clearance to sail '*Coracle*' out of Honolulu for Australia. I've had a haircut and a shave, and I'm wearing the one decent shirt I own in an effort to look something like an affluent yacht owner. Along with my passport, I place all the papers in a folder and walk to the bus stop outside the marina.

Anxiously waiting for the bus, I feel my nerves shredding. To make matters worse, the trip takes me past the Honolulu prison. I stare up at the high grey walls topped with razor wire, and wonder if I might soon end up on the other side.

The customs office at the port of Honolulu is housed in an old cream-coloured building a block from the waterfront. I walk through the glass doors and find myself in a long, dark corridor lined with offices. On the wall opposite the doorway is a board showing the room numbers of the various offices. US Customs is indicated in large lettering with an arrow below, pointing to the left. I head that way and almost immediately see the same lettering on a pane of frosted glass. I enter through the swing doors.

Inside, behind a wooden counter, sit three uniformed customs officers. One glances cursorily at me as I enter, and they all continue writing at their desks. After a minute or so, an officer stands up and comes over to me.

'Yes?' He looks at me officiously. 'Can I help you?'

'I'd like to get a clearance for my boat,' I say, trying hard to muster aplomb. 'I'm sailing for Australia.'

He transfers his attention to the papers I've pulled from the folder.

'It's a new boat,' I explain. 'I've just finished building it.' I gesture towards the papers, though there's in fact nothing to indicate that I own a boat but the fake bill of sale.

'It's at the Ala Wai yacht marina,' I add. I have to bite my tongue to stop myself from pouring out a flood of excuses and explanations.

The officer nods and pulls the papers over. He starts to read them as I watch in silence. The bill of sale, at the top of the pile, he scans and places to one side. The rest of the papers are mere bumph, padding I added to lend some kind of credence to my claim.

I watch, feeling my guts squeezing into a paste of bile as carefully reads through each of the documents. He is obviously suspicious. There can be only one reason for his concentration, for the fact that he is perusing each and every worthless piece of paper. He knows somehow that it is all bullshit. From the frown on his face, a look of bureaucratic malevolence that freezes my blood, I can see I haven't fooled him one bit.

I consider running, escaping while I have a chance. I won't be able to return to the marina, because they'll know I've been staying there. I can hide in the mountains until the search is over, and then maybe I can somehow get off this island. Maybe I can persuade Jack to sail me to another island – Maui perhaps, which also has good surf.

Readying myself for a dash to freedom, I transfer my weight to the balls of my feet, steeling myself to make a grab for my passport, which is lying next to the folder.

Without looking my way, the officer reaches under the counter to grab a gun or handcuffs, and comes up instead with a sheet of paper. My heart does a little flip as I read 'US Customs Clearance – Port of Honolulu'.

He takes all the papers and returns to his desk, where he slides the clearance form into an ancient typewriter. Very slowly, he begins to type with two fingers, eventually whipping the form out of the typewriter and stamping it with the US customs seal.

The clonk of the stamp is a beautiful sound. It seals my owner-ship of *Recluse*. And more than that – it is the sound of my escape. I struggle to control the muscles around my mouth as he hands the papers back, including the precious clearance.

I'm so relieved I almost forget to take note of his name, written on a little tag on his chest: J. Peterson. A nice man. By sneaking covert glances, I've also made a note of the names of the other customs officers: Hitchcock and Mazaruki.

As I place the papers in the folder, J. Peterson gives me a small smile. 'Good sailing,' he says.

'Thank you, sir. Thank you very much,' I blurt, stopping the flow of gratitude with an effort. Then, suppressing my excitement, I exit to the street.

I've done it. I've completed the first and most risky step. I have a form that should ensure that no questions are asked at the first port I enter. I can hardly wait to get back to *Recluse* to savour my new ownership.

* * *

Back at the marina, I take Jack's typewriter and place a sheet of paper with a small mark on it under the ribbon. I hit the number 8 key to see how close to the mark the 8 is. I practise repeatedly until I get the 8 exactly where I want it, and then I slide in the clearance certificate and align it carefully.

Decisively, I hit the number 8 key again, and check the form. Where it previously read 'LOA (length overall) – 33 ft', it now reads 'LOA (length overall) – 38 ft'.

Over the next few days I keep a wary eye out for customs officers around the Ala Wai marina. I am now busy with last-minute preparations. I check my new Timex quartz watch with WWV, the radio station that transmits a continuous time signal on shortwave throughout most of the Pacific. The watch cost me $120 – cheap for a rated chronometer, though I hated to part with that much money. The only other watches that are good enough for navigation are expensive timepieces such as Omegas or Rolex Oysters, at about $2 000 apiece.

I begin to stock the vessel with supplies, first buying all the dry goods and canned foods, and leaving the perishables until the last moment. I fill extra jerrycans with water and tie them to the shrouds amidships.

My money is beginning to run really low, and I have to consider carefully what I can afford. As a cheap food source, I stockpile coconuts in the forepeak. I need to keep a small amount of cash for port fees and emergencies when I reach the other side.

A week has gone by, and I've been keeping a low profile. Apart from a few visits to Jack I no longer go out at night, and during the day I keep my head down, working to get *Recluse* ready. Lack of money is one reason, but I also want to avoid anything that might jeopardise my plans – such as bumping into an off-duty customs officer named J. Peterson.

What am I getting into, I ask myself. I'm about to sail across the Pacific, some six thousand miles, with not much between Hawaii and Australia but some scattered islands, a huge expanse of water, and hurricanes. It is now the time for them, and I will be sailing right through a major hurricane area. I've deliberately not given too much thought to this, but what would happen if I got caught in one? Could I survive?

And what about loneliness? I spent two weeks on my own camping in the Grand Canyon, and I wasn't lonely at all. I'm an independent spirit, capable of enduring my own company for as long as I want. I don't need society – or so I keep telling myself.

I picked up some tips on how to navigate by watching the captain of *Stormvogel* as we crossed the Atlantic, though I have yet to try it myself. *Recluse* has a sextant, and I have bought the nautical almanac for this year, 1973. I also found a book by Mary Blewitt on how to do celestial navigation, which I've read from cover to cover. I have almost everything I need, and I've done almost everything I need to do.

It is time to go.

* * *

I have one more hurdle to overcome, and that is to clear customs again. I first have to make sure that the same officers are not on duty, so I phone the number that I find in the directory at the marina office.

'Who am I speaking to, please?' I ask, ready to replace the receiver with a quick excuse if it is Peterson or one of the other two officers. He gives me a name I don't recognise, and I ask if I can speak to Peterson, Hitchcock or Mazaruki. To my relief he replies that all three are off duty, and I ask what time they'll be in again.

'They'll be on duty tomorrow,' he replies.

Perfect, I think, as a lurch of something – not fear, anticipation maybe – makes my gut tighten. I will be leaving today if I can successfully clear *Recluse* for the American mainland.

Once again, the bus ride into Honolulu is a strain on my nerves, but not as bad as before. I enter the customs building and wait outside the office for a moment to think about what I will say if Peterson or one of the other two happens to be inside. Then I steel myself and enter.

Two officers I don't recognise occupy the seats where Hitchcock and Mazaruki sat before and a third stands at the wooden counter. I hand him the letter from Jim Johnson, and five minutes later I am outside again, a clearance in my possession and nothing to prevent me from sailing away in my own boat.

I make my way to a supermarket and buy the last of the provisions I will need – some fresh fruit and more vegetables. I buy mainland apples and oranges, as tropical fruit from Hawaii spoils too quickly. I struggle with the bags to the bus stop.

During the trip back, I look around me with a new appreciation. This is the last time I will see these trees, the mountains, and for a long time I won't be seeing shops or cars or people. In fact, for a long time I won't even see the earth.

My chest tightens with excitement. But I also feel a sudden tearing conflict between my dreams of being alone upon the ocean with *Recluse* and a desire to stay in the relative safety and comfort of this island.

I find it hard to believe that this is really going to happen. I am twenty-one years old and am about to sail across the Pacific in my own boat, or sort of my own. I am scared, excited, happy and sad all at the same time. I even feel a fondness for the bus transporting me back to my means of escape, the object of my dreams.

At the marina I alight, and after putting the fruit and vegetables inside *Recluse*, I go straight to Jack's boat. I have a letter in my pocket addressed to my parents in South Africa.

Jack is applying varnish with an oversized brush in great messy goops and I am momentarily tempted to correct him and show him how to do it properly. Instead I say, 'Hey, Jack,' and swing myself over the life rail.

'Hi, Rob. All clear? No problems?' He knows where I've been.

'Nope. Not one. I'm free to leave.'

'When are you going?'

'Now. As soon as I've filled up with water.'

'I'll come over and help you with the lines,' he says, putting the can and the brush down on a rag and standing up. 'I'll just clean myself up. I'll be over there in a minute.'

I give him the letter for my parents, and tell him that if I have not contacted him within six months, he is to post it. He nods with sombre attention as he takes it from my hand.

Back at *Recluse* I pull the hose out along the dock and start filling the tanks. I watch as the water flows out of the breathers, making sure the tanks are filled to the brim, and I'm just finishing filling the kettle and a couple of saucepans when Jack arrives. He re-coils the hose as I replace the filler caps on the deck.

The moment has come. I start the engine, the heavy diesel billowing black smoke from under the stern with an enthusiastic roar. Allowing the motor to warm up, I check to make sure that the pin locking the self-steering gear is still in place. I would hate to end my adventure ignominiously upon the sea wall before I even leave the harbour.

Then I shake Jack's hand.

'Good luck, Rob. Hot damn! I wish I was going with you,' he says, squeezing my hand hard.

A sudden dumb emotion constricts my throat, making speech difficult as I squeeze back.

'Thanks, Jack. I'll see you in a few months. And thanks for all your help.'

'No. Thank *you* for all your help with my boat. Go safely now and with good winds.'

He throws the lines aboard one by one as I stand at the controls, and as the last line snakes onto the deck I pull the lever into astern. *Recluse* begins to back out as Jack lifts a hand in a kind of salute. I wave back as I slip the gear into forward, my concentration mostly on manoeuvring my vessel safely past the other yachts in their slips.

My last glimpse of Jack is of him standing with his arms folded, watching as I motor out towards the open sea. He waves again briefly, and then turns away.

Once past the yachts, I turn the wheel to bring *Recluse* into the main channel and ease the throttle forward. She accelerates easily to six knots, moving towards the freedom of the open sea.

I am alone now, alone with my new love, and through the teak spokes of the wheel I feel a warm kinship with *Recluse*. Now it is just the two of us, sailing together at last. At the end of the channel, out to sea, the Pacific looks as wide as the expansive feeling in my heart, which is partly relief from the tension of the past few weeks, partly excitement, and partly anxiety at the dangers we face together crossing this vast ocean.

10

Half a mile clear of the harbour entrance I unfurl the sails, hauling the billowing material up the masts with the halyards. I move back aft and winch them in until the dacron fabric is filled with wind. *Recluse* heels and slowly accelerates as the white dacron spreads its power through the rig. I fiddle with the self-steering until the vessel is on the southeasterly course I'm setting to fool anyone who may be watching from the land, and then I switch off the motor.

The silence is now broken only by the steady hiss of the bow wave and the contented creaking of *Recluse* as she feels the pull of the wind.

I still can't believe that I'm on my way, and I sit and savour all the feelings I'm experiencing. There's a weird mix of emotions within me as I watch the beautiful island of Oahu slowly dwindle astern of us. I feel joy and fear at what lies ahead, sorrow and relief at what lies behind. I already love every plank and screw in *Recluse* as she sails like the thoroughbred cruiser that she is.

I think of Jack and the friends I made in Hawaii, and of Mihai and Mary back in LA. I think of Vlazo, back there as well, and the

Priest, and of poor dead Alex and Bainesfield. I am so glad to be out of there – supremely happy to be alone on my way around the world.

* * *

Oahu is now a mere speck on the horizon. The wind is blowing from the northeast, onto the starboard quarter of *Recluse* as we head now almost directly into the setting sun. I've just changed course, no longer heading east towards the States, setting our direction instead towards Australia. I figure it's too dark and too far from land now for the yacht to be seen. The wind is pushing us along at over six knots through the slightly choppy sea, occasional white caps sprinkled upon its indigo surface. The weather is fine and everything is working perfectly aboard *Recluse* as she slips easily through the water.

I go below and prepare my dinner in the galley, which is on the port side, just forward of the companionway. From there I can see the blue material of the wind vane making its jerky corrections to our course.

Dinner is a can of spaghetti followed by coffee and a piece of bread, all of which I consume while sitting in the cockpit watching the sunset. Although I am slightly nervous about my first night aboard *Recluse*, I also feel contentment, a deep satisfaction at having at last pulled off my scheme.

The sun is a fiery red ball, streaking the sea with gold, and *Recluse* is sharing my happiness with playful leaps down the waves as they pass under her stern. As though inviting me to follow, the sun slips over the horizon towards Australia.

* * *

It is almost completely dark when I remember to switch on the navigation lights. I now have to admit to myself that I no longer feel quite as relaxed. Barrelling through the night, surrounded by strange sounds – unexpected slaps of water against the hull, strange creaking and groaning noises along with some distant clanking – it all makes me increasingly nervous. And then a mournful groan from high above the rigging adds to my fright. I have no depth perception in the dark, and the sounds seem to come from the sea and air around me. I don't believe in sea monsters, but I do move inboard slightly, drawing solace from contact with the cabin top.

I try to read by the light from the companionway entrance, but I am soon forced to give up as my stomach reacts queasily to the roll of the boat. Tense and alert and yet wanting to sleep, I sit and watch for ships – wanting to blank out the night yet unable to allow myself to go below. Too scared to be away from the deck and the boat's black surroundings.

Yawning constantly now, I begin to feel the effects of all the excitement of leaving, the mental stress and the physical activity, coupled with a little seasickness. I am becoming fatigued, but I'm too nervous to doze. I press up against the still warm cabin top with my back to the wind, staring into the blackness of the night.

I worry about becoming overtired, but then the thought suddenly comes to me that I can sleep any time. My routine is completely my own now, and I can sleep all day tomorrow if I so wish. For the next few weeks or months I have nobody to account to. I can do whatever I like. I can even stop the boat – take down the sails and simply go to sleep. As long as my food and water hold out I can keep sailing wherever and whenever I wish. It's a strange thought, though one that holds no reassurance at this moment.

And so I sit throughout the long night, occasional cups of coffee giving me comfort and helping me stay awake.

* * *

By morning I am bleary-eyed, the dawn breaking across an empty grey sea. Fleecy cumulus clouds are following in our track, the wind having swung to almost directly behind us during the night.

As the sun begins to climb up into the sky, filling me with warmth that is not merely physical, I nurse one more cup of coffee. The thought of breakfast brings an onset of nausea.

I stretch out in the cockpit, lying on the leeward side against the coaming, my head sheltered against the cabin as the wind strokes my bare ankles with feathery touches. I doze, dimly aware of the soothing sounds of *Recluse*'s rigging. I am beginning to attune myself to the noises of my boat, every regular creak and groan a signal of her well-being. As I relax further into sleep, I draw comfort from these sounds and also from the rush and slap of water along her hull transmitted through her timbers to my ear against the deck.

* * *

I wake up around noon, sweating, the sun burning fiercely above us. A welcome hunger signals that my seasickness has gone.

My chance of taking a morning sight with the sextant has also gone, but I'm not too concerned. Tomorrow is good enough to start navigating. Today I'm just heading in a general west-southwest direction.

While finishing off a peanut butter sandwich in the galley, I remember the fishing line. I forgot to put it out yesterday, and have probably lost my chance of catching any of the fish around the Hawaiian islands. I go forward and dig through the supplies under the starboard settee until I find the fishing equipment. I tie a lure to the nylon line with a steel trace, and let it out about two hundred feet astern. Pulling a loop of the line back to the stanchion just forward of the stern life rail, I tie a bungee cord to it to absorb the shock of a fish fighting. I also feed a small loop through a steel ring on the stanchion and hold this in place with four matches.

Now if a fish takes the lure, the matches will momentarily hold the line so that the hook can set, and then as they break against the strain they will warn me that I have a fish on the end.

* * *

At about three o'clock I spy a ship on the horizon. I can see only the top of the bridge and its funnels, so I figure it is some eight miles away. It looks as if it is steaming in a direction opposite to my course, towards Oahu. I hope the seamen aboard it are lax with their watch-keeping duties. Although there is no reason why they should report a yacht sailing west, I do not want to take any chances. I consider lowering the sails so that I'll be less visible, but then realise that if they do see me and the sails are down, there is more chance that they will either investigate or report it. I watch a mite anxiously as the ship slowly disappears astern of *Recluse*.

I feel relaxed and happy again. I'm enjoying the fact that I'm enjoying being alone. I clean up the interior of *Recluse*. Then I walk around the deck, adding chafing gear to the jib sheet where it is touching a port shroud. I check everything, making sure the jerrycans are secured and that no pins have fallen onto the deck from the hardware securing the mast. A flying fish is lying on the foredeck, and I consider eating it, but I have no idea how long it has been there so I toss it overboard.

The day ends, a beautiful sunset accompanying my dinner once again. Around nine o'clock I start feeling sleepy, so I go below and lie down on the starboard settee berth in the salon. Within moments I am asleep, my first real rest inside the cosy haven of my yacht while at sea.

* * *

Some inner signal, possibly nervousness, makes me get up every hour or so. Mostly I just check the secondary compass above my head on the bulkhead, to ensure that the yacht is still more or less on course. I have a flashlight handy, so I simply raise my head and shoulders to look at the compass, falling asleep again almost immediately.

But sometimes I go up on deck and check the strength of the wind, making sure that everything is where it should be and that the horizon is clear of ships. I stand in the cockpit and absorb the feel of the boat and the placidity of the sea, staring up at the stars to check the clarity and stability of the night, and then I go back down below again. I have become more accustomed to the strange noises now, and feel far more at ease than I did the first night.

* * *

The next day I try my first sun sight. Bracing myself against the cabin top, I hold the sextant in one hand and my Timex in the palm of the other.

It takes repeated attempts to bring the sun's reflection down to the horizon using the sextant mirrors, and then I am frustrated in my efforts to get the sun to lightly 'kiss' the horizon as I pendulum the sextant. The rolling of the boat, my inexperience and a cloud that covers the sun just as I am about to take a reading all hinder my efforts. My arm holding the sextant begins to tire.

Frustrated, I rest momentarily, careful not to bump a mirror of the sextant against anything. And then I try again. There is no other way to obtain my position, so I have to learn to do this. I eventually manage to get three readings. By averaging these with the time at the moment I obtained them, I have a sight.

At the chart table I use the almanac and the sight-reduction tables to calculate my line of position from the sight I have just taken. This is a line that I know myself to be on. By taking a noon reading, and a third sight in the afternoon, I will be able to effect a cross fix, which will tell me where I am: my position is at the point where the three lines meet – or at least within the triangle they make where they almost meet.

At three thirty I have my calculated position.

I now estimate my position by dead reckoning – the term for figuring one's position using the starting point, the course sailed, and the distance covered. I use an instrument called a taffrail log, at the back of the vessel. And factors such as currents or leeway – the sideways drift of the vessel – must also be taken into account. It's by comparing the estimated position and the one from my sights that I'm able more accurately to ascertain the current affecting the yacht.

It's finally done. My calculated position works out to be eight miles from my estimated position, and I am well satisfied. After two days and nearly three hundred miles, that is pretty damned good. I am a real seaman now, I think to myself, while another part of my brain heaves a sigh of relief that I'm not destined to wander the Pacific, asking directions at any island or ship I might come across.

To celebrate, I open a coconut using a hammer and chisel on top of a winch, and in the process I make a huge mess all over the cockpit. The crisp sweet flesh is delicious, though I suspect that the amount of energy expended to extract it doesn't equal the calories it supplies. I'll have to regard my pile of coconuts as luxury food, and not as nutrition for sustaining me.

* * *

It's the third day, and I've begun to set some sort of routine. After breakfast, which is just after dawn, I complete the log with the course that I sailed through the night. Then I pump out the bilge, counting the number of pumps it takes, and I enter this figure in the logbook too. I learnt this trick when I sailed across the Atlantic – it's to have some idea of the amount of water entering the vessel. A sudden substantial increase in the number of pumps indicates a leak.

Then I tidy the boat and check all the lines, and, of course, the fishing line. I check the sails themselves to make sure there are no tears starting. There are four sails, the jib at the front of the vessel, the staysail between the jib and the mainmast, the mainsail behind the mainmast, and the mizzen – a smaller sail that flies from the mizzenmast, which is just forward of the cockpit of *Recluse*.

After that I read, relaxing in the cockpit or in a shady part of the deck. I have only four books, Henri Charrière's *Papillon*, *Don't Stop the Carnival* by Herman Wouk, and two mystery thrillers. They were all I could afford.

Around ten thirty I take my first sun sight with the sextant, and record the result in the logbook. Then I get busy doing chores, fixing and servicing things like blocks and winches.

A water bottle strapped to the mainmast is wrapped in mutton cloth, which I keep moist with sea water. This cools the drinking water inside, as there is no refrigeration on board.

At about twelve o'clock I take another sight, a simple noon sight, and then I open a can – usually corned beef or sausages – and have lunch. My afternoons are spent in a variety of ways. I read a little, work a little, take the afternoon sight, take a nap, do some exercise – mostly push-ups – and then take a shower. This I do by hoisting up buckets of sea water and pouring it over myself on the foredeck. After that I prepare dinner – canned spaghetti, canned meatballs, canned stew, or canned something else. My small stock of fruit and vegetables is dwindling rapidly, with half of it going bad.

* * *

On the afternoon of the fifth day the wind drops. It has been fairly consistent from the northeast or east-northeast, at around eighteen knots. By sunset the sails are hanging limp and *Recluse* is nearly stationary in the water. Steering becomes a problem because there is no longer enough wind to operate the self-steering vane.

I spend my time jumping around the boat, leaving whatever I'm doing to make continual course corrections with the wheel. But our speed is so slow that even when the boat is way off course it doesn't really matter. We're doing less than two knots.

* * *

The night brings a frustrated restlessness and irritability. Without the wind in the sails to steady her, the yacht is rolling and the dacron is banging and slapping. I eventually drop all the sails except the main-sail, winching it tightly to reduce the rolling of the boat. It becomes impossible to sleep, impossible to relax, with the crack of the sail and the continual pitching as *Recluse* rolls about uncontrollably. Sailboats have a nice steady motion when sailing, the wind on the sails acting as a roll damper, but without this the high mast and low-slung keel create a nasty roll in any kind of sea. The wind has left a steep chop on the sea surface, making *Recluse* roll so badly she is almost dipping her gunwales underwater.

Exasperated by the continual loud slapping of the mainsail and the sense of trying to sleep atop a mechanical bull every time I go below, I eventually give up and sit angrily behind the wheel of the heaving and bucking boat. I attempt to steer her onto a more pleasant course, but soon realise the futility and try to grab some shut-eye in the cockpit, leaving the vessel to her own stupid devices.

I spend a miserable and tormented night.

* * *

Dawn arrives, bringing with it a red sky filled with high, streaky clouds. The sea has flattened, and *Recluse* has become mercifully still, a gentle sway the only remnant of her awful rolling during the night.

Going wearily below, I check the barometer and find that it has dropped radically during the night, and has now begun to rise again. With a sense of strong disquiet, I make some coffee, suspecting that the good sailing conditions I have experienced up till now are about to change — and drastically so.

After breakfast I move around the yacht, checking the lashings on the jerrycans, wedging objects into corners, and dogging the hatches down tight. The air has become absolutely calm; not a breath ruffles the glassy sea. But I am preparing for wind, not sure of the strength or direction, but certain that it will come. I'm still too far north to be in any danger of hurricanes, but I expect that this will be a fairly strong blow. I make my preparations and then I wait, tired and a little anxious.

Around ten o'clock the wind puffs gently from the northeast, the sails fill, and a small bow wave gurgles once more as *Recluse* begins to move again. I am relieved at the direction, and begin to hope that I'm mistaken, that the wind will resume its steady blow to push us westwards.

With gentle puffs the wind increases, and soon we are happily on our way again, a white froth spreading from *Recluse*'s bow and the blue self-steering vane jerkily making its little corrections. The wind is back to fifteen or sixteen knots, and I relax my storm vigil.

And then, without warning, it becomes calm again, the wind dropping so abruptly that *Recluse* is still moving forward on her own momentum as the sails hang slack from her spars. I feel a resurgence of the night's frustration as she begins her listless rolling again, the slap and crack of the sailcloth as the masts swing adding to my irritation at the fickleness of the wind.

Twice, the wind starts to blow again. Each time the puffs last no more than ten or fifteen minutes, teasing me with hope. At midday the heat is intense, baking the deck to a foot-burning temperature and turning the inside of the boat into an oven. I find a small patch of shade on the foredeck behind the staysail where I sit sweltering and waiting, wishing I had enough diesel to use the motor.

And then, creeping over the sea surface with a sibilant stealth, a different wind, blowing from the north, fills the sails and heels the yacht with a new motion.

Returning aft to the cockpit, relief mixed with anxiety, I make adjustments for the new wind direction, trimming the sheets and correcting the self-steering as we begin to move in earnest once again. I make preparations to reef the mainsail, some instinct warning me that we are in for a rough ride.

I don't feel afraid: I am fully confident in the capabilities of my vessel and only slightly less so in my own. But I am nervous about what I suspect will be the first test of rough weather for us on this voyage. Despite its name, the Pacific instils more fear in me than the Atlantic ever did. This is possibly due to its vast size, but more probably because I grew up next to the Atlantic Ocean, familiar with its moods, its storms and calms, knowing what it is capable of. The Pacific is a mysterious and sinister unknown.

* * *

Soon *Recluse* is slicing through waves faster than I have yet seen her sail. I reef the mainsail down to the second reefing point and change the jib to number two, reducing the sails to take the strain off the rig. The wind is now blowing twenty-five to thirty knots – close to gale force.

The vessel's motion is very different from what it has been for the past five days. She is heeled well over, cleaving through the choppy sea with a much sharper movement. Nervously, I move around the decks, checking that everything is secured, and looking out to where the wind is blowing from as if I might see what's coming.

By mid-afternoon the sea has become an endless vista of scudding wave-tops, white horses breaking before a driving wind that has now reached gale force. I reduce sail even more, reefing the mainsail down to its third and last reefing point, and change the front sail to the smaller, thicker storm jib.

I change course slightly, turning the yacht fifteen degrees to port to run before the swelling waves. With a few thousand miles to go, I'm not particularly worried about sailing off course for a while.

The self-steering gear seems to be coping easily with the more intense yawing of the vessel; I feel a deep gratitude to the makers of RVG self-steering systems. Dinner is a hastily heated can of stew, which I bolt down in the small lee provided by the mizzenmast.

* * *

Sunset, and the waves are now so high that I can barely see over the top of them, even standing on the cabin top. Just before nightfall I lower the mizzen and the staysail, securely lashing each to its boom. I know that it is going to be a long night again, and I'm trying to make the motion of the boat as comfortable as possible for both of us.

I haven't used the navigation lights for the past two nights now. I'm trying to avoid running the engine to recharge the batteries, thus saving precious fuel. But I'm tempted to switch them on again, if only for the comfort that I would draw from their feeble illumination.

With a sharp unease, I listen through the dark to the noise of the gale. I hear the moaning of the wind through the rigging and the taut slapping of the sails, and anxiously I anticipate the crashing of the waves against the hull as I hear them foaming and breaking to windward.

The darkness seems to amplify the sound, and a growing roar warns me of an approaching wave that rumbles through the black towards us. Sometimes the wave slips under the hull with merely an upward heave, mocking my anxiety, and other times it crashes against the exposed heeled surface of *Recluse*'s hull with a force that sends her shuddering down the wave face. Spray spatters against my foul-weather jacket and runs across the tilted deck with heavy swishes, then drains gurgling out of the leeward scuppers.

I'm nervous, awaiting the ripping sound of a tearing sail, or the violent flogging of the dacron that tells me a sheet has snapped or a halyard has gone. The tension I feel seems to reflect that of *Recluse*, my nerves stretched like her rigging to near breaking point.

Yet my preparations are done. All I can do is sit and watch, and hope that everything remains intact and in working order, that nothing breaks suddenly, forcing me into immediate action on the pitching foredeck to save whatever sail is violently flogging itself to pieces. Or worse, maybe – losing the whole rig. I brace myself for that larger-than-usual wave to come breaking over the deck, or smashing into the side of my boat with enough force to broach her.

Around midnight I drop the mainsail and alter course another fifteen degrees to port, running even more before the wind to take strain off *Recluse* and myself. Later I manage to nap, wedged between the mizzenmast and the cabin top, my empathy with *Recluse* remaining unbroken even as I sleep. I feel every shudder, every crash and every sudden heel of her, unsure what is dream and what is reality – my awareness of my boat and her struggles twisting through my conscious and unconscious minds in a strange mix of sentience as I doze.

* * *

Dawn breaks across a ghastly sea. The height of the waves has increased far beyond what I imagined during the hissing and roaring of the night. Towering ridges streaked with spume heave past us – endless swells driven by howling gusts, crashing down with a foaming thunder that drowns out the screech of the wind. Overhead, grey clouds rush low, skimming the gigantic wave tops. The horizon is invisible below a foreboding cloud that forms a menacing black line where it meets the tormented sea.

The cold light of day reveals a full-blown storm. Wave tops are sliced off by a wind that is gusting past sixty knots, whipping the water off the surface in a fury of horizontal spray. The sheet holding the storm jib is bar-taut, and the single small sail drives the yacht through the howling sea at eight knots and more as she surfs down the steep wave faces. The swells are now so high that the troughs produce momentary false calms. I watch each impending break with fearful fascination, knowing that sooner or later we'll be caught squarely, a wave breaking just as it reaches us and enveloping us with its full might.

The waves roll by with awesome power. Some break and crash alongside *Recluse*, and others pass her by with just a touch of foamy aggression that heaves against her stern – still forcing me to spin the wheel to correct her course. And sometimes the waves thunder down ahead of her, leaving a boiling wake of foamy water for us to bounce across.

There is no chance at all of taking a sun sight, even if the sun were visible. I can't see the horizon, and there's no way I could use the sextant in these conditions anyway. So I sit and wait, huddled against the wind and spray, wishing I were somewhere else.

Crouched in my position next to the mizzenmast, I watch as *Recluse* careens down waves that are much bigger than any I've ever surfed on a surfboard. The speed would be thrilling if I wasn't so aware of the strain on the rig and the rudder. The vessel yaws heavily, broaching to starboard as a breaking wave slams her stern down. I crawl back to inspect the self-steering gear.

It has occurred to me, more than a few times, to lock the self-steering and to take control of the vessel myself. But everything still looks fine at the back; the storm jib is helping to keep the bow pointed downwind, and the self-steering is still managing to cope with the high speeds *Recluse* is attaining. Also, having the self-steering working frees me up for any emergency if equipment fails. I return to the cockpit and resume my position of waiting and watching.

* * *

I have begun to develop a headache from the tension. A storm is all about tension: tension in the wind, tension in the rigging and sails, tension in every structure of the vessel. And tension in me, as I wait for something to break. Like a stay, maybe, that holds up the mast, parting from it with gunshot violence.

It is the waiting that is the worst, that taut anticipation of another crashing wave, or something breaking or coming loose – and all the while the banshee howling is a reminder of the stress that everything is being subjected to. Hollywood depictions of storms have always amused me, because they never show the single most important ingredient of a storm.

The wind.

It howls and screams and tortures, it blasts through the rigging and bends the mast. It whips across the sea and decapitates the wave tops, leaving frenzied agitation behind, trails of spume and froth strewn across the arcing swells.

It is a constant: never ceasing and never softening, screeching and spitting its anger at everything in its path.

The tempest is buffeting against my back, howling off the sail and spinning away to leeward in whirls of spray, and every now and then a thundering roar warns me of yet another breaking wave coming to crash across the deck in a torrent. Blue sea, mixed with white, sweeps across the tossing boat, splashing and slurping through the scuppers, gurgling down the cockpit drains and cascading over the gunwale.

I get occasional glimpses of a maelstrom stretching to an invisible horizon as *Recluse* lurches off the top of an enormous wave, and I have a desperate fear: I may not have seen the worst of this storm.

Thoughts of America enter my head, and I wish I was back there, safe and dry, my only worries being how to get Mike and Pete to wash the dishes, or escape being murdered by Vlazo. Why on earth did I want to go to sea? There are so many warm and safe adventures to be had on land. What possessed me to think I love this crap?

'THIS IS FUCKING UNPLEASANT!' I surprise myself as I shout, my voice lost immediately to the wind. I try again, screaming obscenities in an attempt to make myself feel better, to show my own strength, but my efforts are whipped away by a cruel, unrelenting might that mocks my insignificance.

How could they name this lousy stinking fucking ocean the Pacific? I wanted adventure, not this shit. Isn't adventure supposed to be romantic, maybe even fun? This has all the romance of a traffic accident. I dream miserably of a ship arriving and hoisting both *Recluse* and me onto a safe, dry deck, and then a hot shower, and a good meal. Maybe followed by ice cream. Do they have ice cream aboard ships? Maybe …

A skidding crash jerks me from my thoughts. *Recluse* has fallen off a wave; she's dropped into a trough – virtually free-falling down the face of a huge wave and landing on her side. Sounds of clattering in the galley, things falling, add to the noise as I cling to the mizzen-mast, which by now is almost horizontal.

I wait apprehensively as *Recluse* rights herself, coming slowly back upright with her beam to the wind and her storm jib flapping with pistol-shot violence, shaking the entire yacht as it slams against the lines that are barely holding it to mast and boat.

Recluse almost comes to a complete halt. I jump across the cockpit and spin the wheel all the way to its stop, trying to help the self-steering haul her away from the wind before the sail shreds itself, or brings the mast down. Slowly, she begins to turn as the jib fills. When she is again facing downwind I re-secure the wheel with the lashing and glance quickly around the boat, checking for damage. I look astern.

The self-steering is gone.

My mind is blank. It is as blank as the space where the self-steering used to be. There is nothing there: the entire self-steering system has disappeared, and my intestines knot as the full implications hit me. How will I sail this boat across the ocean without a self-steering system? How am I going to hand-steer her across six thousand miles of ocean?

Then I see a strange sight. Towing behind the boat is the entire system. The two lines that are used for adjusting it are still attached to it. The thought runs through me like a surge of current that I might yet be able to save the system. At the same time, I notice that *Recluse* is picking up speed again and I remember that the lines are only a quarter-inch thick. They won't hold for long.

Without thinking further, I jump to the back of the boat, where the control lines are so taut over the taffrail that they make the wood creak. I take hold of the thin rope and heave, working the heavy apparatus slowly back towards the yacht with overhand grabs and torturous pulls against the drag of the water.

I can feel the strength going in my hands and biceps, and with a last desperate yank I manage to get a grip on the metal post of the system. For a while I rest, sucking in air and holding the steering gear up from the water with my arms braced on the steel life rail to take the strain off. *Recluse* seems to be steering herself downwind – and I am thankful for this piece of luck.

Through the rushing water, I see a twisted piece of metal that attaches the steering system to the boat. The steel probably snapped as *Recluse* half-fell and half-surfed down the monster wave. Gathering my strength, I try to heave the system on board, but as it comes out of the water its weight increases. Shit. It's much heavier than I thought. How am I going to get it back on board? If I let go now, I'll lose it. I wait a few moments, trying to recoup some more strength, and then give it another heave.

I get about three-quarters of the gear out of the water, but my crouched position against the life rail and the unsteadiness of the deck make it too difficult to lift it any further. I am forced to release the weight into the water again, still holding on to the steel bar with shaky hands. I know that if I don't manage to pull the system up soon, I never will.

Fuck. There is only one way to do it. I'll have to stand up. If I brace myself against the rail and use the motion of the boat to help me, maybe I can lift it. So, keeping my grip tight and my legs tensed against the strain of towing the self-steering system through the water, I stand up carefully and wait for the right moment.

There is a wave towering astern, and as it passes underneath us I feel the bow lifting, pushing the stern down until the gear is almost weightless and my grip is at the same level as the top of the life rail. As the stern starts to rise again I heave mightily, making a last effort to pull it all on board. The stern kicks high into the air at the top of the wave, and the boat lurches, the entire 150-pound system falling from chest level as I lose my balance.

With my own weird cry in my ears, I feel the life rail dig into the back of my knees as I fall overboard. There's a craze of sky, weightless dropping, and the terrible knowledge that I am about to be separated from *Recluse*. And then a crash and a tearing pain across my legs, and I'm lying with my head and shoulders in the water and my legs bent over the rail, trapped underneath something heavy that seems to have torn my shins.

Oh, fucking hell. I'm overboard, being towed on my back, staring up at the transom of *Recluse* as she carries on sailing. I make out the self-steering gear, lying at an angle across the stern, up against the life rail, my legs trapped beneath it. The yacht is sailing at over six knots, way too fast for me to catch if I lose this connection.

Carefully, ultra-cautiously, my heart screaming with fear that I might become unpinned, I twist my body and pull myself up out of the rushing water. I have no idea how securely the gear is lying across my legs, and the lurching of the boat might yet disconnect me from my precarious position.

With a final heart-stopping heave I manage to grab the lower life rail, and then with shaking arms I pull myself back over the railing. I am back on board again. The pain in my legs is intense as I push against the metal to release myself, but I feel a deep, all-embracing gratitude – especially to *Recluse* for not making any violent lurches, and to whatever Supreme Being has decided that it is not yet my time to die.

Blood is streaming down my shins as I tie a quick line around the steering gear to hold it against the life rail. And then I slump back into the cockpit, unlashing the wheel as *Recluse* begins to yaw about violently, as though she had been struggling to keep on course during the whole incident – ever aware of the danger I was in.

I take control of my yacht, helping her as she has helped me.

* * *

The storm is unabated, and I steer through the rest of the day, a quiet desperation growing inside me for it to end. My shoulders ache and my arms are tired from constantly spinning the wheel and fighting the monstrous seas. My legs hurt and I yearn for the luxury of the self-steering system that allowed me to be miserable in peace, huddled against the mizzenmast and not having to face the bleakness of the elements.

Night falls suddenly: no transition from the day, no sunset, no beautiful streaks in the sky, and no lessening of the wind. I am cold and I am hungry, and I'm too miserable even to shout curses against the wind. There are no stars for me to steer by, the compass light is off, and I am too exhausted and sore to go and switch it on. I steer by the feel of the wind on my back, not caring which direction I'm going in, not even caring if this course is taking me back towards Hawaii. All I want is the wind to stop. I try to picture the sea calm again, but I've been in this turmoil for so long now that I can't imagine it placid.

* * *

I don't know what time it is. My whole body is numb, with cold, fatigue, pain and the relentless screaming, moaning wind that I hate with every fibre of my being. How can it go on for so long? A strong storm like this should blow itself out within a day or so, but this has been going on for how long now? Two days? Three? I find it difficult to think, to remember when it started.

Waves crash through the night, rolling out of the darkness to smash against my poor boat. I hate everything in the world but *Recluse.* For her I have only the utmost respect and love. She has not let me down, fighting back valiantly against the vicious seas when even my own spirits are so low that I no longer bother hunching up against an oncoming wave – I simply sit and allow myself to be drenched by the water.

It is wet everywhere, water running off me in rivulets, streaming off the deck, water running off the masts, and water in the air above me. It could be raining, but I wouldn't know. There is too much water everywhere to tell.

I have no idea of the state of the inside of the boat. I closed the companionway – when? One day ago? Two? And I haven't been inside since. It must be a mess, but that is the least of my worries. I begin to fall asleep. My mind and body are shutting down, and I know that soon I will be unable to continue steering.

* * *

With nervous uncertainty, never having attempted it before and not knowing how *Recluse* will handle it, I decide to heave her to, leaving her to her own devices. The wind seems to have calmed a little, and I am going to take a chance, to slow her down a bit.

Wearily, painfully, I lash the wheel again, and then I pull the tie-downs off the mizzen sail. It takes me nearly twenty minutes to tie the reefing lines and to bring the yacht back from her violent yawing. Finally, I haul the recalcitrant shortened sail up the mast until it is tight. Then I take the wheel again, waiting for the right moment, a lull in the swell.

A small wave begins to kick the stern around, and I help it with the helm, the wind suddenly taking the jib from the other side and slamming it back against the shrouds. It is now lying on the opposite side to the mizzen, and the vessel is hove-to.

I no longer have to steer. We are making almost no way through the water and the reefed mizzen and the storm jib now keep the boat's direction more or less stable in the wind, and steady her as well. Her motion has become more comfortable, and I mentally kick myself for not doing this earlier. This is the first time I've been hove-to in a storm. Running before the wind is normally considered the safest and easiest course in a storm, but *Recluse* seems to be handling this new situation well. The biggest drawback now is that the seas hit her amidships, crashing even harder against my poor boat. But she will have to take this punishment. I cannot. I'm too tired to carry on steering her downwind.

With a stiff and sore weariness I lash the wheel and push back the main hatch to go below, to take refuge from the wind and the water. In the salon I switch on the light and am surprised at the lack of mess. A few items from the galley are rolling around on the floor, but everything else is in place, more or less. And she is dry, or reasonably so. The relative quiet down below, away from the wind, is a solace, and, apart from the occasional waves that crash against her hull and pitch the yacht onto her side, it's almost peaceful down here.

Too tired to dress my legs, too tired to care, I strip off my foul-weather gear and lie down on my bunk, the lee cloths I rigged earlier preventing me from being thrown out. I fall asleep almost immediately.

* * *

I awake with a cold light seeping through the portholes. The companionway is closed, the wash boards keeping out the sea and the noise. Lying against the stiff fabric of the lee cloth, my clothes still sodden, I try to sense the movement of the boat. It seems less violent than during the night.

I don't want to leave the bunk. My shins feel stiff with dried blood, my muscles stiff with weariness, and I want to sleep again. I want the oblivion of sleep to shield me from whatever is going on above me. I close my eyes, trying to ignore all the messages that say I should check to see how my boat is doing. I hear sloshing in the bilge, but when I peek over the edge of the lee cloth I can see no water washing over the floorboards. I will have to pump her out, but later. Now I'm still too tired.

* * *

Awake again. I've dozed a while, and now I can definitely feel that it is calmer outside. The wind is no longer screaming through the rigging. *Recluse* is more upright and her motion is easier. There are only occasional thuds and splashes against the cabin top.

Slowly and stiffly I heave myself over the lee cloth, catching my balance with a hand on the grab rail. The cabin floor is still in turbulent motion with the pitch and roll of the boat and my head is spinning slightly. Gathering my strength and my will, I prepare to go up on deck again.

I pull on the still-wet foul-weather gear and feel the blood return to my legs with an agonising pain in my shins. Strips of skin hang loose where they were torn from my legs and I turn my eyes away, unwilling to find out the extent of my injuries.

Pushing the companionway hatch back, I stick my head out and face the new day with weary hope. It still looks miserable; grey overhead and a grey sea, with threatening clouds circling the horizon, and no sign of the sun.

But it is calmer. The wind is no more than twenty-five or thirty knots – a mere whisper compared to what it was before. The waves are still high, but they are no longer breaking with the same force, and *Recluse* is bobbing around happily in her hove-to position. The self-steering gear is where I left it, tied to the stern life rail, and I can see no damage – no torn sails or missing spars – to my yacht. Even the jerrycans of water are still tied to the shrouds.

The storm is over and we've survived.

11

It's nightfall, and the sea is fairly calm again. The wind is a gentle fifteen knots, and there are even signs of the sun breaking through to present an actual sunset – a sight that warms my soul with the promise of a peaceful night.

I have replaced the storm jib with the number-one jib and hauled the rest of the sails up again, managing to set them so that *Recluse* is keeping her course. The wind is on the beam, from the starboard, and she holds a direction that is within ten degrees of the course I want, an unexpected boon. I yearn for the wind to remain gentle and constant, at least through this particular night. I need a peaceful night of rest.

By now I've also tidied up the boat and pumped out the bilge, and retrieved two halyard ends that were trailing in the water. I am amazed at the minimal damage that *Recluse* has suffered. A knife that was in a sheath on the mainmast is gone, a small canvas bag I'd hoisted aloft on the mizzenmast and filled with crumpled aluminium tinfoil as a cheap radar reflector is hanging loose. And the self-steering gear is broken.

But I expected much worse. All the rigging seems to be fine and the vessel is taking no water. I've re-secured the lashing on the self-steering gear and I've dressed and bandaged my shins, using a well-squeezed tube of antiseptic cream that I found in a drawer and an old pillow-case that I cut into strips. My boat is in fine shape, and I move around her as though I am not a day over eighty.

Dinner is a celebratory affair. I heat a can of chicken pie, one of the more expensive food items I bought. This is followed by tinned peaches, a luxury that I savour mouthful by mouthful. Finally, I have my first mug of coffee in three days. I sit in my spot next to the mizzen-mast, cupping the coffee in both hands as I reflect on the reinvigorating comforts of a hot meal.

* * *

The next day I inspect the self-steering gear. The central post, the main beam that attaches to the transom, is broken, its metal twisted and sheared. It will be impossible to reattach it, but I am no longer so full of dread at the loss of my self-steering. I have discovered that it is not particularly difficult to make *Recluse* self-steer using her sails, though this means that I now have to accept a less accurate course.

Sailing upwind is not a problem at all, as she is an extremely well-balanced boat. With the sails sheeted in to the correct positions, they act together to hold her on course. Downwind is another matter – though I have a couple of ideas that may make it possible for her to self-steer.

It is two days, though, before it is necessary for me to try out these ideas. The wind gradually moves from the north to slightly south of west, coming almost directly from the direction I'm going. Eventually I have all the sails sheeted in hard, inclining the vessel sharply as she beats into the wind.

Recluse is now plunging and pitching into the short choppy seas, and my average day's run is reduced to way less than a hundred miles.

My forward progress is dishearteningly slow, off course, and uncomfortable too.

But at least being off course holds no problems as far as navigation is concerned. This is a massive, empty area of the Pacific, devoid of islands and reefs as well as shipping lanes. I haven't seen a ship since I spotted those funnels on the second day. And I haven't seen any aeroplanes or even debris – floating plastic, a bottle, a plank of wood – or any other sign that I inhabit the same planet as other human beings. Every day, the same empty sea surrounds me, and I notice that the ocean is devoid even of the big sea birds and dolphins that I am used to seeing in the Atlantic.

Peculiarly desolate, the Pacific stretches before me in an endless sequence of new but identical horizons. My solitude is absolute.

* * *

By playing with the sails and the poles, I discover I have a fair amount of control over *Recluse*'s downwind course, more than I'd expected. The wind has now come back, blowing from the east – from almost directly behind us – and our speed has increased. The motion of the yacht is also much easier and I am happy, even more so to discover that my steering plans are working – more or less.

I experiment as the days pass and the conditions change, and I produce a format of course stability. A stable course is one where, if *Recluse* sails off the course I have set to the wind, either by wave action or a sudden gust, she will automatically return to that course. An unstable course is one where she continually veers from her course once the delicate balance of wind and water pressure is upset.

It is only with a stable course setting that I am able to relax, read a book or sleep. With practice, I manage to achieve this much of the time and I settle back into my routine, my shins healing and my confidence returning. Once again, the easterly wind is blowing consistently fifteen to eighteen knots, and *Recluse* is making slightly more than 140 sea miles a day – a good speed.

I have finished the first book I was reading, and I now start on *Papillon*. The story of a Frenchman imprisoned for a crime he did not commit, the book describes the torment and loneliness he suffers as a result of his repeated attempts to escape from the infamous penal colony of French Guiana. I empathise with the prisoner, imagining a bond of mutual hardship that connects us somehow through time and the pages of the book. His pain is mine, and his loneliness is mine, and his strength shall be mine. If he could endure five years of solitary for trying to escape, I can endure another couple of months at sea, imprisoned here for a crime that I *did* commit.

The radio receiver on board is a Zenith shortwave radio, and occasionally I catch a voice breaking through the static, so distorted that it hardly sounds human. These erratic reflections from the stratosphere seem to be the only thing I can tune in to, but even this minimal human contact is a comfort to me. I play with the radio endlessly, twiddling the dials and listening for these alien voices, mostly speaking French or Spanish, through the hisses and scratches and squeaks and squawks.

One day I hear a voice say 'South West Africa ... women in solidarity'. My heart thumps with excitement as I tune the radio carefully. The man's voice goes on to say that the women of the Herero tribe near Swakopmund have turned up in force to protest against the imprisonment of a labour hero of the people, who has been arrested by the racist imperialist forces of Pretoria.

It is a signal from Radio Africa, a Moscow propaganda station, but I have no idea what the man is talking about. I have never heard of the labour hero he mentions, and I'm pretty sure that a small gathering of women in some little town in a country as remote as South West Africa is of no interest to anyone. It is obvious propaganda bullshit by our Soviet enemies, but I love the man behind the voice because he is talking about my own country.

* * *

There is a fish near the boat. I spy him one day as I am walking back along the deck to the cockpit. Three feet of silver and yellow, he is swimming alongside the hull, keeping pace with *Recluse*.

He is an albacore, a type of tuna – sleek and tasty. I view him solely as a meal, the fishing line having netted me absolutely nothing so far. There is a speargun on board, left behind possibly by one of Jim Johnson's children, and I duck down below and haul it out from behind one of the bunks where I have stowed it. Back in the cockpit I pull the rubber back, carefully slipping the fork into the notch of the spear and trying not to aim the spear at my feet or the boat. I have no idea what the state of the trigger mechanism is, and I fear the spear might release accidentally.

With a sneaky peek over the side of the boat, I ascertain that my meal is still there, swimming happily alongside what he possibly perceives as a huge new friend. Is he as lonely as I am in this vast ocean?

Silently, I lie on my stomach on the warm teak deck and ease the gun over the side. Slowly, so as not to alarm him, I twist the barrel downwards, aiming at his back as he swims not more than six feet from me. I pull the trigger.

Click and whoosh, and the spear sinks into the sea, still attached to its line. The fish is gone, and I've missed. Damn it. Fuck it. I could do with a tasty fish. I'm tired of canned food and yearn for something fresh to eat.

I pull the spear out of the water. Without much hope, I take the gun to the other side of the boat and look over, sure that the fish has scarpered.

But he hasn't. He is swimming on this side now, refusing to abandon his new mate. Quickly I reload, fumbling in my haste, and then I creep on my hands and knees to a new position. Again, I slowly lower the gun over the side, line it up, and pull the trigger. Click-whoosh, and nothing.

I've missed again.

I can't believe it. I know that light refracts through the water, but not this much, surely? I'm not that bad, am I? I used to spearfish as a kid, and I was pretty good at it then. It can't be that much harder with me being out of the water, can it?

On my hands and knees, I crawl around the deck yet again, casting furtive glances over the side until I find the fish. Now he is swimming next to the bow. For the third time I lower the gun over the side, but this time he doesn't give me a chance to shoot. He just hightails it under the boat, and it is ten minutes before I find him again, this time near the stern.

Again I try to sneak the gun over, but the wily fish slips away immediately, disappearing once more under the hull. He has learnt, the bugger. He knows now what I'm up to, and he is not going to give me another chance. But I have the advantage. I'm a human, and therefore I'm cleverer. He is only a fish; I can outwit him.

I go below, and from the toolbox I pull out a mirror I remember seeing there. It's a woman's mirror, with a plastic handle. Quickly, I find a piece of line and tie the mirror to the dipstick from the fuel tank, angling it so that I can see over the side of the deck without revealing myself. I'll show this fish a thing or two about human ingenuity.

Sliding myself along the teak planking of the deck, I use the mirror to find the fish. He is almost in his original position. Lying on my back, I grip the dipstick between my knees and slowly slide the gun out, struggling to keep him in view in the mirror. When the gun is pointing towards him, as near as I can tell, I gently open my knees and release the mirror so that it lies across the gunwale. Then, in one quick movement, I roll over and push my head through the lifelines, aligning the gun and pulling the trigger as I do so.

Another miss.

I won't give up. I'll show this fish who is superior. I repeat the performance, this time on the other side, near the bow. It takes me more than ten minutes to find him and set everything up again. In the mirror I see the fish disappear the moment the gun appears over the side of the boat. His intellect is obviously not that deficient.

I try a new technique. Deliberately scaring him from one side, I jump quickly to the other and then lie on my back, gun already over the side and the mirror held up. With predatory patience, I wait.

It is fifteen minutes before I see him, and I have almost given up. But there he is in the mirror, cunningly keeping close to the side of the vessel to make it more difficult for me to spot him. His image is refracted through the water and then reflected in the mirror, and I have no real idea of where I am aiming the gun. But I shoot anyway. And miss.

Six more times I pull the trigger, without hitting the albacore once, and the day passes by unnoticed. I'm having fun. And the fish is probably having fun too. Maybe he gets bored swimming around out here. He could easily swim away, and he obviously knows I'm hunting him. But he stays, and for that I'm grateful.

I'm glad I haven't shot him. He has become a companion. I show myself without the gun, and sure enough, after skittering away a few times, he seems to realise that I'm no longer armed. From a distance, I can sit and watch him; once, I'm sure, he turns on his side – the better to view me.

* * *

The next day, immediately after breakfast, I walk around *Recluse* to see if my fish is still with me. I search all around the vessel, but he's gone. The intensity of my disappointment catches me by surprise, and I realise how lonely I really am.

I have, up until now, managed to stave off that acknowledgement, still convinced of my independence from other humans. But now I am forced to admit to myself that this may not be true. I miss human contact. I miss people, and I miss civilisation. My fortitude has become a front, a sham, and suddenly I see my character more clearly than I care to. But this is not the right place or time for my carefully nurtured sense of independence to be breaking down. I have too far to go still. With an effort, I think of other things, turning my mind away from my solitude.

Taking out Mary Blewitt's book on navigation, I learn more about the art, teaching myself how to do star sights and moon sights. That evening I practise with the stars, aiming the sextant in the direction I have pre-calculated, the arc of the instrument set, and I wait as twilight approaches. Like magic, the star appears in the viewfinder, and I take a sight.

Lowering the sextant, I'm not certain if I can make out the star I've just sighted on. There are three stars in that part of the sky, three other possibilities, but I know that the star I sighted on is the correct one. Its appearance in the viewfinder of the sextant assures me of this. Knowing that I can take a star sight renews my sense of confidence.

I'm still an old sea dog.

* * *

The weather has become hotter. I've been sailing in a southwesterly direction for two and a half weeks now, and my noon sights of the sun are close to ninety degrees, which means that the sun is almost directly overhead at midday.

The wind has changed, too. It no longer blows constantly from the northeast. It switches, blowing sometimes from the east, and occasionally even from the east-southeast. Its strength has become fluky, dying to a mere whisper at times and then resuming a variable eight to ten knots.

I am well into the hurricane area now, and every day I monitor the barometer closely. The only warning I will have of a hurricane is a sudden huge drop in barometric pressure, and therefore any anticlockwise movement of the needle causes me immediate anxiety. I hover near the barometer like a mother hen, tapping it fearfully until the needle begins to rise again.

Although my home is a coastline where storms are commonplace, I can only guess what a hurricane would be like. I know the difference between a thirty-knot gale and a sixty-knot storm. But the terrific violence of a wind over a hundred miles per hour is something that I don't want to try to picture. The fury of the storm is not a linear equation of the wind factor. It doesn't merely double in strength – its violence triples, or quadruples, and a hurricane can have double the wind strength of the storm I recently experienced. My overactive imagination conjures up gigantic smashing swells, set in furious motion by a wind so strong that it could blow *Recluse* and me right off the tops of the waves – smashing us into the chasms below and then burying us beneath tons and tons of water, splintering my vessel like a packing crate demolished by a wrecking ball.

I include the barometer in my nightly checks.

I've covered approximately 1400 nautical miles since leaving Hawaii, just over 1600 land miles. I am not yet halfway, or even close to it. My supplies are a bit of a worry. Water is not a problem as I left with slightly more than 150 gallons, in addition to the jerrycans I have on deck. I use sea water to shower, half a cup of fresh water to brush my teeth, and when I cook things like rice I use one-third sea water to two-thirds fresh water, and omit the salt. The rest is for drinking, and I have not even used half of one tank yet. But I have long since finished all the fruit and vegetables, and I don't have all that much food left, maybe enough canned foods and rice to last me another two months. I simply didn't have enough money to buy more.

I'm worried about the fuel situation too. *Recluse* has two diesel tanks that together hold 120 gallons, but I couldn't afford to fill these when I left. I've been running the engine for an hour every third or fourth day to charge the batteries, and the marks on the dipstick show that I have less than thirty gallons left.

Cooking gas is not a concern. I have two bottles, and as yet I have not used even one, so there's plenty left. As long as the wind doesn't disappear and *Recluse* keeps sailing, I should be okay. If our progress remains at this rate, Australia is only about five or six weeks away.

12

The wind becomes even calmer, and I wonder if this is the doldrums. In this part of the world, the almost windless belt lies to the north of the equator, so I may already be in it.

I make preparations for one more bit of subterfuge. I have to change the name of the vessel. In Hawaii I bought brass letters from a hardware store. The letters are slightly larger than those in the name *Recluse*, painted across the transom.

The sea surface is almost perfectly calm, glassy and smooth, without a ripple to indicate wind. It has been like this all morning, so I assemble my equipment. I have a bo'sun's chair – a thick plank with two holes at either end, suspended by two ropes. It looks like the seat of a child's swing. The chair hangs from the stern life rail, so that the seat is inches above the sea. I lower myself off the transom until I am sitting on the seat. My feet dangle in the water and my bottom is gently dunked into the sea as *Recluse* slowly moves with the infinitesimal ocean swell.

I've placed everything within reach on the afterdeck, and I start by applying sandpaper to the letters spelling *Recluse*, erasing them from the painted stern. When I have finished, I sand the rest of the transom and then take a pot of white paint and a brush, and carefully paint the entire back of the boat.

I haul myself back on board to wait for the paint to dry.

Two hours later, the sea still calm, I lower myself once more onto the bo'sun's chair, and now, using small brass nails, I carefully fix the letters C-O-R-A-C-L-E where the old name used to be. Not a hint of the old name is left.

I am not concerned about the new-looking paint because the exhaust fumes from the motor will soon discolour the transom again. To make the brass letters look old, I plan to drip a little sea water onto them every day.

The name *Recluse* is also painted on the life rings, and I spend the rest of the day sanding the letters off and repainting the rings with the same white paint. Using two coats, I completely obliterate any sign of the old name, and use a stencil to paint the name *Coracle* on them.

One last job, to remove all evidence of the yacht's real identity, is to get rid of the registration number. *Recluse* is a documented vessel, and her number is deeply etched into a thick deck beam in the forepeak. With a chisel I slowly and sweatily carve away at the numbers until there's a quarter-inch indentation in the beam, two feet long and four inches wide. Carefully trimming a plank I brought for this purpose, I fit it into the indentation, using glue to fix it in place. When the glue has set I sand the edges of the inset smooth, flush with the rest of the beam, and paint it. The paint is stark white and fresh compared to the paint around it, but this does not concern me much. Maybe later I will paint out the entire forepeak.

I will have to get used to thinking of my boat as *Coracle*. She is *Recluse* no more.

* * *

This now must surely be the doldrums. The wind returned for a while, but in variable light breezes and only for another four days, giving us just under three hundred miles on the log. It is now much more fluky. Sometimes the yacht is becalmed for half a day, with the wind blowing gently for just an hour or two. I spend most of the time waiting, feeling hot and frustrated. We are now making barely fifty miles a day.

Another irritation is the rainsqualls. These arrive with increasing frequency as the yacht moves further into the becalmed area – long fat clouds hanging low on legs of rain, moving slowly across the sea surface like caterpillars. I refer to them as such in my logbook. The caterpillars usually have a wind strength of around twenty-five knots, though the bigger ones often get up to thirty-five. The sails on *Coracle* are old, and if I'm not careful, a sudden squall will rip them. A typical entry in the logbook looks something like this:

> **Time:** *1530 hrs.* **Log reading:** *2026 miles.* **Course steered:** *237 degrees magnetic.* **Barometer:** *1026 millibars.* **Bilge:** *ten pumps.* **Sea:** *calm.* **Wind:** *Nothing to light and variable, mostly east.* **Position:** *10° 31' north, 162° 05' west.* **Remarks:** *Hit by another* FUCKING PISSING SHITTING *caterpillar this morning! Mainsail torn again, and it took nearly three hours to repair. I'm opening a can of peaches tonight. Fuck it!*

Most of the time I can see the caterpillars coming, the squall angling across the ocean on a fairly easy path to read. A few times I use the engine briefly to hasten out of its way, and occasionally I release wind out the sails to slow *Coracle*, waiting for the squall to cross ahead of us.

But now and then I am caught, and if I am taken by surprise, the unexpected wind heels the vessel until her gunwales are underwater. Loud creaking and tumbling objects accompany my hasty scrambling to get out on deck and pull down the violently flogging sails.

At night I take care not to be caught while I am asleep. I reef the mainsail to its second reefing point and change the jib to number two. At times, however, these precautions prove not to be enough, and an unseen squall creeps up on me and flogs a new tear in the old sails, which I then have to repair.

Our progress across this ocean has become irritatingly slow.

* * *

I hear a loud crash as the boom gybes, and feel a stomach-dropping lurch as *Coracle* swings wildly over to starboard. This has me off my bunk immediately and out of the companionway, as I stumble up through the dark and rain to grab the helm.

I work the sleep from my mind as I try to orient myself to the wind, and spin the wheel. The boom crashes back again and *Coracle* surges forward, accelerating rapidly as her sails crack open, filled with thirty-five to forty knots of wind.

Holding her downwind, I struggle to keep the strain off the sails. She is cavorting and gyrating now through the squally waves, reaching speeds of over eight knots as her over-canvassed rig bends and strains under the extreme pressure.

The rain is lashing across me as I stand naked, peering ahead and trying to see the ghostly shape of the jib, which warns me of an impending gybe by switching to the other side of the vessel. Water is in my eyes and dripping off my face, streaming from the mizzenmast above me and running across the decks to collect in the scuppers.

I know that the squall will soon pass, and that I must keep *Coracle* running before the wind to save the sails. This is just another fucking caterpillar, but it's a big one. I settle into a steady rhythm, correcting the wheel every time I feel the vessel's stern lift, holding the helm momentarily against her surging, and then easing it back to its neutral position just before she settles.

My course is a knife-edge line, keeping her facing almost exactly downwind in order to protect the sails. I shelter the jib by keeping it behind the mainsail, which itself has less pressure on it because the boat is running before the wind. But this brings me very close to a gybe, which in this squally blow could damage the rig by violently swinging the boom across. I can hardly see a thing and I steer mostly by touch – the pressure of the spokes against my palms, the wind on my back, and the tilt of the deck under my feet.

It's cold now. The rain is whipping against my bare skin, the wind reducing my body temperature to a chill that I am entirely unaccustomed to in these tropical climes. I start to shiver, clenching my teeth as I work the wheel. How long is this going to last?

Normally, a rainsquall is over within fifteen to thirty minutes. But this has been going on for over two hours now, with no sign of abating. The wind is gusting at what seems like fifty knots or so, and I fear it might get worse.

A thought hits me. I haven't checked the barometer in the last four hours. Could a hurricane have crept up on me? Will the wind keep increasing until it is a full-blown cyclone? And me without any clothes on. But no, hurricanes give more warning than that – what about the sky going all funny? What about that sultry, threatening atmosphere before the storm?

But I was asleep. It was dark, and I was unaware of any changes. Maybe all the signs were there. The wind has reached storm force, and that's too strong for a rainsquall. Oh shit. Maybe this is it. The ultimate storm, a hurricane.

But then another thought strikes me. What about the waves? If this were a hurricane, I'd already be seeing big seas. Hurricanes drive a huge swell before them, and the sea is still flat, though not so flat any more. The waves are now four to six feet. Is this a hurricane in its infancy?

Blinded by rain and shivering uncontrollably, I hang on to the wheel with growing dread, guiding my boat as she charges through the night, and wondering if I am about to face my worst fear.

* * *

The wind has gone. *Coracle* is rolling heavily in seas that are confused by the absence of their master. The waves lop and they slop, peaking and flattening, their power diminishing without the energy from the wind.

I am down below, eating. Two cans of stew, one can of soup, coffee on the boil, and I have opened one of my precious packets of cookies. I am so hungry that my stomach feels like it is trying to wrestle one of my vertebrae loose.

Five hours I spent steering, five hours of misery in the mother of all caterpillars. Five hours of being cold and wet and frightened, afraid that this caterpillar might metamorphose into a massive monster-moth with circling white wings, forcing us to the bottom with its hurricane breath.

* * *

Another week goes by. I have covered less than three hundred miles, and my patience is not so much wearing thin as being abraded by forty-grit sandpaper. I hate the caterpillars for their furtive treachery, and I resent them even more because they have the only wind on this goddamned ocean. For nearly six hours now, I have motored, heading due south in a desperate attempt to find wind and escape the doldrums. Fighting a battle against my conscience over the fuel I am wasting, I eventually switch off the engine.

I am waiting, waiting and repairing sails. I use every bit of breeze I get, no longer avoiding the squalls. I steer deliberately towards them, trying to maximise the distance I can gain from the wind. But *Coracle*'s sails are sun-weakened, the stitching is giving way, and I spend an average of three hours a day repairing the seams. Using a special protective device for my hands, called a palm, I push a thick sail needle through the heavy sailcloth. I protect the thick thread and make it easier to pass through the sailcloth by first pulling the thread through a wax ball. By now I am proficient at sewing, using a zigzag pattern –

a sail stitch – for the seams and patches, and a herringbone stitch for the smaller tears.

My frustration over the lack of wind is aggravated by the loneliness I'm feeling. Forward progress made it easier, giving me a sense that soon it would be over and I'd be with people again. But now I am stuck here making no headway. Stuck on this eternal infernal fucking ocean.

* * *

Unbelievably, our pace becomes even slower. No more than ten or twelve miles a day, and most of that due to the ocean current. On this vast sea, that is negligible; we may as well be completely stationary. The days are long, slow, windless hours of wicked heat, of sweating and miserable waiting. The sun is the only thing that moves in this vast space. There are far fewer caterpillars, and they have become much weaker and smaller, with a torpid breeze that gains us no more than a mile or two if we are lucky enough to catch one of them.

The days drag by. I try to find tasks to occupy myself, to take my mind off my detention on this desolate ocean. I splice lines that don't need splicing. I whip ends that are already done. I take apart every pump on the vessel – bilge pump, galley salt-water pump and freshwater foot pump – then clean them out and reassemble them. I've used up the rest of the paint in the forepeak, painting out three-quarters of the little cabin before the paint ran out. I practise tying different knots and try to invent new ones. These are the only 'knots' I am making, since *Coracle* is virtually at a standstill – but that thought does not amuse me. Reading one of my four books is a treasured occupation, but I have restricted this pastime to just one hour a day so as to ration this precious commodity. I am now rereading *Papillon*.

Navigation occupies and obsesses me. I've reread Mary Blewitt's book, and every day I take star sights, moon shots and sun sights. I would like to practise a North Star calculation but I can't see Polaris from this low latitude. Every day, after I have finished my sights and found our position, I rework my calculations over again in the hope that I might find an error somewhere, and that our position is a mile or two further ahead than the sightings indicate. The crosses that mark our daily positions on the chart are so close together now that they look as if they've run into a traffic jam.

Lying in the shade of the foredeck, I stare for hours over the almost stationary bow. I have a kind of compulsion to catch sight of something that might indicate that I share this earth with another species. A fish, a feather, a bottle, anything at all would make me happy. I try to control the frustration that is eating away at me. I force myself to curb my impatience, my longing to be away from here. I must just wait, I tell myself; other seamen have been through this before. Eventually, currents or the wind will take us out of this doldrums area. I must be strong and just let the time pass as a necessary requirement for my escape. I'll never again feel impatience at having to wait in a queue, or in traffic, or for an unpunctual girlfriend.

Especially that. I think of Joanne with a yearning that is not so much about who she is but what she represents – human company. I fantasise about seeing her again – about calling her from Australia and her flying out to join me there. Dreams that make my mood lighten and then come crashing down again as I'm reminded of how far I have yet to sail to that country, and how long *Coracle* and I have been floating alone and motionless in this windless sea, at a pace almost equal to that of the tectonic plates. I've no idea which direction the Australian continental drift is going, but if it's westward we won't be able to catch up with it at this speed. It's a thought that makes me want to weep.

* * *

There has been no sign of wind at all now for over five days. *Coracle* is sitting with her sails drooping listlessly from her spars; a glassy sea surface surrounds her and I can see my reflection as I gaze into the depths. Some six thousand feet below me is land: mother earth – which connects to dry land, full of people, all going about their happy lives.

I take the surfboard out of the forepeak where I stowed it in Hawaii and slip over the side of *Coracle*, paddling around the near-motionless hull of my boat with a strange sense of alienation. I have been a part of her for so long that this small separation gives me a weird feeling. Strange, too, is the fact that I am floating on my board over such a vast depth.

I paddle further away, partly to look at *Coracle* from another angle and partly in response to some inner dare. I am achingly aware that if a gust of wind comes along, the yacht will take off and leave me stranded on my surfboard. I could never catch her.

Sitting on the board, my feet dangling in the warm water, I take a slow scan around the sea, checking for caterpillars and looking for telltale cat's paws of wind. I see nothing, just a smooth surface baked flat by the sun. I paddle out further.

Now I am about a hundred yards from *Coracle*, and I sit on my board again and study her. She looks white and beautiful. Perched prettily upon the sea surface as she waits, the lovely sheer to her deck line momentarily overcomes my nervousness at being so far from her. She is exactly duplicated by her reflection, with not a ripple disturbing the lines above or below the water. It is a picture of stark perfection.

My appreciation crumbles as I visualise an unseen wind creeping up and filling her sails, and her graceful hull sailing away from my futile efforts to paddle after her. I imagine a slow and horrible demise on my surfboard, as *Coracle* gets smaller and smaller and eventually disappears over the horizon, leaving me absolutely and truly alone.

I paddle back and my relief is almost tangible as I reach her side. I sit for a moment and contemplate my fear. Now that I am holding on to her, my thoughts seem ludicrous. There is no wind for miles around, and even if a gust did come, I would see it, wouldn't I?

I push myself from her and slowly paddle away again. This time I am over two hundred yards away before I stop. This is weird, me sitting here and her sitting there – separated after so long together.

What about sharks? I become conscious of my legs in the water. I tell myself that this is ridiculous, that the chances of a shark happening to be in this patch of sea right now are extremely remote. Still, I lie flat on the board with my legs out of the water, the notion adding to an almost uncontrollable desire to be back on my boat.

I paddle back to *Coracle* once more.

As I reach her I again feel the easing of my tension, the diminishing of my fears. My heartbeat slows to normal. And yet, despite my urge to be back on board, I make no move to climb back onto the security of her deck.

'What are you trying to prove?' I berate myself. 'Who do you think is going to appreciate your little act of daring, out here?'

What does it matter? What do *you* matter? It's as though somebody else is answering me. I push myself away from the hull again, and a strange sensation spreads within me – an abandonment of fear, of my quest to reach Australia, and maybe even of life.

I've come to a decision. I'll show what I can do. I'll paddle out until I know I have conquered my fear. If *Coracle* sails away, so be it.

I paddle forcefully now, pulling myself further and further away. My heart is beating strongly and I am light-headed with alarm at the absurdity of what I'm doing, yet I feel weird pleasurable warmth at my own carelessness. I might die, and I don't really care. At least I won't be lonely any more. There's nobody out here to miss me, and nobody will give a damn. I won't have to face any more thoughts about my future.

I stop paddling. I am at least a quarter of a mile away, and even if I saw wind approaching I would not be able to get back to her in time.

Coracle looks small on the empty expanse of sea. She is a tiny remote island, stuck like me in the middle of this ocean that never ends. We are a million miles away from anyone, from anything at all.

We are not even together any more. She is sitting there without me, as empty as my own heart, nobody caring for her, nobody to drive her, and no one to show her the way to civilisation.

I paddle back again, pulling myself through the water as though a shark is chasing me. The surfboard is cleaving a small bow wave and my shoulder muscles begin to ache with the effort I put into my strokes, but I don't stop paddling until I reach *Coracle*. I grab onto her gunwale, gasping for air, gasping with relief, gasping at the glimpse of my own insanity.

I pull myself on board with trembling arms.

* * *

The wind has come back at last, though it is light and variable. We are still occasionally beset by the caterpillars, but at least we are making progress again, even if it is only fifty to eighty miles per day. The sound of water lapping and sloshing along *Coracle*'s hull brings me instant happiness when I wake during the night. It is the sound of our freedom, freedom from the doldrums, freedom from our torment, freedom from this huge empty prison.

As the days pass, the wind settles into a light easterly, pushing us slowly westwards towards that elusive horizon. I steer sometimes, when the wind is too light or when our course is almost directly downwind and I cannot get the sails to guide her in that direction. But we are now at least moving consistently, eating up miles.

During the daytime I read if I have to take the wheel. I am able to steer her now while reading, with only an occasional glance at the compass – most of the time steering with my feet, my back propped up against the cockpit-coaming, and my book in my lap. Still carefully rationing each book, I read no more than a hundred pages a day.

I force myself to read slowly, absorbing every word, and sometimes even rereading certain parts if they are well written or exciting. My biggest regret is not bringing more books – at the time I regarded them as a superfluous luxury I was unable to afford. Apart from sleeping and navigating, reading is the only thing that helps pass the time.

And time *is* passing, as are the miles. Every day now we cover an appreciable distance on the chart, with a two-inch gap between my daily positions instead of the totally disheartening eighth of an inch, or less, while in the doldrums.

Australia no longer seems such a long way away. I begin working out how long still to get there. When I started off, the distance from Hawaii to Australia was too vast for me to consider how many weeks and days it would take. Two months, two and a half months – maybe even more. I thought then only in vague terms about voyage duration. But now, if I can maintain this speed, I'll be in Australia in about four weeks – only twenty-eight days or so, maybe less. I feel very happy.

And then the mast falls down. The crash jars me awake ...

13

Dismasted.

It's been two days now that I've been trapped in despair, unable to plan my way out of this. But I must. I still feel anger and frustration, though now that has more to do with myself than my circumstances.

Willing myself out of my funk, I decide to make a jury rig. Anything, just to give us propulsion. Other dismasted sailors have done it. There are sails and spars on board; I just have to think of a way. Even if it makes the yacht go really slowly, at least we'll be moving. This is a setback, but we're not totally helpless.

First I have to do something with the fallen rig. If I do get a jury rig together it will be virtually impossible to tow the mast, so I have two choices – either ditch it or get it back on board. If I ditch it, I have no idea how I'll get another one. It'll be horrendously expensive getting a mast and all its accoutrements out to some island here in the Pacific. I'll just have to abandon the boat wherever I land and get myself to a place where I can find work – without a proper rig I can't see a way to continue. But if I can get the mast back onto the deck somehow I might be able to re-rig it somewhere, and in that way carry on to Australia.

So I set about preparing to lift the mast onto *Coracle*'s deck.

I dive into the warm ocean and swim out to the mast to strip it of the sails and spars and all the running and standing rigging. The water-filled sails are heavy, billowing lazily in the swells and difficult to handle, exhausting me by the time I've pulled them all onto the deck. The mast is also rolling about and surging with the waves, tangling me in wires and ropes and sailcloth, and almost drowning me. A gashed and bleeding knuckle raises another issue. Sharks. Although the chances are pretty remote, I can't help staring into the blue depths for a glimpse of some hungry lurking monster, hoping to see him before he shoots up to grab his meal. And the fact that it's getting dark by the time I finish doesn't help matters either.

At last, all the components of the rig are back on board, the mast now a stripped-bare pole.

* * *

In the light of dawn I begin the next step: lifting the heavy spar out of the water. To do this I use the mizzenmast, plus the spinnaker pole that I set upright where the mainmast was, held in place by four ropes. A block tied to the top allows me to run a rope through and back to a cockpit winch. By a series of winching moves, seesawing the mast upwards, I eventually have it level with the top of the boat. The next step is tricky. Relying on the weight of the mainmast to keep tension on the starboard rigging of the mizzen, I undo the port shrouds – the side stays – of the little mast, and then swing the mainmast inboard until it lies askew across the cabin top. I then re-secure the mizzen stays and remove the spinnaker pole so that I can lever the heavy mast until it rests on the steel railings in the front and back of the boat. The middle I support with a bucket and a piece of wood. Finally it is done. The mainmast is back on board, and darkness comes again. It has been a long day and I sleep deeply.

At first light, I jump up and set about preparing a jury rig.

The mizzenmast is too far aft and too small to be of any use by itself. A sail on it would just turn the boat into the wind. I need to set up something forward. While stripping the mast and getting it back on board, I had some thoughts on how to do this. The spinnaker pole is too short by itself to be of any use, as is the main boom. But what if I tie the two together, making the one sort of like the topmast on a schooner? Then I'd have a reasonably lengthy mast again. But to withstand the pressures of sailing they would need something like the steel bands that join the masts on tall ships.

There is just such a band on board: in one of the lockers of the cockpit, attached to the side and holding the gas bottle in place, is a metal ring. I measure the ring – it's just wide enough to go around both poles, but I need to flatten it a bit to make it more oval. Wedges all the way around will make it tight around the poles.

These I fabricate out of bits of wood I have in the forepeak. Then I set about constructing my new mast. After laying the spinnaker pole and the main boom along the deck, I slide the flattened hoop over the two poles at the point where they overlap. Next, I push the wedges underneath the hoop and smack them in with a hammer, driving the wood until it starts to splinter. And finally I wind two lengths of rope tightly around the two poles above and below the hoop.

There. My new mast is ready, and I use a halyard on the mizzenmast to raise it, controlling the swinging of the new mast with ropes to the side. It is tricky with the rolling boat, but eventually the new mast is upright and secured, the gooseneck fitting of the main boom fastened to the mainmast step, held in place with a strong lashing. The top of the spinnaker pole is now nearly twenty feet high, almost as tall as the mizzen. Three rope stays secure the top of the new mast to the deck.

Now I raise a jib, sideways. The sail reaches all the way back to the stern of *Coracle* when I sheet it in, and the lower edge hangs down almost into the water like a gigantic floppy bloomer.

But it works: with the mizzen up as well, and the storm jib rigged as a mizzen staysail, *Coracle* leaps forward at a stunning four and a half knots. Maybe not quite the speed I would like to be doing, but a lot better than just drifting around with the current.

With this new rig I know I'll have to steer myself all the time, and this means that at night I'll have to stop the boat to sleep, considerably cutting down the distance I cover each day. I'm not looking forward to the upcoming weeks of sitting behind the wheel, but I'm on my way again and I have just over three thousand miles to go to Australia. At nearly five knots that shouldn't take me more than five weeks, barring mishaps like meeting a hurricane, or running out of food.

* * *

Five days pass, and I cross the equator. I've been anticipating this event for some time now, but it turns out to be rather anti-climactic. I'm back in the southern hemisphere, and it looks just like the northern one.

I'm totally weary of steering day after day for up to sixteen hours at a stretch, and I'm frustrated at having to stop at night to rest. I even have to stop the boat to take sun sights. I am making only about seventy to eighty miles a day, and the daily positions I mark on the chart show a line of crosses depressingly close together. They head now towards a group of islands called the Ellice Islands. I've decided that I am going to stop at Funafuti, one of the islands, where I may be able re-step the mast. Sailing to Australia with my jury-rigged vessel is not really an option that I care to consider any more. Fortunately, I have a chart of Funafuti that I bought in Hawaii, having allowed then for the possibility that I might have to stop for emergency repairs. Funafuti is the main island of the Ellice group, and it is a coral atoll.

I'm less than five hundred miles away now, and if the wind stays like this I should reach it in just over a week.

This central part of the Pacific is virtually devoid of islands, a big barren expanse of water that is surrounded by the ring of fire, the volcanic islands that have formed along the tectonic plate lines on the outer edges of the Pacific. The only other island I have passed is Johnston Atoll, way to the north and east now. The normal route for yachts cruising the Pacific is to sail south to the Marquesas, and from there along the South Sea island chain, making landfall every few days or so. Very few yachts choose the route I have taken, passing through the near-uninhabited middle of this enormous ocean. I decided on this way for two reasons: firstly, because any investigation would be unlikely to look for me here, and secondly because I don't have the funds to cruise through the Pacific. I need to get to a place where I can make some money.

The onerous hours of steering, together with my despondency over the slowness of our passage, are taking their toll on me. Will this voyage ever end? Although my line of marks across the chart tallies with the dead-reckoning positions I calculate, I now begin to doubt them. Are we really where they say we are? It is a silly thought, and my logic tells me that my navigation is fine. I know that my adeptness with the sextant has greatly improved. I have no reason to doubt where I am – but I have not yet seen the proof of it.

Every day the scene is the same as the previous day's. I find myself wondering: What if this is all wrong? Or there's something I haven't done? What if there is some fault with something – my calculations, or the compass, the sextant, or maybe the whole goddamned theory – and all these positions are just hogwash?

Maybe I'm sailing around in circles. Maybe the reason that all the horizons look the same is because they are. But wait. What about the doldrums? What about the fact it has become much hotter since leaving Hawaii? And the sun is to the north of us now. What about that, hmm? What is your answer to that piece of intelligence, you illogical idiot?

Wow! Now I'm not just talking to myself, I'm arguing with myself – over some idiotic thought, some miserable fantasy borne out of my insecurity about my own ability, or my solitude. Okay, stop it. I know where we are. We're heading for Funafuti where there are people. I think.

The island must surely be populated. It is, after all, the main island of the Ellice group. There must be somebody there. But what if there isn't? What if there has been a nuclear war? What if Russia has lobbed a missile at America? And what if America fired back and a full-scale nuclear war has been going on while I have been sailing along, oblivious of the radioactive fallout and the carnage – the entire population of the earth dying in a frenzy of combat? What if I am the only person left on earth? It sure feels like I am. I haven't seen a ship or plane since I left, and although I know this is an unfrequented part of the ocean, isn't that a bit unusual? Is it because of a war that there's been a complete absence of anything related to human existence all these weeks? Is that why I don't even get any distorted voices on the radio any more? Everybody is dead, and I am completely alone in the world.

Ah, fuck! Stop it! I remonstrate with myself, realising that a huge weight of depression lies like a thick coating of lead over my heart. This fantasy of being alone in the world has allowed a heavy sorrow to creep over me with insidious stealth.

This is stupid, first the navigation and now this. Get your mind out of it, Rob. You're making yourself upset with your own ridiculous childish imagination. I feel somehow disgusted with myself, at the loss of control, as if I am a still a kid. What am I anyway, a man or a boy?

Mentally I give myself a huge kick in the butt. I'm away from Los Angeles and Vlazo, I've crossed the doldrums, I'm sailing again after losing the mast. I've got this far, haven't I? Think of other things, think of cities, buses, cars, commuter trains. Think of a happy, easy world filled with people. With an effort I try to clear my head of stupid thoughts. But it is slow, and my sorrow envelops me like a cloud of African flies. I brush them away, but they keep coming back as I steer my crippled boat through the waves.

* * *

We're nearly there. Funafuti is less than eighty miles away. It is late afternoon and I've just finished working out our position. We're doing a little over four knots, and according to my calculations we crossed the International Date Line early this morning, longitude 180 degrees. We should be at the island mid-morning tomorrow, if the wind holds.

Actually, it is tomorrow. Or is it yesterday? I have to think for a moment. When the sun crosses over the date line the day starts at Greenwich, so time-wise the western hemisphere is behind the east. Therefore, since I am sailing from the west into the east, it is now yesterday. No, how can that be? How can I be in a day I have already been in? This is like travelling back in time, and my voyage has just become longer by a day. Or has it?

I give up, turning my thoughts to something more pleasant, to my arrival in Funafuti, to no longer having to sit behind this fucking wheel any more. My insides feel squeezed, I am so excited. Will I really see land tomorrow, and people, and grass and trees, and maybe even houses? I wonder if they have houses on an atoll. Well, huts maybe, I don't care. I just want to see people again.

There may be a shop to buy food. They must have some sort of shop, surely, or how do the inhabitants get food? Maybe they just grow it: bananas, papayas, even mangos, possibly. What other tropical fruits could there be? My mouth waters as I try to remember other tropical produce. It is so long now since I have eaten anything fresh that the thought of biting into fruit makes my salivary glands squirt like fire trucks having a water fight.

I don't lower the sails and go to sleep as I usually do. Instead, I steer and stare through the dark towards the bow of the vessel which is dimly visible under the starlight, the sideways jib faintly illuminated by the greenish glow of the phosphorescence. A curling green glow spins off the rudder ten feet below the wake, laying a double trail behind us as *Coracle* ploughs slowly towards Funafuti.

Apart from my eagerness to reach land, I have another reason for staying on deck. I must watch for ocean currents, or an unanticipated increase in our speed, or a mistake in my calculations.

I must watch to make sure that we do not arrive with a crash.

* * *

I dare not take my eyes off the horizon in front of us. The sun has been up for four hours now, and we are very close to land. I know that Funafuti, as an atoll, is only about twenty feet high, though buildings and trees should increase its visibility. My dead-reckoning calculations place me within ten miles of the island, and now I am worried that I might miss it. It is so small that a mere five miles out of position could cause us to go sailing right by it.

It is time for a sun sight.

I lower the jib and carefully remove the fragile sextant from its box, then get myself into my usual position – butt against the after part of the cabin top, legs spread wide, and facing out towards the morning sun.

After I finish the calculations I draw my bearing line on the chart and study it carefully, trying to work out my position in relation to Funafuti. Unfortunately, a single sun sight gives only a position line, running at ninety degrees to the direction towards the sun. I have no idea where on the line I am. Also, because it's so early in the day, this line is running almost north to south. Since I am heading almost due west, it doesn't give me a good indication of what course to steer, though it does tell me that I am very near. I pull the sail back up and resume my steering and staring.

I don't know if my course is taking me north or south of the island, but feel that I should soon be able to see it. We are less than ten miles from it now, according to my calculations, and although from a small yacht the horizon is only about three miles away, tall objects such as trees and buildings might be visible if they were a hundred feet or so high. How tall is a coconut palm? Mentally, I try to measure it against the horizontal mainmast, which is forty-eight feet in length. A palm, I guess, is not a hundred feet tall.

I keep staring, narrowing my lids against the glare as I gaze longingly towards the empty rim of the sea.

I see it.

There it is, a long, low smudge of land along the horizon. Oh wow. Oh boy. Funafuti. I stare intensely, trying to make out more. There are small hills, a wavy silhouette that is sand-coloured, sharply defined against the blue sky. I let the sheet of the jib go and rush below to study the chart, seeking to identify the hills from the contour lines on the chart to see exactly what part of the island I am viewing.

But there are no contour lines on the chart, only a single building – a church – shown as an identifying mark. I jump back up the companionway to see if I can make out the building.

The island is gone.

No. It can't be. I stare towards where I saw it, but it is nowhere in sight. The empty horizon taunts me, mocking my efforts to find the island again. I rub my eyes to clear them, and wildly scan the sea. There is no land. There is nothing – it must have been a trick of my eyes. I've been staring too long into the bright sunlight. Maybe it was some sort of low cloud, my enthusiasm and longing causing me to mistake it for land. Disappointment and frustration mingle to become a festering bubble in my chest, making me want to scream out loud, to vent my fury at nature's hoax. Whatever I saw, it is no longer there.

One hour later, and I have still not seen the island. I feel sick. A wrenching conflict has started inside me. Should I stop sailing my westerly course and begin some sort of search pattern, or just keep going? I've taken another sight, which has put my line of position almost through Funafuti – but I still don't know which side of the island I'm on, north or south. If I miss the atoll I'll have to sail back upwind, and I doubt my jury-rigged vessel can do that. I'd have to use up the last of my diesel trying to find it. Or be forced to carry on to Australia.

I jump from the deck to the chart table, calculating and recalculating, comparing my dead reckoning to my sights, and then scramble back to my vigil, standing and steering and gazing out towards the unrelentingly empty horizon. A rain cloud about two miles to port blocks my view, but the rest of the ocean is an immense water-filled void, the same vacant sea that has surrounded me for so many weeks now.

Where is it? Have I missed it? Maybe my fears about everything are correct. Maybe it's all a lie, the sextant, the compass, my charts, the whole damn theory of celestial navigation. Or maybe nuclear bombs have blown the whole island off the face of the earth.

The rain cloud lifts and I am looking at palm trees.

PALM TREES?

Holy fuck! It's palm trees. It's the island. I can't believe it. Palm trees. Growing out of the ocean. No, there is land. I can see the land now. I can't believe I'm so close. Funafuti is no more than two or three miles away, and I think I can see the building marked on the chart – something white, anyway, something made by humans.

Trembling, I go below to check the chart again. My heart dances.

* * *

I am on the southwestern side of the lagoon now, sails down and my smelly Bukh diesel running, motoring slowly parallel to the coral reef.

Funafuti is shaped like a curved pipette. The main part of the island is one mile long and about a third of a mile wide, with long, thin arms extending about three miles from either end. Where the land ends the coral reef begins, forming a circle around the lagoon.

My chart shows a single entrance into the lagoon, a narrow channel midway along the southwestern side of the coral. It is buoyed, so it should be easy to find. *Coracle* and I are about a quarter of a mile away from the waves breaking heavily along the perimeter reef. I look for the buoys.

Scanning carefully over the mainmast towards the edge of the surf line as we motor along, I see no sign of these markers, just an unbroken line of crashing waves. Finally, having neared the far end of the coral reef and now almost at the other side of the island, I turn *Coracle* around. We motor back along the reef, closer to the coral, my search now a little more anxious.

Still no buoys.

After about six miles we are nearly back at the western part of the island, and still there's no sign of the channel. I stop the boat and study the chart carefully. There is no other way in; an unbroken line of coral circles the lagoon, an impassable barrier of shallow spiky reef and thundering waves, with only one entrance.

The chart indicates that the channel, though narrow, is deep. It can't have filled in or just disappeared. But where is it? Where are the buoys, the channel markers?

There is a tiny island – a sandspit really – with half a dozen palm trees just inside the coral reef, marked on the chart and fairly close to where I am. From it, I can ascertain my position exactly. I motor *Coracle* towards it and stop the boat when I am directly opposite the spit.

I take a log reading and then motor carefully along a course I have set from the chart. After precisely one and a quarter miles I stop *Coracle* again. I should now be exactly at the mouth of the channel.

I climb up onto the cabin top and straddle the mast, straining my eyes for a glimpse of the buoys. But I see nothing, just the backs of the waves as they curl away and crash down onto the jagged reef with heaving roars and sprays of white froth. I come to an inescapable conclusion.

The buoys are gone.

The chart probably hasn't been updated in ten or twenty years. It is such an isolated area – who knows when a yacht or a ship last came here? I'll have to find the channel without the buoys.

I'm pretty sure that my position is correct. We should now be exactly at the channel entrance, even though the surf line is unbroken. I start motoring *Coracle* straight towards the surf, watching with trepidation the powerful breakers in front of us.

Closer and closer, engine idling and propeller spinning slowly, and I still cannot make out the channel. Waves are breaking on reefs either side of the boat now and I am almost on top of the surf. What is in front? Where is the channel? The sound of the waves smashing onto the coral is frightening – heaving masses of water that crash down onto an unseen reef. I can't give up. I have to find the channel. There's no way I can even think of continuing my voyage onwards.

With less than eighty feet to go until we are in the breakers, my hand is closed tightly around the throttle, ready to plunge it into reverse. I study the waves coming up behind almost as closely as I watch those in front. Seventy, sixty, fifty feet – the pounding of the surf stretches my nerves tight. The waves are thundering onto the shallow razor-wire coral just ahead of us.

Then I see: the surf in front looks different. The waves are breaking further in, without the force of those on either side of us. They are peeling away from the coral to the left and right, and meet in front of *Coracle*'s bows.

An unusually high wave lifts the boat, and there, almost directly in front of us, is the channel. A deep blue-green, flecked with foam, it leads tantalisingly into the calm lagoon. I pull the throttle back into neutral and wait, watching the waves and waiting for the right moment to enter.

In quick succession, three large waves pass under the boat, allowing me a view each time of the entrance as they crash with sickening force on the coral on either side. Broken surf rolls into the channel and meets in the middle – foaming white water right across the mouth of the way in.

With a final tweak of my nerves I push the throttle, the flat sea behind us signalling that it is time to go. Waves break as we reach the entrance, peeling from the reef that lies only fifty feet away on either side, a foaming crest reaching *Coracle*'s stern as we motor towards the calmer water ahead. I fight the wheel as the three-foot wave pushes us forward, slewing the yacht around until we are heading almost directly towards the vicious-looking coral.

I spin the wheel hard and gun the engine to get her back on course. Holding the spokes against the force of the rudder, I tense as the wave passes underneath. Then the bow comes around with a jerk, swinging sharply away from the reef – *Coracle* is clearly as scared as I am. And then we are in.

We motor past the reef's submerged vertical sides, fear-sweat running down my face, and relief at our safe passing transforming the menacing coral into a beautiful playground for small fish. There are colourful fronds and pretty polyps along the sides of the channel, and the aquamarine lagoon in front of us is calm and welcoming. And I am as happy and excited as any person on this planet.

* * *

It is almost four miles across the lagoon, and I keep a careful watch for coral heads. As I near the land I can see huts and objects on the beach, and then one of the objects moves. I realise it is a human being, a person, walking up the sand and disappearing between the huts.

I control my urge to speed up, to push the throttle to its maximum. I want *Coracle* anchored and I want to be on that land so absolutely inviting, to feel the sand under my feet. To stand once more on the earth, solid and stable, smelling the musty odours of plants and soil. I want to hear the sound of human voices, no matter what language they speak.

I want off this boat.

* * *

With the throttle in neutral, *Coracle* gently noses towards the beach only three hundred feet in front of us. I go forward to drop the anchor I have made ready. As we come to a stop I let go, the rattling sound the chain makes as it runs over the bow roller signalling some deep inner contentment in both of us. We have arrived. We are safe at last within this lagoon, safe from the unpredictable moods of the Pacific, free of caterpillars, and food shortages, and storms, and interminable sitting behind the wheel.

I walk aft to switch off the motor and prepare to go ashore. I notice a small boat being pushed off the beach. There is only one person in it, and I watch as he rows towards us. Going below, I pull on a shirt and prepare myself for human contact, my first in over eight weeks.

14

As he draws alongside, my smile stretches unaccustomed muscles in my face. He is Polynesian, copper-skinned, and is wearing only a sarong and a hat – a white peaked cap. The man is about forty, as far as I can judge, and is carrying a battered briefcase as he beams up at me from a round friendly face.

'How do you do? Are you fine? Please welcome to Funafuti.'

I almost laugh: his English is a bit strange, but I am also hugely relieved. Does he sound strange simply because I haven't heard a human voice for so long?

'Hello,' I answer as he hands me the line from the bow of his boat. I tie it off.

Nimbly, he jumps aboard *Coracle*. 'I am Hu'ati,' he says, placing one hand flat on his chest and lifting his cap with the other. 'Chief immigration officer of Funafuti.' He grins widely and I catch a mischievous glint in his eyes as he puts his cap on his head again. Is he perhaps mocking himself? I grin back, taken with his antics.

'Please, come on down below.' I gesture towards the companion-way, trying to match his weird courtliness.

'No mast,' he says cheerfully as he looks up at the stowed pole. 'Fell down, yes?'

'Yes, I'm afraid so.' In the salon I offer him my passport, which he studies with interest before hauling out an oversized stamp and stamping it officiously, carefully aligning the stamp with the corners of the page. Then he reaches into the briefcase, and with something of a flourish, produces another cap, this time khaki. He places it on his head with a broad smile.

'I am also customs man.' This time there is no doubt. He is as amused by his performance as I am. He fills out a form and stamps it, and then hands it to me along with my Hawaiian clearance that I have presented to him. I am relieved to get it back; even though the form from Funafuti is a proper entrance form, the Hawaiian clearance paper is much bigger and more official-looking. I don't want to relinquish it until I have another big official form to replace it.

After the formalities are completed I accompany him back onto the deck. There is no jetty visible on the island, something I was half hoping for, with maybe some sort of crane to lift the mast back into place. But there is only beach. I am about to ask him if he has any ideas how I can re-step my rig, but before I do so he turns to me.

'You come ashore now?' He points towards the beach. 'I show you island. Yes?'

'Yes, sure.' My problem with the mast can wait till later. At the moment I just want to go to the island and stand on land. I take my surfboard so I can get back; Hu'ati seems amused that I don't have a dinghy.

Once ashore, he leads the way up the beach. I carry my sandals, revelling in the feeling of the sand crunching beneath my feet. I absorb everything around me with the greed of deprivation. I fill all my senses with the land, with the sights, smells and sounds, the total warm substance of it.

We pass a few islanders as we walk through the grass-hutted village – the men lean and friendly, the women also friendly but shy, and not quite as attractive as I imagined Polynesian women to be. The older ones are mostly overweight, the backs of their necks sunk into a thick fold of flesh. But now and then, among the huts, I see pretty young girls sneaking bashful glances at me.

Hu'ati introduces me to his island with pride.

'There is our church.' He points towards a simple stone building, its spire topped by a wooden cross. This is the building I identified on my chart. It is the only permanent identifying mark on this otherwise flat atoll.

We walk some more. The village is small, and apart from the church it is all huts, spaced out along the beach on the lagoon side of the island.

'Most Funafuti people live in village,' Hu'ati tells me. 'Also a missionary.' I ask about this missionary and he explains. 'White woman missionary, from America.' I am interested to meet her.

Funafuti is an airstrip. The entire island has been turned into a landing field. My tour guide explains to me that during the Second World War Funafuti was used as a refuelling base, a jump-off station for American bombers on their way to Japan. Because of the depth of its lagoon and the single deep entrance, bunker ships were able to come in and offload fuel and supplies.

The Americans actually extended the island, bulldozing the middle and pushing the earth off at both ends, in this way lengthening the runway so that it could accommodate the bombers. The old runway is still there, cracked and overgrown.

We walk to one of the narrow arms of the island and Hu'ati shows me the trenches that were dug for extra soil. I am intrigued to see that they are filled with rusty machinery and ancient earth-moving equipment – remnants of the war.

'Hu'ati, why are the trees like that?' I point to a clump of palm trees, all angled at about a forty-five-degree tilt. No wonder I had difficulty seeing the island.

'Hurricane,' he says. 'Come, I show you.'

He takes me to a coconut tree. Pointing to what looks like a small branch near the top, he says, 'Look.'

I realise that what I'm looking at isn't a branch at all. It is a thin stick, about an inch in diameter, jutting out from the dead trunk of the tree.

'Hurricane push it in,' Hu'ati says.

I'm amazed. I know that hurricanes are powerful, but what I am seeing is a piece of wood that has been driven at least an inch or two into a trunk that is extremely hard. It must have hit with the force of a bullet – a scary reminder of the winds I'm dealing with.

Hu'ati tells me more, answering my questions with relish. The islanders all took shelter in the church during this particular hurricane, two years ago. The church was built of coral stones, under the direction of some long-gone missionary, and was the only structure left standing – minus its roof – after the hurricane swept through. All except five of the islanders took shelter within its walls, battered by waves rolling right across the atoll. They survived, but the five who remained in their huts did not.

There are no shops on the island. The inhabitants grow most of their own food, exchanging vegetables for fish, and swapping other things in an age-old bartering system.

I've seen nothing on the island that might help me get the mast back up, even though I've kept my eyes open for some machine or structure that might do it. Eventually I explain my predicament to Hu'ati and ask him if he has any ideas.

'Hmm,' he says, staring out towards *Coracle* in the lagoon with her decapitated rigging. 'There is a ship to come soon, maybe two weeks, maybe three. It has the, um, the …' He extends his forearm at forty-five degrees, moving it up and down, then he makes a grabbing and lifting motion with his hand.

'Derrick,' I say, but the Polynesian looks blank. 'A crane, a crane on the ship – for lifting cargo?' I am hoping that this is what he means. A ship's derrick might be just what I need.

His face clears as though I have just supplied the answer to his problems, instead of the other way around.

'Ah, yes,' he nods happily. 'Crane, yes. For ship.'

I try to contain my excitement as Hu'ati haltingly explains that a supply vessel is due in from the north, from the Gilbert Islands, in less than a month. It will bring medicines and food that the islanders barter for copra – dried coconut flesh – the only product made on the island for trade.

We pass a solitary hut with bars across the window openings, and a barred door. 'That is jail,' Hu'ati says, noticing my interest. His expression becomes mischievous again.

'I also chief of policemen. Only one,' he says with a kind of fake pride. 'Also chief of island,' he looks smug. 'Also postman,' he adds as an afterthought.

'Do you ever get any crime here?' I ask.

'Ah, yes. Not much often,' he says earnestly. 'We have prisoner now.'

I glance over at the obviously empty jail. The door is open.

'So, where is he?' I ask. 'Has he escaped?'

Hu'ati answers my smile with one that is even wider.

'Nowhere to escape,' he says, gesturing around the island. 'He at home now. Come back at night.'

His amusement is as great as my own.

* * *

It's dusk, and I paddle over to *Coracle* on my surfboard using one hand, and with the other I hold up my shirt and sandals to keep them dry. The next day I explore by myself. Apart from Hu'ati, there doesn't seem to be anybody else on the island who speaks English. Except for the missionary, that is, who rather surprisingly has made no attempt to contact me. I'd have thought that any Westerner here would welcome the chance to chat with someone from the same culture.

I wander to the far end of the atoll, along a spit of land so narrow that I can throw a stone into the sea on either side from where I am standing. Mosquitoes rise from the water-filled Second World War ditches, and soon I am slapping and scratching. I try to run, but my legs give out after a few yards. My muscles have atrophied after long periods of sitting or lying around aboard *Coracle*, so I resolve to use my time here to regain some fitness. But for now, all I can do is walk quickly to escape the irritating little bloodsuckers.

Near the end of the spit, away from the mosquitoes, I sit under a lone palm tree and stare out over the Pacific, across the sea that I have travelled. Hawaii lies nearly three thousand miles away, and I ponder my being here on this isolated and beautiful little atoll. I feel deeply content, taking pleasure in the thought of being so close to other people, and in the knowledge that my boat is safe within the lagoon and may soon be fixed.

I allow my thoughts to wander to my time in Los Angeles. What has happened to Mihai? Is he okay? It all seems so remote now, those events, so reassuringly distant from where I am now. When I set off from Hawaii I held off recollections of Mihai and Vlazo and the shooting, feeling that it was a distraction I needed to avoid to keep my mind strong. I felt too disturbed by the images, so I deliberately squashed any remembrances of the incident.

Dwelling on those events now, my mood turns sombre again, so I deliberately push them away. I don't want to think about it in this setting; I don't want any harshness to spoil this perfect serenity.

Instead, I savour the whisper of the wind through the fronds above me and the gentle roar of the surf, rolling across the coral to leave broad white spumes trailing across the clear aquamarine lagoon water. The warm clean sand against my skin reassures me of the proximity of the earth and its people, and yet I am strangely reluctant to be with them, or to talk to them. I am happy to know that they are there, close to me, and that I can be with them if I want to, but for now I feel more comfortable in my solitude.

Twisting around, I can see *Coracle* anchored near the beach, the huts lined along the sand behind her. She looks small from this distance, and perfectly natural in her tropical setting. I think of my dreams in Hawaii, my fantasies of sitting on a palm-lined beach, watching my boat at anchor.

It seems strange to think about it now. *Coracle* and I have been together for such a very long time – or so it seems to me; we've been through so many trials that she feels like an extension of myself. Before, she was just a means of escape and an object of my desire, but now she has become a personality to me. We have become so much a part of each other that I miss her, being away from her. When will I be able to make her whole again?

In the distance, across the lagoon, I see a small shape. As it comes closer I realise it is a pirogue with a sail, and I guess it must be coming back from a fishing trip. It is almost dark when I return to the village, to stroll through it and watch the activities of the islanders. They accept my curiosity with grace, smiling and waving, and I smile and wave back.

* * *

I wake up with flu symptoms. My whole body is sore, a deep ache running through the muscles of my back, extending to every limb. It hurts to bend over and even to stand, and all I want to do is lie down. I have a shitty headache that starts at the back of my neck and spreads upwards and over like a leaden cap on my skull. I take to my bunk, lying down with relief.

As the day goes on it gets worse, with feverish chills passing through me in waves, and a deep muscular ache at the core of my being. I am eventually so weak that it is an effort to prepare dinner, which I have to force myself to eat. In a daze, I return to my bunk, barely aware of when it gets dark. I'm feeling really, really sick.

* * *

My legs hang over the side of the bunk, and the interior of *Coracle* is whirling around. I am dizzy and weak and I'm trying to push myself from the bunk, but the effort is proving too much. I'm so weak that my legs will not support me. I rest, seated on the edge, breathing heavily with my chin hanging on my chest, struggling to get air past a dry, swollen tongue and mouth. I need water; my thirst is closing my throat, making me concentrate my thoughts on getting to the tap in the galley.

When I feel a bit stronger I try to get up again, holding on to the grab rail for support. My legs are trembling and I'm afraid to let go for fear I will fall. With a careful shuffle-step I move shakily towards the galley.

It's a mess. Banana peels and cracker crumbs lie around, and there is a pot on the floor with some sort of congealed mess in it. A dank, lingering stench of rotten food and old dirty clothing assaults my nostrils and I can smell the odour of faeces somewhere. I think maybe it comes from me.

I've been lying here on my bunk for some days now, maybe weeks. A fever has had me drifting in and out of consciousness, and I've had only a hazy awareness of my surroundings, even when I've been lucid. Most of my memories of the past few days are vague and disturbing fragments of feverish dreams.

And sweat. I have perspired in floods, drenching the bedding. The sweat has gathered in pools on my body and on the bunk. It seemed to spring from the nightmares that have tormented me – dreams like huge Salvador Dali paintings viewed through the wrong end of a pair of binoculars. I have a sort of remembrance that I was shouting, in delirium maybe, but I'm not sure when.

I reach the galley and drink straight from the tap, the tepid water tasting wonderful. I have to stop and breathe occasionally, drinking in spurts while my legs and arms shake from the effort of keeping myself up, slaking my thirst with eager slurps from the running water. My leg aches as I pump the foot pump, and when I am finished I allow my body to sag down onto the bottom step of the companionway.

I've never been so sick in my life. Not from measles, flu, chicken pox or any other illness I suffered as a child. Whatever hit me has left me weaker than a starving kitten. Actually, I am starving. I can feel the hollowness inside my ribcage, as though my intestines and other organs have been entirely removed. I look down at my legs and I am shocked at what I see.

They look like they belong to somebody else. They are so thin. How could they become like that in such a short time? I normally have strong legs, although the crossing did take away some of that strength. But the legs I'm looking at are wasted beyond any comprehension. How long was I sick? I have no idea.

With difficulty, stopping often to rest, I open a can of spaghetti and eat it cold. I don't have the energy to cook it. Unable to face the stench from my bunk I ease myself onto the floor, the timbers surprisingly cool and comfortable. Allowing myself to sink back into a doze, I lie and breathe in the comforting smell of *Coracle*'s bilge.

* * *

The first thing I say when I see Hu'ati is, 'What is the date today?' I discover that I have been ill for just over two weeks. His brow wrinkles when I tell him that I've been sick.

'Ah, you alone on boat, long time. You not fix mast?' Then he frowns. 'Maybe you sick with dengue fever.' I've never heard of it.

We are sitting together outside his hut, facing the beach under the shade of a palm tree. I am still weak and woozy but feeling better, my strength returning slowly. He speaks to me of a yacht that was here before me, the last one to visit the island, and tells me about one of the crew members, a child who also contracted dengue fever here. And how the child nearly died.

'Oh, yeah?' I say, perking up with interest. 'When were they here?' Maybe they are off visiting one of the other islands of the Ellice group, and are about to return here. I would love to see another cruising yacht, to have yachtie company.

'Three, maybe four years past,' Hu'ati says.

I look away towards the horizon as I contemplate the utter remoteness of this atoll that his information implies. As if to contradict this impression, I see a ship steaming slowly across the lagoon.

'Hey, look,' I point.

'Yes. Ah ha. It is supply ship. From Gilbert Islands.' He gestures northwards.

We watch as the ship weaves slowly past the coral heads. It is an old and rusty coaster, with a tall funnel behind a rounded old-fashioned bridge. Small and decrepit, it is not much more than a hundred feet in length, but it has a derrick boom mounted behind the high fo'c'sle, stowed across the cargo deck.

This may be my salvation, this old lady of the sea, hiding out here, away from the necessity of complying with the seaworthiness regulations that would be imposed upon her in some First World country. Hope mixes with uncertainty as she anchors a few hundred yards from *Coracle*. Will the ship be able to help? Will the captain be prepared to help me?

Hu'ati jumps up to get papers ready for the new arrival, and I sit, controlling the urge to swim out and talk to the captain. I wait under the palm tree, watching the ship anchor. Finally, a lifeboat is swung out on davits from the side.

There's a fair amount of shouting and struggling as the crew cling to a couple of old hemp ropes running through twisted blocks, and then the boat is lowered jerkily to the water. A rope ladder is flung over the side and two crew members climb down into the tender, one depositing a large sack in the bow. Then another man, heavily built and wearing a singlet, a peaked cap and rolled-up trousers, swings himself nimbly from the ship into the boat. From the way the two crew members hold the vessel steady for him as he jumps aboard, I guess he is probably the captain. A crewman fiddles with some controls, and soon a clattering, smoky little diesel engine is propelling them towards the beach.

With an effort, I get to my feet and go down to where a large crowd has gathered, waiting for the tender to land. As I near them I catch a glimpse of the missionary lady. This is the first time I've seen her, and with the same instinct that makes dogs sniff each other out in recognition of one another, I focus my concentration on her.

She appears to be in her late sixties. Tall, thin and rigid, and dressed in dark, shapeless clothing, she ignores the activity around her. She is, in a single word, austere. I walk along the beach to where she is standing, her bonneted visage fixed upon the approaching launch.

'Hello,' I say as I draw near. 'I'm Rob Fridjhon. From that yacht over there.' I point towards *Coracle* to make sure that she knows which yacht I am referring to.

'How do you do.' While not exactly cold, her tone is indifferent. She bestows barely a flicker of a glance at me before returning her stiff gaze to the tender as its bow scrapes onto the sand. Then, wordlessly, she walks away from me towards the beached vessel.

I am dumbfounded. Here we are, the only two white people for a million miles around, and she snubs me. The captain of the ship hands a small parcel to her and she thanks him with barely a nod, and then walks away without a glance at me. I wonder at her antisocial behaviour. Maybe this is why she's here, isolated from a society she probably hates, her only allegiance to God, and her interaction with native people probably no more than an unfortunate necessity. What hurt has this woman suffered?

Forgetting the strange missionary lady, I stand and watch as the jovial captain hands out mail and parcels, good-natured joshing and ribald shouting accompanying his efforts. This is obviously a big event for the islanders. Nearly everybody on Funafuti appears to be here. I wonder if the prisoner is also present.

When the last of the packages has been handed out I approach the dirty, scarred little boat to speak to the captain.

'Excuse me, sir,' I say to the swarthy man who is about to issue instructions to his crew nearby. 'I have a problem with my yacht.' I point towards *Coracle*. 'My mast fell down and I wondered whether you might be able to help me put it back up again, with your ship?'

He studies me for a disconcertingly long moment. 'Ah so. You are the one with the dismasted yacht?'

I nod. 'Um, unfortunately yes. D'you think it might be possible to use the derrick on your ship to help me lift it back into position?'

He folds his thick arms across his belly and leans back onto the gunwale of the tender, looking quizzically at *Coracle* and then back at me. I wonder if he is going to ask me for some exorbitant sum of money. He can have all I've got left, about thirty dollars. If it's not enough I'll clean his ship, scrape the barnacles off the bottom, paint it from stem to stern, anything.

'Sure.' He beams at me. 'No problem. Just tell me when you want to do it.'

* * *

The mast is back up.

We've managed to re-rig *Coracle* using the rusty old derrick on the *San Cristobal Tres*. It was a bit tricky, as the derrick had only hand-operated winches and not quite enough height, but with Juan – the Filipino captain – and his three crew members helping, plus extra aid from Hu'ati and some of the islanders, we were able to raise the mast back into position and re-step it.

With *Coracle* back at anchor and the rigging all in place, I turn my attention to the broken self-steering system, and cobble together a makeshift splint for it. When I have managed to repair the gear to the best of my limited capacity, I use the halyards of the mizzenmast to lower the self-steering into position. Still fighting the effects of dengue fever, I struggle to reattach it to the transom. It is much weaker than before, so I will have to baby it, steering the boat myself if the wind gets up. But at least I have a self-steering system again, as well as a mainmast.

Barely finished, admiring my handiwork and feeling the satisfaction of having a more or less fully operational yacht again, I see the tender from the ship heading towards me. It comes alongside, and as I move to greet the seaman steering it, he shouts above the popping noise of the diesel as he reverses to stop the boat.

'You come,' he shouts, 'come, talk to captain.' He points at the ship. I jump aboard, curious and only mildly disconcerted at the apparent rudeness of his demand.

Juan is in the wheelhouse of *San Cristobal Tres* and he immediately calls me over, placing a fat finger on the chart. 'Look here: hurricane Francisca is to the east of us, heading west-northwest at twenty-five knots. It is very strong, maybe category three.' I stand transfixed as he pulls on a cheroot, if that's what it is. Pale yellow and thinner than usual, it's unlike any cigarette I've ever seen. I breathe in its pungent but strangely pleasant odour as Juan continues, 'You must go to Suva. It is a good place, good hurricane hole. I've been to Suva many times.'

I nod, feeling distinctly agitated as we stand next to the chart table with its small-scale chart showing at least a third of the Pacific. This hurricane is going to come close, with wind strengths of around a hundred knots.

'Much better to go to Fiji instead of Australia,' he tells me. 'Better you stay there until the hurricane season is over.'

'Is Suva easy to get into?' I have no charts of the Fijian islands, never having intended to go there.

'It is not so bad. You must follow many buoys for the channel. Go in only when it is daytime.'

'But do you think I can sail to Suva without a chart of the area?'

Sensing my worry, he hands me an old chart of the Fijian group. 'Here, take this one. I have another.'

The chart covers the whole archipelago and therefore doesn't show much detail. But it's clear that if I sail right around the island group to Suva in the south, I should be able to keep clear of the dangerous areas.

'Thank you very much, Juan.' Yes. I have decided: I'm going to Fiji. It is only about a thousand miles away, and I'll be safe there. And who knows, maybe I'll even find work there.

* * *

The ship has left, and I must go too.

Though I've made the decision, the actual leaving is hard. If I stay, I should be safe on the island. But *Coracle* won't – I'll definitely lose her if the hurricane does come this way. And yet, if it catches us out at sea I could lose more than my boat. I could lose my life.

I take my leave of Hu'ati and wave goodbye to the other islanders. Between my teeth I hold a Funafuti clearance, wrapped in a plastic bag. I paddle slowly back on my surfboard to *Coracle* as she pulls gently against her anchor chain.

Raising the anchor depletes my remaining reserves; I rest whenever I can, trying to ease the pain where my muscles used to be. My weakness scares me, and the wisdom of going back to sea so soon after my fever would be in doubt even if a hurricane were not headed this way. But at last I haul the flukes aboard and secure the anchor to the deadeyes on the foredeck. Breathing heavily, I move aft, using the support of the cabin top to supplement my meagre strength.

The ride through the lagoon has a tearing effect on me. I'm loath to leave, loath to return to the emptiness of the ocean, away from my newfound companions here, and scared of what I might have to face with a hurricane wandering the ocean nearby. To add to this, I have a newly repaired and therefore untested rig. I resent not being able to spend more time in the calm and beautiful lagoon of Funafuti. But I do have a mast again, and it is only about ten days or less to Fiji. Soon I will see shops and houses, and planes and people, lots of people. I take heart from this. Soon I'll be back in civilisation again – as long as the hurricane doesn't take a turn to the south.

15

The Bukh diesel chugs steadily as we pass through the channel. Juan has kindly given me ten gallons of diesel and some cans of food, and my gratitude towards these people of the Pacific is as wide as their ocean.

The sea is calm, and the entrance to the channel is almost flat. Hu'ati told me that the buoys disappeared some ten to fifteen years ago in a hurricane; I assume that the charts have never been updated because of the paucity of visitors. The sea looks beautiful and inviting, and for that I am grateful – though still mistrustful.

I pull sails up my re-erected mast and soon we are churning through the sea at over six knots, the blue wind vane making its jerky corrections to our course once again. It takes less than an hour for Funafuti to disappear astern of us.

We are alone once more.

My trepidation and reluctance to be at sea have not disappeared entirely, yet I revel in the beauty of *Coracle* in full sail again. Her sails are swollen with wind, pushing fatly against the lines that hold them.

Her leeward scuppers are only inches above the water that is sluicing past us; a bow wave crumbles steadily beneath her bow, fanning out behind us, leaving a broad white swathe. At this rate we may be in Fiji even sooner than I figured.

Night falls, another beautiful sunset that has yet to show me the famous green flash – the streak of green across the sky as the sun dips below the horizon. Dinner is soup and a can of stew, a sudden onset of fatigue making it difficult for me to finish my meal. The effort of readying *Coracle* for the voyage and then pulling up the anchor and the sails has exhausted me, and I am looking forward to my night of rest, with the self-steering doing its duty and *Coracle* eating up the miles while I sleep. Before I retire I check the barometer carefully.

As I lie in my bunk, I listen happily to the gurgle of the sea a mere six inches from my head before sinking into a weary, achy unconsciousness. My slumber is broken only four times as I raise myself briefly on my elbows to check the compass on the bulkhead, and of course the barometer, before slumping down into sleep again.

* * *

On the second day after leaving Funafuti a heavy groundswell arrives, travelling southwestwards. The waves heave slowly past, lifting and lowering *Coracle* as though we are on a giant see-saw. The barometer has remained fairly steady though, dropping only slightly. I hope and pray that the storm system is moving away to the north of us, that it's just the swell that has travelled all the way southwards, and that it is therefore not a prelude of things to come.

When the rain arrives, it falls in heavy, solid downpours. I use the runoff from the sails to have a freshwater shower, squatting under the boom near the mast as I lather the soap in lovely white bubbles.

The swell disappears after a day and I breathe more easily, in a flat benevolent sea. The hurricane has missed us.

* * *

Two days later the self-steering breaks. Hearing a loud crack from *Coracle*'s stern, I see the blue vane sink to a strange angle. My repair job is not quite up to scratch.

'Ah, shit! Fuck it!' I go aft to try to retrieve the system. I've released the sheets, allowing the sails to flog slightly in the twenty-knot breeze, slowing the boat down and making it easier for me to lift the self-steering back on board. Bugger it. I'm back to hand-steering.

This time I use a halyard from the mizzenmast, attaching it to the system and using a winch to haul the gear up. Soon it is lashed against the rail, back in the position where I have become so accustomed to seeing it.

I get back to my old routine with the sails, my 'stable' course setting allowing me the freedom to sleep or relax around the boat. A 'neutral' setting means that I have to keep a relaxed eye on the course, and an 'unstable' course setting forces me to stay in or near the cockpit, making constant adjustments with the wheel.

There are long periods where I have to steer the vessel myself, but by now I can virtually steer her while I sleep. Once, after inadvertently dozing off, I woke to find that we were perfectly on course, my hand still on the wheel and making unconscious adjustments just by the feel of the boat in the wind.

I have another problem, though. I am not healing. Every scratch, every cut, is turning into a suppurating sore. The boat is covered in blood – wherever I sit, or whatever I brush against, I leave a blood-stain. The pages of the logbook are blotted red, and on the chart I have marked a large bloodstain that I can't remove as 'Blood Island'. And my teeth are beginning to ache.

It was on Funafuti that I first became aware of the problem, though it was slight then. I ate bananas a couple of times, but felt inhibited about asking the islanders for anything else. I saw very little fruit on the island, and eventually gave up my quest for something fresh to eat. The fact that there were no shops there, with food shared in a kind of bartering system I wasn't part of, precluded me from obtaining fresh vegetables or fruit, or even fish.

Apart from the bananas, Hu'ati never offered me anything else; I suppose he thought I had everything I needed aboard the yacht. I have been relying on my stock of coconuts, which I replenished at Funafuti, to supply the vitamins I need, but I'm beginning to suspect that coconuts, though plentiful in vitamin E, have no value at all as far as vitamin C and the B group are concerned.

It looks like the early stages of scurvy.

* * *

I have with me the single chart of the Fijian islands, the one cadged from Juan. It is an extremely old British Admiralty chart, and shows the entire group of islands. Because of the scale, smaller details such as inshore reefs are omitted, so I will have to be very careful in my approach to Suva.

My plan is to sail right around the western side of the island group, approaching Suva from the south in deep, clear water. Suva is on the south side of the main island of Viti Levu, the southernmost of two big islands of the huge Fijian archipelago. The barometer has remained nice and steady – no sign of the hurricane turning and chasing us south.

Two days to go. We are now only 250 miles from Suva, and making roughly 120 miles per day. The northern Fiji group is only about sixty miles away to the southeast, and I hope to catch a glimpse of the islands before nightfall. I am fantasising about the fruits I will eat, the people I will see, and the sights and sounds of cars and shops.

My condition has become worse. The sores extend now over my entire body, with pussy blood on my arms and legs and back. Taking my deck shower has become an arduous and painful task. In fact, every task has become painful now, as the slightest bump touches a sore on some part of my body and causes me to bleed. I am moving around the deck like a wounded animal – slowly and carefully, with every movement an effort.

* * *

Damn. What the hell is going on with my navigation? I can see land ahead and to starboard of the bow, but not on the port side, where it should be. I can't understand where I made such an error, even allowing for a current setting eastward around the islands. We're way over to port from where we should be.

Have I been using the wrong date? I redo the calculations, using a date one day ahead of the one given to me by Juan. Crap. The new position puts me heading straight for the middle of Vanua Levu, which is what I figure we're now doing.

I'm about thirty-five miles too far to the east, adding at least half a day to the trip; I'll have to steer closer to the wind and against an unexpectedly strong current. Shit.

Instead of sailing around the island group, I could sail through it though, across the Koro Sea. I study the chart again, more carefully this time, and I figure that there is only one real obstacle. It is an area where almost impassable coral reef lies scattered between two larger islands – Vanua Levu and Taveuni, about five miles apart. But the chart does show a passage through the reef, called the Somosomo Strait. It's a narrow channel about half a mile wide and three miles long – easily deep enough for *Coracle* to pass through. Beyond the strait lies a clear stretch of water with just a few small islands further on that might be a hazard to navigation.

If we get there in daylight it will be no problem to pass through the strait. We are doing six knots, and it is about one thirty in the afternoon. We should make it before dark. So I set a new course, to take us towards the eastern tip of Vanua Levu, the second-largest island of Fiji.

* * *

The Bukh diesel is thudding. Vanua Levu lies abeam of us now, to starboard, and the channel is about five miles away. But the sun is also close to setting. The wind calmed as we approached the mountainous islands, and as the sails drooped our speed dropped. I am wasting precious fuel to reach the channel in time.

The coral reef makes it dangerous to stay in this area at night. If we don't make it to the strait entrance before dark we'll have to turn northwards again, to the open sea. I am not keen to spend hours sailing back to get into clear water again, and then wait for morning.

There is less than one hour before nightfall and the sun is a huge orange orb on the horizon. The land has grown dark with shadow. I try to get us into a position near the entrance to the channel, close to the middle, before it is too dark to continue using the land to navigate, as I am now doing – using a cape on Vanua Levu to check our position every ten minutes or so. Once we are lined up with the middle of the channel I will go through it, keeping us carefully on course with the compass, so that we stay in the centre and avoid the reefs.

But the sun is going down fast. In the dusk, the cape is a dim silhouette to starboard as I use a hand-bearing compass to see exactly where we are. On the chart table I plot the bearing – we are getting close.

* * *

We're stationary in the water, engine idling. *Coracle*'s sails hang limp as I make my final calculations, bent over the chart table. A moment ago I managed to get one last sight of the cape, peering through the near dark at a barely visible outline. I have to confirm that we are where I think we are – right at the entrance to Somosomo Strait, and equidistant from the reef on either side.

Satisfied, I return to the deck. Even though I'm pretty sure of our position, I re-engage the propeller a little nervously. We head down the channel towards the clear water only three miles ahead of us. Night surrounds the boat, and the black masses of land have disappeared into the darkness. The sea is flat, the surrounding reef and islands sheltering the inside water from the ocean swells of the Pacific.

I am looking forward to the open waters of the Koro Sea on the other side of the channel, where I can relax and get a bit of shut-eye. For a while now I've been too keyed up about making landfall to get much sleep. Rest is just a short distance away.

After about twenty-five minutes I check the log. We should be nearly through the channel now, and I relax a little. I turn slightly to starboard to avoid running into the reef off Taveuni and accelerate to six knots. In another few minutes we'll be in the Koro Sea, and if there is wind to sail with I'll be in Suva in just over twenty-four hours, gorging on fruit and vegetables and ridding myself of the festering sores that cover my body. I want to rest and recuperate, regain my strength and vitality, and enjoy my illicit ownership of *Coracle*.

There is a bump against the keel. A brief, hard knock.

Oh no. No no no. Oh shit. Don't let us be on the reef. Please.

I'm yanking the throttle back into full astern and my brain is electric with fear. A loud sucking gurgle accompanies the roar of the diesel as the propeller starts to spin in reverse.

Coracle heaves and slews, grinding her thirteen tons to a crashing halt against the coral and throwing me hard against the spokes of the wheel. The clatter of falling crockery and the shaking and twanging of the rig accompany other horrific sounds of our grounding.

I lie in a tangle, one leg over the wheel and my body wedged between the cockpit seat and the compass binnacle. *Coracle* rests at an angle on the reef, her engine still roaring and shuddering in reverse. I struggle up and see fountains of sand and water thrown out from under the hull by the prop, illuminated by the red glow of the port light. With trembling hands I pull the motor into neutral and switch it off, and then I stand in the sloping cockpit, aghast at this debacle of navigation.

Fucking buggering shitting hell. What now? I've run the boat onto a coral reef. Is she lost? Have I wrecked her? After everything I've been through, is this the end to my adventures, my dreams, and my boat?

As these thoughts spin through my head I'm galvanised by another. I must check out the bilge: see if we are taking water and stop any inflow, if necessary. I jump down below, a throbbing pain in my ribs where I hit the spokes. The floorboards come up easily, wrenched out by my frantic hands. I scan along the bilges, looking for the welling pool of water that would indicate we're sinking. Nothing but normal bilgy dampness. I pry and search wherever I can gain access to the hull. At last I am satisfied – though not without a slight sense of disbelief.

The boat is dry.

After all the tearing, grinding, cracking noises of our grounding, she is taking not a drop. Hope seeps slowly through my despair and I investigate further, carefully inspecting her frames and planking. There's no sign of breakage, no cracked timbers or loosened joints.

I can still barely believe it. Our crash seemed so hard. But apart from a smashed plate or two and a few pots and pieces of cutlery lying on the floor, I see no sign of disintegration. She must surely have exterior damage where she hit the coral, but if she is still intact in all her frames and planking, then maybe I can save her.

The sea is relatively calm, with just the slight scrape of the hull against the sand indicating a swell across the reef. As long as the waves don't increase in strength I might have a chance.

Up on deck I switch on the deck lights and look overboard. The sand and coral are visible about five feet below, swirling colours of green and black-brown, dark shapes illuminated by the pool of light around the boat.

Coracle's decks slope even more steeply now, and I realise that the tide is on the way out. I have no chance of freeing her from the reef until the next high tide. I also realise that the tide might go down until she is lying on her side on top of the reef. And although the waves are very small it is still possible that a piece of coral might pierce her hull.

There's no time to lose. I must dive under the vessel and check to see what is below, pull out all the loose coral if possible, or try to get fenders under her. The reef seems to be mostly small coral rocks and coral fronds on the sand, and if I can get all the lumps of coral away she can lie safely on the bottom. Apart from a mask, I have no other diving gear on the boat. I grab the mask and jump over the side, standing in the warm water lapping around my shoulders.

It takes me nearly an hour to clear the coral pieces from under my boat. The last five to ten minutes are increasingly difficult and dangerous as *Coracle* descends closer and closer to the reef. I am swimming underneath her hull, which is bobbing only inches above me as I scour the sand in front of my nose for coral pieces; her thirteen tons could easily crush me, or pin me against the bottom and drown me. The illumination from the boat lights is weak; the water dissipates it, barely allowing me to see anything.

Exhausted, I eventually climb back on board, hauling myself from the water that is now only about three feet deep and onto the gunwale, which is level with the sea surface. My only fear now is that the sea might yet become rough and destroy my vessel as she lies helplessly in the predicament I've landed her in.

Low tide comes, and *Coracle* bounces her side gently against the sandy bottom. I'm trying to sleep, lying against her hull. The insistent thuds as she bounces on the sand keep jolting me awake. Eventually I slumber, only to be woken by a disjointed nightmare, with *Coracle* stuck on top of a reef, surf crashing all around her, and me riding my surfboard on the waves at her side. Bainesfield is on the deck and seems to be waving at me, only he has a gun in his hand, which he keeps pointing to. And then both my boat and Bainesfield are gone, leaving me alone on my surfboard in the middle of the Pacific.

* * *

It is morning, and *Coracle* is almost upright and level again. I step onto the deck to take a look around. On either side of us the islands lie verdant and beautiful. Taveuni, about three miles to the east, is a low-lying island with shadowed white beaches. Vanua Levu, to the west, looks deceptively closer. This is because the dawn sun is illuminating the larger island, shining directly onto its steep green peaks, bathing them in iridescence.

I climb up onto the pitched cabin top, and from there I have a clear view around the yacht. In front of the boat the reef extends in a wide arc towards the west. *Coracle* is lying on a spit of sand and coral that bulges into the channel. Had I been a mere hundred feet to the left, we would have missed it and passed right through the strait into the Koro Sea. It is a bit of a dogleg of reef that we've hit, something that wasn't apparent from the chart – the paper has been folded and creased so many times over that particular spot that the markings of the channel have been almost obliterated. I can also make out that the reef we're on is a barrier reef. Further in, towards Vanua Levu, the coral disappears and the water is a darker shade of aquamarine, becoming deeper.

We're about a mile from the nearest shore of Vanua Levu, opposite a large bay. I can see the northern peninsula and another cape. Because of yesterday evening's failing light, I sighted on the wrong silhouette of land – a careless and disastrous error. But looking around I can see that I was in fact lucky; further ahead is solid coral, a reef that would probably have torn the bottom out of my boat. Where we've hit is mostly sand, with lumps of scattered coral.

This luck is undeserved, I know. I give myself a mental kick for my stupidity, for not allowing for the fact that I was fatigued at the time. I should have gone slower, taken more care, or waited till it was light, but I was too eager to reach the Koro Sea and the final stretch towards Viti Levu. I'd now be nearing Suva, if only I'd been more cautious. I'm paying for this wretched mistake by being stranded here on this reef.

I shrug off these thoughts and busy myself with trying to free *Coracle* from her stranding. The water is about five feet deep around her now, so I make preparations. First I tie rubber fenders on the anchor so it floats, then I lower it off the bow; using the surfboard, I tow it towards the deeper water in the channel. It is difficult, the drag on the anchor rope as it pays out from the foredeck increasing as more of it slides into the water. When I can't get it any further, I release the anchor so that it lies about eighty feet from *Coracle* on the sand, at an acute angle to the bow.

Back on the boat, I wind the anchor rope on the winch, heaving and pushing the winch handle, forcing *Coracle*'s bows around inch by inch, until finally she'll turn no more. But she is at least facing almost back towards the channel. With the engine roaring at full throttle, I try to motor her off. Sand and water swirl together and boil astern of her, the push of the propeller causing her to tilt first one way and then the other. At the same time, I apply more force to the winch, trying to haul her forward by using the anchor too.

For fifteen minutes I battle with my boat. But it's futile, so I switch off the engine. The tide is now receding, and the deck begins to tilt further as the water level drops again, and there is no more chance of freeing her until the next tide. I'm wasting diesel and I'm tired and hurting and frustrated. But the daylight and my efforts have at least put me into a more positive frame of mind. As long as the sea remains calm I won't lose the boat; I just have to find a way to get her off the reef.

Lunch is a dismal affair. I boil coffee on the gimballed stove, the only level surface in my boat, and then I perch uncomfortably in the tilted cockpit, eating a can of cold sausages for which I have no appetite. The rest of the afternoon I sit and gaze at the land, wishing *Coracle* and I were away from it and still out at sea. But wishing, too, that I was on the land.

The next day, at full high tide, I try again. No luck. I try everything I can think of. Hauling the sails up for extra push even though there's hardly any wind, swinging the rudder around with the helm to redirect the push from the prop. I try running from one side to the other in a silly attempt to get her to sway and lift her weight off her keel. But nothing works; she's hard aground, stuck like a helpless whale up on a beach.

I consider emptying the boat of all her contents to lighten her, but apart from the fact that she doesn't have much removable heavy gear, there is nowhere to put it. There's also no point in emptying her tanks as she's nearly out of diesel anyway, and the water tanks don't have too much left in them either. I'm running out of ideas and I don't know what else to do. I'm becoming more and more fearful for *Coracle*'s safety.

Night comes again. And again it's even worse than the day. I try to sleep as the boat pounds gently upon the sand, a ceaseless irritating reminder of our predicament. The only bright spot in all of this is that *Coracle* is showing no signs of any real damage. She's still taking no water, and I can't find any internal breakage. She's a strongly built yacht, but this heavy construction isn't helping at all to get her off the sand.

We're stuck. Really stuck, on this godforsaken reef.

What if I paddle the surfboard to the island? Although there is no sign of civilisation, I could walk around the coast until I find something, people who might call the authorities perhaps, and send a rescue party out to haul the boat off the reef. But drawing attention to the boat and myself would be pretty risky as far as my crime and my identity are concerned. So the only alternative is to abandon *Coracle*, slip onto the island, and try to find some way off, by boat or plane. To sneak away anonymously. But this I won't do. Can't do. Apart from the fact that I have no money, I cannot just abandon my yacht.

16

It's the third day, and I'm taking a break from my labours. My back is against the decking as I sit on the side of the cabin top; *Coracle* is heeled so far over that there is no level seating. I've begun to dig a trench towards the channel. It's slow going, since I can only dig at low tide. And I suspect that at night the sand will simply drift back in and fill up the depression again. But it's something to do, at least.

I'm still considering taking the surfboard to the island, if only to walk about on the beach and explore this deserted area. Maybe I'll find a tree with fruit on it.

While I'm studying the shoreline, something snags my attention, something moving close to the shore, a speck appearing and disappearing on the small swells closer in. It moves slowly, and then seems to stop. As it becomes more visible, I realise it is coming towards me. It's a small boat or canoe or something, with two people in it. I watch them approaching, coming to investigate me.

It is a dugout canoe with outriggers, similar to the pirogues on Funafuti, and it draws alongside my tilted yacht. The occupants are about my age, Fijians, with strong faces and strong builds. With their frizzy black curls and darker skin, they're a bit more African in appearance than the Polynesians on Funafuti.

'*Bula! Iko vinaka so vei, beka?*' one of the paddlers says to me with a smile. Seems like a good question – though I haven't a clue what it means.

'My boat's stuck,' I say, pointing towards the sandy bottom. 'I'm stuck on the sand.'

We exchange some more words, not communicating much apart from our desire to talk to one another. The paddler gestures towards Vanua Levu, where he came from. He motions with his hands, pointing to himself and me and the island. They bring the canoe no closer, so I realise that they do not expect me to go with them. I shrug and point to myself and the boat, opening my hands, palms outwards, to indicate that we're going nowhere. He chortles and answers in his own language, neither of us understanding a word of what the other is saying, yet with a vague grasp of the other's intent. Eventually, he and his companion wave and paddle away in the direction he pointed towards. I watch as they slowly pull away, becoming smaller and smaller, a speck disappearing from my sight and leaving me with a fragile hope, as well as a fear that they aren't coming back.

* * *

Hours pass, and I spy approaching pirogues, this time two of them. When they draw alongside, I recognise the two Fijians from before. In the other boat, there's a young man and an older person who lifts his paddle in laconic greeting.

'Hello. I am Penaia,' he says. He has a handsome face, with wide cheekbones and deep furrows running from his nostrils to his mouth. His hair is cut shorter than that of the younger men, and it is flecked with grey.

'You need some help, yes?' He inclines his head towards the other canoe. 'These fellas say you have a problem on the reef.' I catch the hint of an Australian or New Zealand accent in his carefully enunciated words.

'Yes. I mean, I do need help. My boat is stuck. I hit the reef about three days ago. A bit too hard, I think. I've been trying to get her off, but the motor isn't powerful enough.'

'Your boat is very heavy, I think, and she is high up on the sand. It will be difficult to move her.' He studies *Coracle* as she leans on her sandy bed. My enthusiasm fades with the knowledge that he might not be able to help; these two canoes are not going to be much use in getting my thirteen-ton vessel off the reef.

'But there is a boat nearby, a big boat with strong motors,' he says. 'Maybe it can help.'

I smile at him. This is just what I need, a bigger boat. I wonder how big the motors are, and where the boat is. I see no harbour, and there's nothing on the chart showing one nearby.

'Where is this boat?' I ask.

'It is over there, at that island.' He points towards Taveuni. 'But first we have to get permission from the governor.'

The guv'nor? Seems quaintly English to refer to his boss, or chief, or overlord, or whatever, in this way. A bit out of place on this South Sea island, I'd say. But maybe it's some sort of legacy from Fiji's colonial past.

'I'd be very grateful if you and he could help,' I answer. 'I don't know how to get the boat off the reef by myself. If the boat you're talking about has big enough motors, maybe she can tow the yacht off.'

'The boat belongs to the governor-general of Fiji. He is now making his tour around the islands. Once every year he does this, and he is now at Taveuni. We must go there to ask him.'

The governor-general of Fiji? Wow. I'm impressed. Also nervous. We're going to ask this most important official if we can use his boat to rescue my stolen yacht?

'Okay, then, can you hang on a bit?' I say, mustering enthusiasm. 'I'll just grab some shoes and put on a T-shirt.' And change to my best tatty shorts. I don't have any decent clothes; all my T-shirts are bloodstained and pretty much the worse for wear. Not exactly the sort of gear I'd choose to meet the governor of Fiji, and hardly likely to convey the impression of a genuine yacht owner. But I have to get *Coracle* off the reef, and I don't see any other way. Maybe, just maybe, I won't actually have to meet the governor.

* * *

The trip to the island of Taveuni takes nearly an hour. The pirogue containing the first two Fijians goes off in the direction of the shore, while we head across the channel to the reefs on the other side. Both Penaia and his fellow paddler row tirelessly, their pirogue cutting through the water. Their strength amazes me. We pass large coral heads, some showing above the sea surface, others lying just below the transparent water. My knees begin to hurt from kneeling. Squashed between Penaia and the outrigger pole, I shuffle about in an attempt to find a more comfortable position. I'm trying hard to be unobtrusive, and feel a bit guilty at not helping with the paddling.

'You speak English really well, Penaia,' I say to him, partly out of curiosity and partly to make conversation.

'Yes, I learn English in Dakuniba. In the town,' he answers. 'I go there to buy things for village. Tools, fishing stuff, things we need.'

'Don't they speak Fijian there?' I feel a little foolish asking the question.

'Many shopkeepers are Indian; they speak English. Very little Fijian.'

Penaia explains that there is a large and influential Indian population in Fiji – descendants of indentured labourers who worked the sugar-cane fields in colonial times.

Eventually we approach a pearly-white beach fringed with tropical vegetation and elegant palm trees. A row of thatched huts appears, strung out along the beach in front of the jungle perimeter. Some distance back, on a hill, a forest rises a few hundred feet into the air.

But my interest is more taken with the appearance of a launch that is anchored less than a hundred feet from the beach. It is about forty-five feet long, newly painted, and – happy days – has two big blackened exhaust ports, indicating large motors. The launch appears modern and possibly powerful enough to pull *Coracle* off the reef.

The pirogue noses gently onto the sand and we all climb out. I help Penaia and his companion to haul the little vessel further up, and then we cross the sand to the nearest hut. Its walls seem to be made out of coconut palm leaves woven together; it has a thatched roof, and the entire structure stands on stilts, about three feet off the sand.

Inside, sitting on a mat made of woven palm leaves, three men are playing a game using bean-like objects and a small mat. They all stare at us, or rather at me, with bemused expressions.

Penaia rattles on in Fijian, explaining, I suppose, my predicament and the need to use the launch. One of the men rises and comes towards me, a tall, powerfully built individual with a lined face and a fierce expression – features apparently typical of the Fijian men around here. A tad anxiously, I watch him approach. He doesn't look at all amenable.

'This man is Tanuki,' Penaia says. 'He is the captain of the launch. You will go with him to meet the governor.' Tanuki's face splits into a smile.

Though relieved, I also feel renewed alarm at the prospect of meeting the governor of Fiji. Leaving Penaia and the others behind, Tanuki and I set off on a footpath. After a short walk through a copse of trees, we pass through another coconut palm village. A few villagers are about, and they stare at me curiously. I stare back, just as curious. We carry on up the hill, the jungle closing in on the path, and then, in a clearing set about halfway up the hill, we come to a larger hut – a house, in fact. It has real windows with glass panes, and a brick porch instead of rickety stairs. Some parts of the walls are also made of brick.

Tanuki knocks on the door. I wait with him, nervous and yet also eager. Help for my beleaguered yacht might be close at hand now. The door opens, and an elderly bespectacled man peers out at us. He is dressed in a clean white shirt buttoned to the neck, a sarong, and sandals.

A conversation ensues and my captain friend's deferential manner indicates that this is either the governor himself or some other high-placed official. The man turns to me and politely smiles, offering his hand, which I take.

'I am Ratu Gamura, the chief of this island,' he says. 'Come in, please. This man says you need to ask the governor-general for you to use his launch. Governor's name is Ratu George Cakobua. Please, come with me. I will take you to him.'

I thank him, and Tanuki and I follow him through the house, which is furnished in a strange mix of Western and island furniture. A modern, fully upholstered settee sits next to three chairs made of raw wood and tied together with some sort of thong-like material. The floor is covered with palm-leaf woven mats, and fabric curtains hang in the windows.

In a large room, seated on chairs around a table, are three men, talking and smoking. Once again I hover in the background while an exchange takes place between Ratu Gamura and one of the men at the table, a big man in his mid-forties perhaps, dressed also in a clean white shirt and a sarong. He has a large head, wide shoulders and a large belly, and he exudes authority. He is without doubt the governor-general of Fiji.

His attention is almost completely on Tanuki as the latter explains, with occasional gestures towards me, that this unlikely-looking yacht owner has betrayed his credibility by parking his yacht on top of a reef. The big man nods thoughtfully as Tanuki speaks, glancing only occasionally in my direction and not saying anything at all. I am uncomfortably aware of my bloodstained T-shirt, frayed shorts and old sandals, as well as the suppurating sores on my arms and legs.

Eventually the big man turns to me and breaks his silence. 'Hello, young man.' His voice is deep and well modulated. 'I understand you are in trouble with your boat.'

'Yes, sir,' I say, and repeat my story. 'I got stuck on the reef coming through the Somosomo Strait the other night. I can't get the boat off and I thought maybe I could use your launch to help me, if you would be so kind.'

He smiles and steps forward. 'Come,' he says, clapping his hand on my shoulder in a surprising gesture of cordiality. 'Let us go and take a look. Let's try to see your yacht from the top of the hill here.'

He turns and says something to the others in the room. Everybody rises and heads out with us, smiles all round. The atmosphere seems lighter and friendlier. We walk up a path, and on top of the hill we enter a clearing that offers a panoramic view across the water to Vanua Levu. The sea sparkles with turquoise congeniality, and far in the distance across the Koro Sea are the hazy shapes of other islands.

'There.' I point towards the angled masts of my boat, barely visible about four miles away. 'There it is,' I say, verifiable proof that I have not been lying to them.

Merry chatter breaks out between the governor and his entourage. They ask questions which the governor translates for me, returning my answers to them in rapid-fire Fijian. It is all pretty much about my grounding, how it happened, and how long I've been on the reef. I answer their questions humbly, and smile dumbly as they all laugh at a joke made by the governor. I am perfectly willing to endure any ridicule as long as I get the use of his boat.

'You are very young to be sailing all alone,' he says to me with a kindly smile. 'And perhaps not as cautious as one should be, no?'

I shrug, trying not to let my smile become goofy – which of course it does, immediately. 'It was night-time, and I wanted to get into the clear water so that I could sleep,' I say.

My reply seems to have amused them again. There is more chatter, friendly laughter, and I feel a bit more relaxed. I am being treated with a kind of ribald respect, and though I understand not a word of what they are saying, I sense that their intentions are not at all unkind.

'We will try to help you,' the governor says as we go down the path to Ratu Gamura's house. 'We will leave early in the morning, for tomorrow I must be at Dakuniba, on Vanua Levu, before lunch time. But we will use the launch to try to tow you off the reef.'

'Thank you very much, sir. I really appreciate this. I'm sure it won't take too long.' I would say more, express further gratitude, but I need to be careful of showing disrespect by my very effusiveness.

* * *

Back at the beach I find that the canoe is gone, presumably back to Vanua Levu. I wish now that I showed more appreciation to Penaia and his companion for their help. I didn't realise they weren't staying.

I spend the night in the grass hut where I met Tanuki. He indicates by sign language that I should take one corner of the hut – he calls it a *bure* – while he and the other two men sleep in the other corners. For most of the night I'm kept awake by concern for my boat, the strangeness of my surroundings, and the snores of the other men sleeping in the hut.

Breakfast consists of some strange starch-like substance and bananas. In the early morning light, I get ready to go to the launch with Tanuki and the other two men, who turn out to be his crew. Once aboard, I'm reassured by the solidity of the immaculately kept boat. After a short wait, the governor and his entourage appear on the beach. One of the crewmen rows the tender ashore to fetch him, and, in our respective languages, Tanuki and I bid him good morning as he boards.

The launch heads out to the reefs, the deck thrumming with the sound of two powerful diesel engines. As Tanuki expertly manoeuvres the vessel around the coral, I watch the reef and also try to catch a glimpse of my boat, hoping she's still where I left her.

'You are worried about your yacht?' The governor has appeared back on deck, and stands next to me.

'Yes, sir. But she should be okay – as long as the waves don't get bigger, and bash her about on the reef.'

'Well, it is generally calm in here,' he says, waving towards the Somosomo Strait. 'It is only when the wind is from the northeast that the sea gets rough.'

'I've been lucky then, I suppose.'

'Not so lucky, I think,' he says with a grin. 'Not at this point of your voyage.'

'No, I guess not.' I smile back.

'Where did you sail from? Was it a long trip?'

'From Hawaii. I left a few months ago.'

'A few months ago? That's a long time. And did you have much bad weather on the way?'

'Um, no, sir. I mean, not really.' I'm more concerned about what I might let slip than actually answering him. 'Although, in some ways it was hard. I was in a bad storm after I left Hawaii, which damaged the self-steering, but not much else, really. I guess altogether the weather wasn't so bad.'

He questions me some more about the trip, and I tell him about the broken mast and limping to Funafuti. I tell him about the calms in the doldrums, and my concern for my dwindling supplies.

'It seems to me that you are a very courageous young man, to do this at your age.'

'Well, no, not really, sir.' I'm hoping this line of questioning isn't going to turn to how I, at this young age, could afford a boat like *Coracle*. 'I've had a lot of experience sailing.' I say this hoping to fudge the age issue, relying on the fact I look a little older than I am.

'Yes, but to handle the boat all alone, facing such storms. That takes a lot of fortitude, I'm sure. You must have a lot of confidence in yourself.'

'Actually, before I left I had a lot more confidence in myself. I've had a few sharp lessons on this trip.'

He laughs. 'Well, I admire your spirit. I do. I think it takes guts to do what you've done. Courage to face such a journey.'

'I think it was more a courage borne out of ignorance,' I say. 'A misguided sense of my own invulnerability and abilities.'

'But still, I'm sure it must have been hard. Managing the yacht all by yourself.'

'No, sir. Actually, the sailing wasn't hard at all. It's not that hard to sail a yacht by yourself. And I trusted in the boat too. I never felt that she might sink. But it's other things that are hard, like not being able to share your feelings with anybody, and sometimes, like when you're approaching land, the watch-keeping gets quite difficult. You can get a bit tired.'

'And that's how you came to hit the reef, then?' he says with a gentle smile.

'I guess.' I smile too. He studies me with a quiet air of concentration. I'm slightly uncomfortable under his scrutiny.

'How did you cope with the isolation, being all by yourself on the ocean?'

'Not that well, I guess.' I think back to my silly fears when I thought the world wouldn't be as I left it, my irrational thoughts about atomic bombs and the end of civilisation. 'There were times when I was a bit depressed.'

'I can't imagine how one must feel, so far from land and humanity. I think you must be a remarkable young man.'

We talk some more, and I find him to be charming and down to earth. He has a fine sense of humour. And his flattery is soothing. No suspicions. I find myself relaxing as we chat. Our conversation ranges from politics in South Africa to sailing and fishing. He has me laughing with his descriptions of his island and its history. And I amuse him with stories about the Caribbean.

* * *

We reach *Coracle* and find a horde of islanders around her. She's completely surrounded by pirogues, mostly overloaded with Fijians wearing colourful sarongs. There's a festive air. Many women are in the canoes too, also wearing sarongs, tied just under their arm- pits. Children are in the water, diving from canoes, swimming around my boat, all shouting happily. Many adults wave their paddles at us as we pass, and there is an excited mood around the yacht as Tanuki brings the launch closer. The news of *Coracle*'s grounding has obviously spread, and the islanders have turned out in force to watch the rescue.

I'm pleased to recognise Penaia, waving vigorously at me from his dugout as he sits with the same fellow he was with yesterday. I'm also pleased to see that the tide is almost full high again. Our timing is excellent. I wave back at him.

Unable to approach any closer, Tanuki stops the launch in deeper water, and one of his crewmen and I cross to *Coracle* in the tender, towing a rope. A load of children swarm onto the deck with me as I board, clambering over the cockpit and deck, turning winches, swinging from the booms, scooting down below to investigate, and popping up out of hatches everywhere. A number of adults accom- pany the children, all in high spirits. Everybody, it seems, is looking forward to a good time. I'm concerned about the extra weight though, but I have no idea how to order them off without coming across as an ungrateful ass.

I carry the towline forward and make it fast to a cleat as the tender returns to the launch. Governor Cakobua stands near the stern of the launch, watching the proceedings with interest.

When we are ready I have to brush a bunch of kids from the wheel, clearing them away good-naturedly as they laugh and shout around the deck. I start the motor. The old Bukh throbs steadily, vibrating through the teak planking, and after a quick look around to make sure there are no swimmers near the boat, I signal Tanuki with a forward wave of my hand. The towline becomes taut as he manoeuvres ahead, and then turbulent water heaves out from under the launch's stern as he gives full power.

I engage *Coracle*'s propeller and push the throttle forward. Pistons hammer, black smoke swirls, water boils, kids yell, but nothing happens. I feel the strain mounting steadily within me as *Coracle* sways and dips but shows no sign of moving forward. I push my hand lightly against the throttle lever, trying to coax more power out of my roaring Bukh.

Another two or three minutes go by, and much shouting and excited laughing accompanies the roaring efforts of the launch's diesels. But *Coracle* remains firmly in place, her thirteen tons immovable upon the sand even though I can see the powerful wash thrown out from behind the governor's launch and feel the shuddering of *Coracle*'s own prop spinning at maximum power.

The decibel level lowers as Tanuki brings the power off the launch's two motors. Shaking his head, he walks out from the wheelhouse.

I pull the Bukh back into neutral as well, despair settling inside my chest like a collapsing balloon. This is not going to work. The launch apparently isn't powerful enough. Also, there are too many children and adults aboard *Coracle*, adding extra weight. I need to get them off – but how? Then another idea strikes me. Maybe I can use that extra weight.

Quickly, I swing all three booms over the starboard side, stretching the spars as far outboard as the sheets holding them will allow.

I secure them with lines, and then I turn to the forty or fifty young guests who have been watching my preparations with interest. I'm aware that Tanuki and the governor are also watching, probably with some perplexity at what I'm trying to do.

'Okay, out you go.' I turn to the kids and gesture towards the booms, making scooping motions with my hand.

'Out there. Out you go. Go on out to the ends.' Encouragingly I tap the main boom, as far out as my hand will reach, and they all look at me with eager bewilderment, not moving. I make a revolving action with one hand while pointing down at the deck with the other. Their expressions remain pleasantly blank. I try pointing my finger at the kids and then out to the ends of the booms, making tilting motions with my body. One of the adults breaks into a broad grin. He shouts something rapidly to the kids and they all clamber out onto the spars. He understands what I want.

Within minutes, the booms are holding about fifty excited children, all hanging out over the water. They wriggle and squirm along the poles, some losing their holds and dropping with a splash, swimming quickly back to the boat and climbing aboard again to hoots of derision from their peers. Anxiously I study the topping lifts, the lines that support the weight of the booms from the top of the masts. Half-inch dacron rope with a breaking strain of about a thousand pounds, they are stretching dangerously thin.

Coracle lists sharply to starboard, which lifts some of the weight off her keel. Once again I wave to Tanuki. He waves back, disappears into his wheelhouse, and moments later the stern of the launch dips as he applies power once again. I push the throttle forward and wait hopefully on my slanting vessel – the children clustered around the boom ends like bees on a honey stick.

For long seconds, nothing happens. *Coracle* is fast upon the sand. Then I feel a tiny sliding bump, followed immediately by another.

We are moving.

Hope and trepidation vacillate within me. I want to shout encouragement, I want to laugh and whoop, but I'm afraid, afraid that it was merely a single movement, maybe a false start caused by the dip in the sand where I tried to dig the channel, or maybe a wave bump that seemed like forward movement.

I wait – tense, fearful. But I feel another bump, and another. I see the sand sliding past us, slowly, almost imperceptibly, an inch at a time, but definitely passing by. We are moving towards the channel in a series of slow lurches and scrapes, the duration of the lurches becoming longer and the impact of the scrapes lessening as we creep into the deeper water.

Then we are free.

Coracle is floating once more, light and easy, back in her element; off the sand that has imprisoned her. I'm also feeling light and easy now that my boat has been rescued. I reduce the engine power, allowing the launch to tow us forward, and join in the laughter of my crew as they cling tenaciously and tenuously, shouting and waving at their friends in the dugouts. Everyone is sharing this moment of triumph. Even the governor gives a cheerful wave.

Tanuki slows the launch, allowing both vessels to come to a stop, and I throw off the towline. He and his crew haul it in as Penaia and his companion paddle alongside.

'Thank you, sir,' I call to the governor across the gap that separates us. 'Thank you very, very much. I'm really grateful.'

'You are very welcome, Rob,' he says. 'I just wish you'd had a kinder welcome to Fiji.'

'Actually, I've had the kindest welcome I could ever hope for. Your generosity, sir, and all the help I've had couldn't have given me a better impression of your islands.'

'Then I thank you for those kind words, Rob,' he says, inclining his head. 'What are you going to do now? Carry on to Suva?'

'Yes, I guess so.'

'Why you don't come back to our village?' Penaia says from his canoe nearby. 'The water is deep and it is safe there. We can show you the way through reef. You stay with us for a while.'

For a moment I'm undecided, unprepared for this further offer of kindness, as I think of Suva and civilisation. But why not? This is civilisation enough and I can relax for a while. And I need to go over *Coracle*, check her out more carefully before I travel on.

'Thank you. I'd like that.'

I say my goodbyes to my rescuers, thanking them again for their generosity and help. As the launch containing the governor-general of Fiji departs southwards towards Dakuniba, I turn *Coracle* around and follow Penaia's dugout to where a channel runs through the reef, towards Vanua Levu. The rest of the pirogues head straight back across the reef, loaded down with their merry passengers.

* * *

We pass a headland, the southern headland that led to my grounding, and I see another bay ahead of us, about half a mile further on and much smaller. We enter this bay, passing pirogues still heading in from the reef, and the two Fijians stroke strongly towards the shore at the head of the inlet, with me following closely in *Coracle*.

We draw closer to the beach, where the tops of huts are visible above the greenery. The jungle isn't nearly as dense here, consisting mostly of coconut trees and bushes. A plume of smoke rises from the village, and on one side mountainous granite boulders hoist their smooth grey sides skywards. A narrow river emerges from the jungle near the boulders and a greenish-brown finger of sediment probes into the water of the bay – water so clear that I can see the corrugated sand patterns thirty or forty feet below us.

Some of the adults and children who've already made it back are waiting on the beach. I anchor the yacht, switch off the engine, and then slide my surfboard into the water. I paddle ashore, and Penaia is there to greet me as I step onto the sand.

'Come, I take you to meet *Turaga-ni-koro*,' he says. 'Our headman. He is in his *bure*.'

We walk through the village, followed by a small crowd of children and curious adults, and Penaia stops before a largish hut and calls into the interior.

'*Io?*' An answer floats out. We step through the doorway.

The headman is sitting cross-legged, sewing. He has a fishing net over his knees, and he's pulling a needle through a bunch of mesh with careful concentration. Somewhere between fifty and sixty years old, he has a large belly, and though he still carries signs of the strong musculature I see in all the male Fijians, he is sagging a little. He has a grizzled face, and like everyone else he wears a sarong – called a *sulu*, as I later discover.

'*Ia, curu mai*.' Glancing at me amiably, he pats the floor in front of him.

The floor of the *bure* is covered with a grass mat. The thatched walls are hung with a strange cloth that has a coarse, irregular weave unlike anything I've seen before. The hut has no furniture, and I follow Penaia's example and sit cross-legged before the headman.

He considers my person a moment, and then addresses me in a warm, friendly fashion. Penaia translates, telling me that the head-man is glad my boat is safely off the reef, and that I am welcome to stay in the village for as long as I like. They will provide me with whatever they can to help repair any damage to the vessel. I thank the headman. Then he invites me to eat with the villagers tonight. In my honour, they will have a dance.

'It is called *meke*,' Penaia adds, when he has finished translating. 'It is Fijian dance.'

I am a little overwhelmed by all this hospitality. 'Thank you very much,' I say to them. 'I'm very glad to be here, and I look forward to seeing the dance.' My statement doesn't quite do justice to the intensity of my feelings.

* * *

The meal is in a large *bure*, the largest hut in the village. It is about forty by twenty feet; there is no furniture, and the floor is covered with a coconut-leaf mat. The *bure* seems to be a kind of village hall, a communal meeting and eating place. Men sit around a coloured mat that runs down the middle, which has foods of all description placed along it. But where are the women?

Fruits and strange-looking vegetables are piled upon large leaves, and also fill wooden bowls; gourds are filled with nuts and berries and other foods, most of which I don't recognise. Yams I do recognise, from the Caribbean, and also bananas. My stomach gives a jolt of delight and I'm forced to swallow the saliva my glands are producing. And then women come into the hut, bringing wooden boards containing fish and a turtle – which is still in its shell – and steaming bowls of a starchy-looking substance.

The men eat and chat, helping themselves liberally, and I do too. Penaia translates occasionally, trying politely to include me, but I'm not too worried about being unable to participate in the conversation. I'm more concerned with the food. It's all delicious and I cram it in. I suspect that the strength and muscularity they all have is a result of this bountiful diet.

The meal winds to a close, and one by one the diners move to the back of the *bure*, lying on their backs as they continue to talk. The conversation begins to die, replaced by snores as the men gradually fall asleep. The sun has hardly sunk behind the hills, but with such a full belly I lie back too, thinking: What a civilised way to eat.

Penaia wakes me after a while.

'Come, it is time for the *meke* now; the women will dance.'

Around the centre of the village are torches, which illuminate a ring of people who are waiting. Penaia and I sit near the *Turaga-ni-koro*, and more men join us. In a cleared space I see five drummers, each with a hollowed-out half-log. Everybody is talking and laughing, and then the drummers begin to play – a sort of syncopated rhythm.

Fifteen women enter the arena.

Wearing long sulus and grass skirts, they move forward with undulating hips. Shell bangles rattle as they shake their arms, and their skirts rustle like a breeze through a cornfield.

One girl in particular takes my attention. She is young and beautiful, and dances sinuously. She moves with a smooth, almost haughty grace. Her eyes are half closed. I find it difficult to take my eyes off her.

'That is Laisa,' Penaia leans over to whisper in my ear. I'm a little mortified that my attention was that obvious. 'She is daughter of *Turaga-ni-koro*.'

I watch, fascinated by the spectacle, but even more so by Laisa. A couple of times she glances at me, a flash from under lowered lashes, inscrutable. Is she perhaps irked by my unwanted attention?

The beat changes and the women dance towards the ring of bystanders, hauling grinning men out to dance with them. Laisa takes a young man by the hand. He is powerfully built and handsome, with an arrogant air. As they dance, their bodies separate and come together again, pelvises almost touching. She slides me a look that seems to say 'this is who I choose'.

I feel chastised, but what the hell; I don't figure I can dance this dance anyway. I'll just sit back and enjoy it all.

17

Coracle is almost unscathed. A careful scrutiny of her hull reveals only one shallow gouge. When she hit the reef she took the full force on her keel, a twelve-foot piece of lead with a steel shoe on the front and eight feet of deadwood at the back, filling it in to the line of the boat. The steel took the brunt of the impact as she slid over the coral, her survival a testament to her strength and superior construction.

My sores have all cleared up, and my gums are no longer tender. I've eaten well and become fit and healthy again. But even more remarkable is the total renewal of my emotional well-being. I feel happy and relaxed, and totally safe here.

If a hurricane comes, the river is deep enough to take my boat up for protection, and the barrier reef will stop most of the swell from reaching the shore. The slow pace, the idyllic surroundings and the hospitality of the villagers make me feel I could live here for ever – but I'm aware that I cannot live off their bounty indefinitely. I need to contribute somehow.

* * *

On the morning of the third day, Penaia greets me as I paddle my surfboard ashore.

'Rob, today we will hunt. Do you want to come?'

I don't hesitate. 'Yes, sure, Penaia. Thanks.' I will help any way I can, maybe even catch whatever it is they're hunting.

The leader of the group of five hunters is a man called Ramanu – the guy Laisa danced with on the night of the *meke*. They all carry spears. Penaia informs me that we will be hunting wild pig. I have no idea of the size of these animals, or whether they pose any threat to us. Exhilarated, I carry my own spear, a four-foot shaft with a barbed iron tip lent to me by Penaia. I follow the party as they trot barefoot into the jungle. I'm revelling in my new role as intrepid aboriginal hunter.

But I soon discover I'm not quite as intrepid as my comrades. Clouds of mosquitoes hover over us, landing on our bare backs in a speckled mass. The Fijians run on heedless, in an easy rhythm, following each other on soundless feet. My back crawls and shudders at the knowledge of the mosquitoes drilling through my naked skin. I slap involuntarily, barely disturbing the bloodsuckers that are emptying me of plasma. But I'm disturbing my fellow hunters, who turn and make shushing gestures with their hands and mouths. I'm scaring the animals with my feverish slapping and clumsy thrashing through the undergrowth. Tormented, I try to shoo away my attackers without making any noise.

The paths or animal tracks we're following are barely discernible to my inexperienced eye. Ducking under heavy greenery and easing through clumps of tangled undergrowth, we follow a hidden route on the loamy earth that takes us way up onto the mountain. Even though we are now at a fair elevation, I'm unable to catch even a glimpse of the ocean through the leaves. The forest is too dense; broad-leafed boughs heavy with blossoms create foliage that cuts visibility to a few feet. My fate is completely in the hands of these Fijians. Without them I wouldn't have a clue how to get back. I'd die here in this jungle, unable to catch a pig, with no idea what fruit and berries are edible. Dying a bloodless husk sucked dry by these infernal fucking mosquitoes.

But these considerations apart, I feel great, like some sort of wild primal being, an atavistic hunter in a prehistoric forest in search of a savage beast. Oops. I almost ran my primal being into the back of Penaia. They've stopped and are studying the ground.

Penaia points to what they're looking at. All I can see is decaying leaves and grassy shoots. He points again, closer to the soggy earth. I stare at the soil. An indentation becomes visible, a vaguely semi-circular shape with a slight ridge in the middle. What the fuck is this? A pig track? The hunters head off into the jungle, following whatever it is they are observing. I follow. We're on another trail now, an even narrower one.

I try to run as soundlessly as the others, watching the ground for twigs that might snap. Concentrating so hard on being stealthy, I again almost crash into the man in front as they all stop next to a huge creeper-covered tree.

Ramanu has his hand up, and with the other he is pointing ahead. I gather that the prey is close. Like the others, I stand still, focusing my senses and peering through the leafy mass of plants. I hear a faint sound, a slight snap and a snuffling.

It must be a pig.

There's a hot feeling in my belly. Ramanu touches Penaia on his shoulder, then taps another villager called Ralu, and then me. He gestures, and the three of us move off to flush the pig towards the other three hunters. Penaia leads, with Ralu in the middle, and I bring up the rear. We step off the path and, like the hunters ahead, I push and edge my way through the foliage, holding the branches apart and closing them slowly behind me. Eventually, we are in position.

Penaia indicates that I should go to the right and Ralu to the left.

Forming a pincer movement, we move towards our quarry. Penaia is carrying his spear above his shoulder now, ready to throw. I copy him. I hear a rustle, a movement ahead of me, and the faintest of snorts. Sounds like the pig is on the move.

My heart is beating faster now and I am determined that the animal should not slip through past me. I hear a shout and a thud. More shouts follow, accompanied by frenzied squealing and a crashing of branches. I stop, straining to hear. Near-human snorts now – the panicked animal may be heading my way.

It *is* heading my way. I break to the right, jumping across a small clearing as I run in the direction of the sound, which is now coming from a thicket of fern-like plants ahead of me. I raise my spear, ready to throw.

A grey-black cannonball crashes into my legs, barrelling out of the bush so fast that I have only the briefest impression of coarse hair, a round body and beady eyes. As I'm flung into the air I think I can maybe catch him with my legs. This optimism is shattered as I reconnect with the earth, separated from my spear. The leafy humus and damp earth cushion the blow somewhat, but I am jolted, and only vaguely aware of the receding sounds of the pig's squeals as it escapes into the jungle.

I become aware of something else. The other hunters have all gathered in the clearing – and where I may have expected maybe a little concern for my well-being, all I can see is amusement. Ramanu is snorting, Penaia laughs, and the others slowly start chuckling. This turns into howls as they slap each other's backs and double over with mirth.

We move on, and occasional laughter floats back at me as we resume our search for a pig. I feel tempted to point out that their hilarity makes for a lack of focus and is a warning to our prey, but I suspect that this would only make for more merriment.

* * *

That night we have a feast. There's no pig, but there's a big fire on the beach. The women cook fish in a makeshift oven made from hot stones piled into a pit in the sand. During the meal, Ramanu entertains the others with the tale of the hunt, and my role in it. I can tell this from the way he simulates my attempt to catch the pig. Although providing general amusement, I'm uncomfortably aware that my poor hunting skills may have something to do with the fact that there is no pork with the fish. I'm aware, too, of Laisa watching Ramanu closely as she brings in the food. She does not even glance my way.

* * *

At dawn we go fishing. I wield a paddle in a dugout containing four people including me. Penaia is in another, and the two canoes move out swiftly over the sheltered water of the lagoon, towards the seas that break over the barrier reefs.

At the edge of the coral we wait for a lull in the surf, paddling gently to hold our position against the waves coming across the reef. The seas further out thunder down onto the razor-wire reef, sending a line of foaming breakers towards us. We wait for the right moment.

Somebody yells a curt command, and scarcely a second behind the others I dip my paddle, pulling with all my strength. I am determined to acquit myself well in my own medium, to compensate for yesterday's ineptitude. We streak forward, the dugout dipping heavily over the seas that foam towards us, shipping water over the bow. With no time to bail, there is already about two inches in the bottom. One wave could easily swamp us.

The back line of the surf is flat as we approach, but then I see a lump forming further out, a swell that quickly becomes a large wave, sucking a trough ahead of itself as it builds into a wall of water. Shouts behind urge me to even greater efforts, and my paddle bites through the water.

The wave has formed fully now, a steep face about six feet high, poised to smash down and fling us back onto the reef. We are moving in a silence of effort, a quiet void filled only by the slap of the paddles and the grunts of our breathing. I am aware of nothing but the strain in my shoulders as I heave against the paddle, the boat sliding forward, the sea bearing down upon us.

The bow rises sharply as the wave reaches us, and then we are surging triumphantly over its crest, our victorious cries drowned in the crash and roar as the wave breaks behind us. I turn to look for the other dugout – there they are, slightly ahead of us, to starboard. Gasping for breath, I give a wild laugh. The faces of my fellow crew members are serene as they smile back at me.

We fish near the outer part of the reef and I catch two, not as many as the others, but I'm not entirely displeased with my efforts. Our return over the reef is much easier, as we surf in on a small wave. I feel elated; I'm revelling in this island life.

* * *

I take my speargun and mask the next day, and paddle my surfboard near to the outer reef. There I tie the board to a piece of coral and swim further out. I shoot five large fish and paddle back to the shore with my catch balanced precariously on the front of the board. I show the fish to Penaia, explaining that this is my contribution to the village.

'Give them to the women,' he tells me, indicating a *bure* I know to be the cooking hut. Just behind it I find a group of women busy cooking – four older women and Laisa. The sight of her makes me pause, but I gather myself and walk up to the women, offering my catch. I keep my eyes away from Laisa, from her smooth brown skin and her rounded breasts under her sulu, not wanting her to see the attraction I feel.

There is some hesitation as they stare at me and my offering, and then one of the older women smiles and nudges Laisa, saying something under her breath. Laisa doesn't respond, occupied with a breadfruit she is cutting, and ignoring me. Another woman pushes her and takes the vegetable from her as she does so. Hesitating a moment, and with apparent annoyance, Laisa walks up to me and takes the fish, without meeting my eyes. I hear her mutter '*Vinaka*' before turning back to the other women. She says something as she places the fish on the table and they giggle and nudge each other, throwing glances at me. I stand there like an idiot, feeling my cheeks getting hot.

I walk away, strolling along the beach towards my boat and wondering about Laisa's attitude towards me; she's the only cool one in the entire village, it seems. But the sun is warming me after my long dive, and I'm happier about my status in the village. I am now contributing to life here with my new friends. I'm not so inept, just not a pig hunter.

18

We're on our way to Mbenua, the village nearest us, to play games – important events in an age-old rivalry between the two villages. There will be a spear-throwing contest and *anoi*, a game involving two balls, which I've learnt to play with Ramanu and other villagers. *Anoi* is a cross between rugby and basketball, and is played with two crude balls made of woven leaves. Each team tries to get its ball past the other team so that it can score first by depositing the ball into a basket at the other end of the field.

I see Laisa laughing and chatting as she climbs into one of the larger canoes, already crowded with festive villagers. I join Penaia in another boat, and we follow the one containing the chief's daughter.

The river isn't more than twelve or fifteen feet wide here, and it flows sluggishly towards the sea. We are heading upstream. The opaque green water is bracketed by thick jungle and mangroves clutching the river with spider-leg roots. Parts of this waterway are completely overhung by trees and the sky is almost obscured by the forest canopy.

We pass the smaller dugouts on the way, and shout and splash water playfully at them as we go by. I worry that the extra movement might overturn our heavily laden boat, but the Fijians seem unconcerned.

After about three miles the jungle on the left bank thins, and I see the thatched roofs of many *bures*. It is a larger village than ours. Canoes line a sandy bay next to an open field in front of the huts, and along the far bank are coconut palms. Between the trees, I catch glimpses of deep blue. It's the Koro Sea. Though close to the ocean, the village is separated from it by a narrow isthmus.

Many people are scattered about, and smoke spirals from two fires – barbecue spits, it looks like. We join the throng and my presence causes some curiosity. A few villagers speak a kind of pidgin English.

'We play games now. Come.' Penaia motions me to join him, breaking into a conversation I am attempting with a man from Mbenua.

'Me? You want me to play?'

'Yes,' he says. 'You play *anoi*.'

'Thanks, Penaia. Thank you very much.' I'm pleased and proud to be included, and more than a little excited. I grew up with rugby, and some of the tactics of *anoi* – especially the tackling – are very similar. Also, I've already learnt that there aren't many rules in this game, so I needn't worry too much about infringement.

'Come, we join the other players.' We head towards the side of the field where some of the younger villagers have already gathered. A group of men sitting on logs are having their chests and faces painted by women. Ramanu is close by, near a group of players. He is standing alone, and has a broad orange band painted across his face with a white line above and a black line below it. He looks fierce.

Penaia addresses the team members, who smile at me and tilt their heads backwards in a gesture that is the local equivalent of a nod. They seem pleased enough to have me on their team, but when I catch Ramanu staring at me, I wonder if he's also happy about it.

Feeling a hand on my arm, I turn. It is Laisa.

'*Curu*,' she says softly, which I think means come.

She leads me to a log and gently tugs at my arms. I sit down and she places small earthenware jars at my feet, then kneels down, leans forward, and begins to paint my face. Her fingers move slowly across my cheeks, and she is so near that her breath is like a whisper on my neck. I'm very aware of her ribs against my legs, the closeness of her face, and the closeness of her breasts.

I look at her eyes, but they remain averted as she concentrates on her task. Why is she doing this? Is it just so that I'm painted like the others? Or is this something else? I wish I knew, but her face is closed to me, not exactly unfriendly, but impassive and remote.

She begins now on my torso, drawing her fingers slowly across my chest in what is almost a caress. Her head is bowed. It's a strange intimacy; she is so close and yet so distant. I'm a statue being adorned by an artist whose fingers are trailing black lines – slowly, deliciously – over my skin.

I shiver involuntarily, and where her fingers linger they leave a hot spot where my blood runs thick through my veins. My heart pounds as I sit, scarcely daring to breathe, surrendering totally to the pleasure of her touch.

I feel I should do something, have her acknowledge what I'm feeling, somehow. But I don't, and she's finished, turning away abruptly and collecting her jars of paint. I expect, or hope, for her to look at me at least once, to inspect her handiwork perhaps, or let me thank her, but she leaves without a backward glance.

* * *

A drum beats and we all run out onto the field. There are about twenty players in each team, all with faces and bodies painted, looking extremely fierce. We stand in two lines in the middle of the field, waiting for the balls to be tossed in. I've been picked as a runner, not a blocker or tackler. This is probably because of my relatively small physique. Though I'm over six foot tall and weigh eighty kilograms or more, next to most of my teammates I'm a lightweight. But I am fast. I've always been a sprinter, and I usually played wing in my school rugby team.

A signal is given, and each side tosses a ball into the middle of the field. I charge across with my teammates, whooping and yelling as they do, hoping I won't disappoint them or myself. Or Laisa – for I can't help feeling that she has, by her artwork, conferred her own expectations upon me.

A teammate scoops up the ball but is hit almost immediately by three burly opposition players. He is flung down but manages to toss the ball backwards. Ramanu lunges over, knocking one of the tacklers aside as he scoops up the ball. He sprints to the left, aiming for a gap in the wall of bodies ahead of us. On one side of the gap there's a wild skirmish around the other team's ball, and on the other side five players are closing in. I accelerate, seeing already that he won't make it – the gap is narrowing too fast, and the opposing forces are determined to stop him.

'Ramanu, here!' I shout. He pops a quick look in my direction, checks the players almost upon him, and shoots the ball to me. I catch it and duck away from the outstretched hands of a massive opponent. I feint to my right, and then lunge to the left again, straight into the wall of bodies around the other team's ball.

But I've seen an opening, a tiny gap where nobody is aware of me because of the action around the other ball. I lunge through, and as I feel a pair of hands grip my shoulders, I slip away and sprint upfield.

Two players converge on me, and I weave and dodge past them, almost slipping as I do so. The basket is close now, but there's no way I'll have a chance to throw the ball in; more players are already upon me, running up from both sides. I get the briefest glimpse of an orange-painted face shouting to my right, and I toss the ball.

Ramanu catches it, ducks his head, and barrels through two players. He moves with incredible speed, weaving around two more players, and then lunges for the pole. He chucks the ball into the basket. One point for us. Ramanu gives me a grin as we trot back down the field.

We win the game 10-8, with Ramanu scoring two more goals. I have a cut above my eye that blurs my vision, and one of our team members was carried off semi-conscious after a blow to the head. It's been a rough game, and though I'm sore I'm jubilant. We strut back to where the food is. A young girl from the other village bashfully hands me half a coconut shell filled with water, to wash the blood from the cut above my eye. Grabbing hunks of food, we slap each other on the shoulders and josh with the other team members. There are no hard feelings. It was all good sport.

The other team wins the spear-throwing competition, and afterwards we enjoy more feasting. A drum begins to beat, and an older man wearing an immaculate white shirt and a sulu steps onto a log to make a speech. Penaia tells me he is the *Buli*, the district headman, and also *Turaga-ni-koro* for this village. He finishes his short speech and hands something to our own *Turaga-ni-koro*.

'It is a *tabua*,' Penaia whispers to me. 'A whale's tooth. The prize for winning.'

I catch glimpses of Laisa during these events, but she is always busy, laughing and talking to others, unaware of my presence. Later, we paddle back to our village and I see her leaning close to Ramanu in another boat and saying something to him. He laughs.

* * *

We come ashore and, like an anxious mother fussing over her child after a prolonged absence, I decide to check on *Coracle*. But she is fine, sitting prettily on her anchor in her picturesque setting. The sun has disappeared over the treetops and the sky is streaked with pink. I feel full – gastronomically and spiritually, buoyed by the beauty of these surroundings and charged by my team's success. And still remembering Laisa's touch.

* * *

Night falls, and the villagers hold a special ceremony called a *yaqona*. Inside the big village *bure*, a group of younger men sit facing a line of village elders. In the middle of the elders is our *Turaga-ni-koro*. The younger group consists of all the players who took part in the sports today. Other men and women stand around, and I look for Laisa among them. I don't see her.

I move to join the players, but Penaia takes my arm and guides me to sit near the elders. I wonder why. I also wonder about a large wooden bowl with stumpy legs that has been placed in the centre of the two groups. In it, there's a fibrous cord with a single white shell, a large cowrie, attached to the end.

The ceremony starts with a speech by the chief. Penaia leans towards me and whispers a translation. It is about our victory, the kudos gained by the village and the valour of our players. He finishes, and a woman steps forward and dips a cup made from half a coconut shell into the wooden bowl. The bowl is filled with a liquid, which Penaia tells me is *kava*.

I've seen this *kava* before, men drinking it in our village and also at Mbenua. Penaia has told me that it is made from the juice of the pepper plant, which young maidens chew on before spitting the juice into a bowl; water is then added to make the ceremonial beverage. I'm not sure if he's having me on, and I don't dwell too long on it.

The chief takes the cup and says, '*Bula.*'

Everybody claps once and he downs the *kava*. They clap again, and the cup is filled and passed on to the next elder who in turn empties it, and so on down the line until it is my turn. The men watch as I take big gulps of the muddy-looking fluid, trying to down it quickly. They clap when I finish.

After all the men have drunk from the bowl Penaia makes a speech, which I gather is about the games. He gestures towards me, and as he does so, everyone looks at me, tilting their heads backwards with a smile.

The *kava* is passed around once more, starting with the *Turaga-ni-koro* again. When it is my turn I take a deep breath and swallow, draining the cup with a gasp. I take the collective clap as applause for my effort.

By now, my mind is having a little difficulty keeping up with my ears. Actually, most of me seems to be having difficulty keeping up with anything. My limbs have become heavy, numb appendages, hanging from a torso that also seems to be losing all feeling.

I drag my eyes around to Penaia, who is saying something to me. I think it is my turn to drink again. I nod at him and lift the bowl to my lips. It's not so bad now – my tongue is also numb. I pour the liquid down my throat, but clapping my hands together as the others take their turn has become a bit of a problem, though.

The chief makes a final speech. I realise that I am the subject again. I try to concentrate as he babbles on – then Penaia tells me that the chief has just declared me an honorary member of the village. He translates some more: I am welcome to return to the village any time in the future, and can live here as long as I want.

I try to focus my paralysed eyes and look appreciative. I'm not really sure what expression I am in fact wearing, since I have no feeling anywhere on my face. I lift a hand to pull at my cheeks, but dimly realise that this might look odd. Letting my hand fall, I manage to fold it into my other one as the assembly claps again at the end of the speech.

'*Vinaka*,' I say to them – thank you. It is one of the few Fijian words I've learnt. '*Vinaka* very much.' I wonder if they feel the same as I do: numb all the way through. Not exactly drunk or stoned, but more sort of paralysed.

Penaia claps me on the back as I ponder my new status. My brethren, my fellow villagers, countrymen – does this make me Fijian?

* * *

I'm happy here. Everyone seems so content, unfazed by the passing of time, oblivious to the demands of the world, unconcerned about what somebody else has or doesn't have. Even the *Turaga-ni-koro* lives simply, fishing with the others, tending the fields, helping to sun-dry coconut flesh to make copra. They are a truly communist society, equal in every way and genuinely sharing what they produce together.

It is four days since my new status has been conferred on me, and Penaia greets me on the beach one morning as I am coming ashore on my surfboard. He tells me that the villagers will have a celebration tonight. Once again, torches are set up around the central area of the village and drums are lined up along one side. When I first came to this village, I had a vague notion that life here would be, well, sort of boring. No movies, no bars, no proper entertainment. But the reality is pretty different: these people party and play, creating their own entertainment with more vigour than anything I've ever experienced before.

The drums start to beat, and another *meke* is performed. The dance is a bit different this time; the women – Laisa among them – form a circle and jiggle their hips as they twirl their grass skirts, their breasts bouncing to the rhythm of the drums. Their arms move sensuously, and a sheen of sweat glows on their skin. As before, each woman chooses a partner, dancing in front of the man before taking him by the hand and pulling him up to dance with them.

Laisa dances slowly towards me, twisting her slender arms with a look of concentration as I watch. She dances until she is directly before me, still moving with rapt attention. Then she holds out her hand. I take it, surprised and apprehensive, wondering how I'll acquit myself in a dance I've never done before. But the drumbeat carries me – that, as well as the woman who dances so close to me, close enough for my limbs to feel the sinuous rhythm of her body.

Later, she dances with others, but the connection remains. Every now and then she casts a glance towards me. I feel a thrill of pleasure, but what to do about it I'm not too sure. I know nothing about local courtship protocols, especially where a chief's daughter is concerned. And though I'm an honorary member of the community, this doesn't really make me a Fijian. How would a relationship – if that's what's on the cards – be accepted by the rest of the village?

I dance with Laisa again. She smiles and moves with me, dreamily. The evening is drawing to a close, and most of the villagers have left. The drumming is less fired up too, as the drummers are clearly all tired.

Finally they stop, and the party is over. The only sounds are those of a few villagers still clustered around the *kava* bowl.

I study Laisa's face, looking for clues, uncertain what to do next and wishing for the hundredth time that I could speak Fijian. This is the point where I'd usually ask the girl for her telephone number. Or try to persuade her to have coffee with me somewhere. I don't want this moment with Laisa to end, but I have no idea how to prolong it.

Then she reaches forward and takes my hand.

'*Curu*,' she says, leading me to a *bure*. We go inside, and I'm not sure what I'm going to find. Never having been into one of these female sleeping quarters before, I naturally expect it to be full of women. And I wonder how they'll react to my presence.

But it's empty. The hut is as devoid of women as it is of furniture. Sleeping mats are placed in neat rows along the walls, but no one is using them. We're alone. Won't anyone be coming back to the *bure*? Most of the women have already gone to bed, I think. So where are they? Was it all pre-arranged, that this hut would be empty?

Does this mean that a relationship between Laisa and me is perhaps sanctioned? I turn around to face her, trying to ascertain whether this could possibly be true.

She has dropped her sulu and is wearing nothing but a smile.

* * *

Over the next couple of weeks I go out and fish in the mornings, sometimes on my own with the speargun, and sometimes in a canoe with Penaia or Ramanu. Afterwards, to warm up, I play beach games with the younger villagers, or explore further along the coast.

I spend a lot of time with Laisa. Although our lack of spoken communication is frustrating and a bit of an impediment, I enjoy her company. We laugh and clown around, not understanding much of what the other is saying, but not caring much either. She has a fine sense of fun, which surprises me, as I initially thought her rather aloof and serious.

We enjoy paddling to the inner part of the reef, where we catch waves and shout with delight as we surf over the coral. Sometimes we walk along the beach, finding deserted spots and making love on the warm sand. I've tried to learn more of her language, but it's slow going. I suspect that Laisa has picked up more English from me than I've managed to learn of her tongue.

And it's fun helping Penaia to build a new canoe. Together we go into the jungle and choose a small tree. He cuts it down with an axe and strips it of branches, and we drag it back to the village. Using an adze, Penaia shapes the log so that the top is flat. We make a fire, and for the next seven days we transfer hot coals onto the top of the log. The coals burn away at the wood, hollowing it slowly in a carefully controlled process. When it is the right shape, we use rough coral stones to smooth the interior, and then attach the outrigger using strips of bark.

* * *

I have a decision to make. No, not exactly a decision, more like a commitment. A commitment to go. I've been at this village for nearly six weeks now – and it's over four months since I left Hawaii. I don't know exactly how long it would take for a letter to get to Honolulu, posted from Suva, but if it takes much more than a month then I have a bit of a problem. My instructions to Jack were that if he didn't hear from me within six months, he could presume I was dead. He would then inform my parents. Apart from the grief this information would cause them, I'm concerned that they might make inquiries in Hawaii, which could lead to the uncovering of the disappearance of *Recluse* – a yacht supposedly lost on its way to America captained by one Rob Greene from Portsmouth in England, and not in fact Rob Fridjhon from South Africa. I need to leave, to continue my voyage to Suva and get a missive off to Jack.

But I'm loath to leave, to abandon this beautiful life here and my new friends. I'm also loath to leave Laisa. I've become very close to her, despite our differences in culture. But I know that I cannot stay. I have commitments: parents to be in touch with, a life in South Africa, a boat to sail around the world. But most important right now, I have to get a letter off to Jack. I have to go, and soon.

* * *

So I say goodbye to my friends. It is hard, especially with Laisa. What makes it harder still is that I'm unable to tell her exactly how I feel, that I don't want to leave but I must. She doesn't cry or look hurt or sullen, just smiles gently, and I suspect that she's known all along that this moment would come. Penaia shakes my hand warmly, as does the *Turaga-ni-koro* and many other villagers. Even Ramanu.

With a heavy heart, I paddle out to my yacht. They're all standing on the beach as I lift the anchor, and after a lengthy two-handed wave I slip the engine into gear. They're still standing and watching, waving at me, when I eventually clear the headland and turn towards the reef that forced me to stop me here – so fortuitously, I now feel. It feels like just yesterday that I ran aground here, but it also seems so very long ago.

A day or two ago, Penaia took me in a dugout to show me the channel back into the Somosomo Strait, warning me to keep close to the shore, away from the barrier reef until I got close to the northern headland of the big bay. He told me to turn to starboard and to watch carefully as I negotiated the channel back into the Strait.

This I do, watching ahead for the reef and trying not to think too hard about the life I've just left. Instead, I force myself to think about Suva, trying to reawaken some excitement about seeing civilisation again, people of my own culture, and buildings and shops, a town, and movies maybe.

But I can't. None of that seems important to me any more.

19

It's been a long, sleepless night, and now I'm tired. Suva is six miles ahead and I must negotiate my way through the entrance channel without the benefit of an approaches chart. To make matters worse, the water is green and opaque from the rivers coming off the land, and I can't see where the shallows are. I'll have to watch the channel markers carefully in order to stay away from the many reefy areas surrounding the entrance to Suva Harbour. The trip across the Koro Sea was hard. I had to beat all night against a near gale-force wind, watching for reefs in the dark. My recent experience on Vanua Levu has made me especially skittish, and I wasn't able to get any rest.

Coracle's sails are down, lying across the deck in large untidy heaps of white dacron. I don't have the energy to furl them now; maybe later in the calmer water after I stop the boat. Above me, on the mainmast, the yellow Q-flag flaps in the stiff breeze. Even raising this small flag was an effort, but until I get clearance I need to signal to the authorities that I'm here, and that there are no contagious diseases on board.

It's hard to concentrate, to push through the fog in my mind and make sense of the buoys in front of me. The channel switches direction and also divides, and the buoyage system is confusing to my exhausted brain cells. I need to negotiate the entrance channel to the port of Suva and find a place to anchor.

We creep up the channel; compensating for my fatigue I slow *Coracle* to a crawl, so that she matches the speed of my brain.

* * *

The huge green mass of land ahead draws closer. Beaches become visible, and then houses, and then I see movement just above the shoreline, fast-moving specks which I realise are cars. I can smell the island now; a tangy odour of decomposing vegetation, exhaust gases, markets and gutters. It is cologne to my nostrils and I inhale deeply, reacquainting myself with civilisation.

The Bukh thuds faithfully as we nose into the harbour, past a couple of small ships tied to a wharf where two cranes are lifting palettes. The harbour is tiny compared to any port in America, but it looks wondrously grand to me. The mountains rise steeply behind the Victorian buildings of Suva, which is set deep within a beautiful bay. It is the busiest port in the South Pacific.

I see people moving about, and I can hear the sounds of the town; occasional shouts, car horns, the bark of a dog, a loud clanking rumble from deep within the hold of one of the ships. I watch a bus come to a stop further ahead and disgorge passengers. I'm re-entering a barely remembered world.

Just off the bow, almost directly ahead of *Coracle*, I can make out masts, and as we draw closer I see five sailboats and a small dock with tenders tied alongside. It looks like some sort of sailboat marina. A small white building stands on a cleared space near some trees and has a flagpole in front – maybe it's a yacht club. I head directly for this.

In an open piece of water, about a hundred yards or so from the little dock, I release the anchor. The chain rattles over the bow roller as the anchor plummets to the bottom, securing *Coracle* to her new home in the muddy depths of Suva Harbour.

I switch off the Bukh and prepare the papers I have, my passport and the clearances from Funafuti and Honolulu. As I wait for customs and immigration, I return to the deck and lower my fatigued body onto the mainsail; it's a comfortable place to lie, but it's also a way of holding the sail down onto the deck since I can't be bothered at the moment to secure it to the boom.

Almost immediately, I fall asleep.

* * *

A voice – intrusive yet distant – pushes in and out of my soggy consciousness like an irritating fly. I'm aware, too, of my shoulder moving from side to side. Sleepily, I wonder why, but don't really care.

Sharper now, the voice is in my ear. I want to brush it away but I'm loath to move any of my limbs. My shoulder is still moving, and now I feel a warm, heavy object on it – a hand. Somebody is shaking me.

The voice is urgent and concerned, but I don't know what he's saying. What's he doing in my bedroom, anyway? Why is my head off the pillow?

Still groggy, I allow myself to be helped upright. I blink at my foreign surroundings. Intensely green foliage descends to a palm-lined road along a shore. Houses made of palm fronds are scattered along it and a yacht is anchored near me. I turn my head and see two ships tied to a wharf. It all seems too acutely vivid. Where am I? Who is this person holding me?

Everything comes back in a rush. I'm in Suva. We're anchored. I see a white launch alongside *Coracle* and two men standing before me in uniforms, also white. A third is kneeling next to me and supporting me as I sit upright. They're all wearing expressions of grave concern, and I guess they are health officials, always the first to come aboard a foreign vessel in a port.

'Are you okay?' The man supporting me asks this. 'Are you sick? What is wrong with you?'

'No, no, I'm fine.' My voice is scratchy and slurred and I wipe drool from the side of my mouth. 'I'm just tired. I haven't had enough sleep.'

I take them below to fill out the forms, and after they've left the customs officers arrive. They board the yacht looking stern and officious, and I'm nervous. But I don't need to be – there are no questions about my ownership of *Coracle*, or any hint of suspicion concerning our identities. They depart, leaving me with an entrance form into the port of Suva. No problems there at all. It's all working perfectly, my plan, and I'm much relieved. It seemed to be the final obstacle, coming here into Suva, a large port like this with proper officialdom. But I'm free and clear now. The only thing left is to find some way to make money.

I'm cleared to go ashore, so I paddle my surfboard to a little jetty close by, keeping my sandals, T-shirt and passport dry in a plastic bag, and then make my way to the immigration shed, as directed by customs.

That done, I go to the white building to arrange a berth for my yacht. It turns out to be a little yacht club, ambitiously named the Royal Suva Yacht Club, and they allow me to stay anchored for free – a welcome surprise and a huge relief, with my limited resources.

I return to *Coracle* to write two letters.

One is to Jack. He no longer needs to be concerned about informing my family of the circumstances of my disappearance. The other letter is to my parents. I tell them that I am in Fiji, having sailed here on a yacht from Hawaii. I don't mention that I am single-handing, instead giving them the impression that I am crewing on a larger yacht across the Pacific.

I set off for town, walking along the road that leads to the centre of Suva. The tar and cement feel amazingly solid under my bare feet. I haven't yet slipped my sandals back on, since I'm still a bit wet from my paddle ashore.

The post office in Victoria Parade where I post my letters is tiny. I feel happy as I walk out onto the streets, taking in the old colonial buildings, investigating shops and markets – being surrounded by civilisation again.

20

I need to make some money. I've bought a few vegetables and fruit at the local market, but the small amount of cash I had is almost gone. I will soon be back to eating canned foods again, digging into my virtually nil supplies on board.

My plan is to approach the holiday hotels to see if I can offer *Coracle* for day charters. I've spoken to a couple of yachties, a young-ish guy called Clint, who sailed out from New Zealand and is currently running a tourist bar in Suva, and a grizzled old Swede called Jan, who is waiting for his wife to return from Sweden so that he can carry on cruising. I suspect that he is waiting in vain – his rust-streaked thirty-five footer and morose personality not much of an inducement for her to come back. But Jan has been helpful, telling me which hotels I should try and how I should advertise. He has even offered to lend me his camera to take a picture of *Coracle* for the flyers I'll distribute. And my Kiwi friend has promised to pass on my information to tourists who frequent his bar and who often ask about hiring a boat to visit outlying islands.

Things are looking good.

* * *

Six days later, wandering through the museum in Suva and studying the weaponry used by the Fijians in their earlier forays against the Tongans and each other, I meet an Australian family out on holiday and keen to do a bit of sailing. I charge them eighty dollars for a day trip to a nearby island. Over the next couple of weeks I take out two more groups, and my financial situation eases somewhat. But I still have to re-provision for my trip to Australia in a month or two, so I need to increase my advertising and do more to promote *Coracle*.

I'm busy inside the galley, cooking myself a dinner using curry powder I bought from an old Indian woman at the market. Since I've never tried making curry before, this is something of an experiment. I carefully measure out the curry powder, mindful of its strength.

A shout diverts my concentration. It sounds like it's somewhere close by. Another shout follows and I realise that it's coming from a boat right alongside *Coracle*. I put down the spoon and make my way out onto the deck, to see who is trying to get my attention.

I see a large white boat, a very official-looking launch, much bigger than the one that brought out the health inspectors. It is stationary, about ten feet from my boat, its bow pointing towards her and towering at least six feet higher than *Coracle*'s deck.

Standing on the foredeck is a group of men: immigration men dressed in white, customs men dressed in grey, port officials dressed in khaki, and policemen dressed in blue. They are wearing identical expressions – grim anticipation, curiosity, and a focused concentration on a single object. Me.

A strange sensation wells up in me, making me feel light-headed.

I am caught.

I know this, without any doubt. My face is frozen and random thoughts are flitting inside my head in panic – futile hope crushed by unwelcome logic. I hear a voice and see lips moving on the face of one of the men. But I can't make out what he is saying; my blood is pounding too loudly in my ears.

'Are you Robert Fridjhon?' He repeats the question.

'Yea …' I clear my throat. 'Yes, that's me.'

'May we come aboard?' This is not a request.

Through a jumble of conflicting thoughts I consider my options. My emotions are churning as I realise that the need for caution is lost. I could try to escape. But how? Dive over the side with my surfboard and paddle away? Swim underwater from boat to boat until I reach the shore? Point my speargun at the men and hope they'll surrender?

No. There is no way for me to escape at this moment. Maybe later … maybe later.

'Um, yes, sure. Come aboard.' I indicate with my hand. I'll be gracious to the end. Surrender without a fight.

The launch noses closer and I help hold it off, trying to avoid damage to *Coracle*'s paintwork. It strikes me, though, that this proprietary concern is no longer valid.

The men clamber down, looking around the yacht with unabashed curiosity. It occurs to me that I could deny everything. Show them my papers and insist that this is my boat. Deny any knowledge of Rob Greene, whoever he might be.

I face the policeman who first spoke to me.

'We are going to take a look around,' he says. 'We have to look at some things, you understand?' Once again, this is not a request, and I nod dumbly. I notice that he has bushy sideburns.

They tramp down below and I follow. The policeman takes a piece of paper from his pouch and studies it, apparently comparing the layout of my boat with some description on it. They speak to each other, but in Fijian. I am aware of the triumphant tone of what they say. My heart, almost impossibly, shrinks even smaller. They know exactly what they are looking for.

Four policemen squeeze into the forepeak. From my position behind them I can see that they are studying the beam where the official number used to be. The number that is now covered over by a very white, very new-looking piece of wood.

'This is the yacht *Recluse*, yes?' The spokesperson twists around in the confined space, speaking through a gap in the bodies that surround him. He has addressed the question to me, catching me off guard as I struggle through a swirl of useless thoughts.

'Yes,' I answer.

There is no point in denying it. They obviously have a full description of her. We all back out into the salon, and I face the policemen. For a long moment nobody says anything; it's as if they are waiting for something, a directive to be given for the next step. But then the sideburned officer addresses me again.

'Robert Fridjhon, you are under arrest for the theft of this yacht.' His tone has become stilted. 'You will come with us now … to jail.' For a moment he seems uncertain, as though inviting me to a place he suspects I might not be all that enthusiastic about visiting.

I nod, a hot sensation spreading through my gut. The backs of my eyes feel prickly and I swallow hard.

'You can put your shirt on and bring any valuables from the boat.' His voice seems gentler.

'I must turn off the cooker,' I mumble, gesturing towards the simmering pot.

'Ah, yes, you may eat your dinner. We will wait.' The policemen seem friendlier, as though they have relaxed, knowing that they have accomplished their mission.

'Um, well, I don't know if it's any good.' I don't know what else to say. My brain is in limbo. 'I've never cooked curry before.'

'It is easy, but you should cook the powder with oil first, with your meat.' His concern is touching. I cling to their friendliness like a drowning swimmer clutching a lifebuoy.

* * *

I swallow the last of my dinner. I may as well be swallowing pieces of cardboard. Under normal circumstances I may have enjoyed the meal, but now I am eating mechanically. I've been arrested; it all seems a bit surreal.

The police wait as I wash the dishes. They're conversing amiably with each other and with me, as if this is some sort of social occasion. Maybe they'll let me go; maybe in Fiji they won't think it's that serious a deal that I stole a yacht.

I grab a T-shirt and my sandals, wondering what else I should take. Nothing. What else do I need in prison? What else will I need for the next few years of my life? The thought slams into me like a body blow, and I almost throw up the dinner I've forced down with such effort.

I'm going to jail. Reality washes over me like a fetid flood. My life is over for the next however many years that I'll be in prison. No longer will I cruise the world on my own yacht. No longer will I decide which road to take; no longer will I go surfing, enjoy my own meals, befriend villagers, or see Laisa again.

Doors are closing inside my head yet still I wonder: if I were to escape, would I be able to get back to Vanua Levu, find my way back to Laisa's village? Maybe I could hide out there until the police stop looking for me. I could fish for them and help them build their boats. But what happens if they learn of my crime and my arrest? No, they wouldn't turn me in. Or would they? Who am I kidding, anyway? I'm a thief.

The present comes crashing back into my brain, sweeping away my fantasy. No, I'm fucked. On my own now, even more alone than when I was out at sea. I'm going to jail. Definitely.

I hoist myself aboard the launch, assisted – without any appreciation on my part – by two customs officers. Silence descends as I walk aft. I resent being the centre of attention like this. I can sense their curiosity at my thieving foreignness.

Standing in the after well behind the pilothouse, surrounded by uniformed men, I look back. The launch throbs as she draws away from *Coracle* – or *Recluse*, as she is to be once again.

A desolate sense of separation tears my heart as I watch her in our wake, so elegant and so stately, riding her anchor with pride at having proven her mastery; a trans-Pacific sailing boat capable of riding out any storms, crossing any sea. She is one of the most beautiful yachts I have ever seen, and she has brought me safely across the ocean.

This is the last time I will ever see her.

21

My cell is six feet wide and twelve feet long, a stone-walled dungeon with a solid door. In one corner there is a bucket, with a lid that doesn't quite fit. It is my toilet and it leaks odours. My bed is a dirty grey mattress on the stone floor. The fabric is sparsely filled with coconut husk that collects around the edges, no matter how I try to shake it around. I basically sleep on two thin cloth coverings on the floor.

Apart from the clothes I've been issued – a too-small blue denim shirt and too-large denim shorts – I have a water jar, two blankets and a towel that may once have been white.

The cell smells of urine. In fact, everything in it stinks of urine. The rank odour of piss is in the mattress, in the towel, in the blankets, and it's even seeped through to the stone walls – the residue from maybe a century or so of prisoners.

I've been here for three days now, in the remand block of the Fiji prison. After my arrest I was taken to the police station, where I sat and waited in a room with a steel table, two chairs, a scuffed green linoleum floor – and a locked door. Everything in the police station seemed hard: the chairs, the lights, the boots echoing on hard floors, as well as the people in it. Eventually I was fingerprinted and photographed and taken to a courtroom to appear before a bewigged judge. He was an Indian, and in a short and bewildering judicial process, he informed me that I was to be remanded to Her Majesty's prison to await trial.

Her Majesty's prison. Why's it still called that, I wonder? Fiji's been independent for three years or more. Why would Her Majesty want to retain possession of this mean construction of massive stone walls topped with broken glass, with damp and stinking cells – the whole place a malignant reminder of harsher colonial times?

For the umpteenth time, I wonder how exactly I came to be caught. Obviously, the American authorities gave the local police information about the boat. But when? I cleared in successfully, and from this I deduce that some notice was subsequently given that I was in Fiji. But by whom? And how did they know I was here?

A clanging of gates interrupts my reverie. Boots echo along the passageway outside my cell and then my peephole is swung open, startling me. An eye studies me as I stare back, seated on my mattress with my back against the wall.

A key turns the lock and the door swings open. It is one of my jailers, a heavy-set Fijian with a fierce scowl and a scarred face. He motions with his hand.

'You come,' he says, the sum total of his English. None of the jailers speak my language.

I follow him through the gates as they are opened, one by one, and we go out of the remand block into the prison area. The main block consists of four tiers of cells, each with a heavy solid door behind a barred landing. The landings face onto a terraced vegetable garden where the prisoners work. This garden separates the main cell block from the administration section, which is at the entrance to the prison complex. We walk past the vegetable patch and I endure the curious stares of other prisoners as they lean on their rakes and hoes. But I am just as curious; they are likely to be my fellow inmates for the next few years.

We reach the administration block, and a guard indicates a small, bare room. Seated behind a desk is a man wearing a grey suit. His tie is loosened and he is reading something.

'Sit, please,' he says. I obey, somewhat apprehensively. With a frown of concentration, he looks at the sheet of paper in his hands. Then he continues, 'My name is Lieutenant Naidoo. CID.' He's a detective. He must know who I am. So I merely nod.

'You are Robert Paul Fridjhon, from Cape Town in South Africa, yes?'

I nod again. 'That's right.'

'You were living at number fourteen, San Pedro Street, in El Monte, California, with Mikhael Krasnopoli and Peter Deerfield. Is that correct?' He reads again from the sheet of paper. 'You lived there until you went to Hawaii to sail a boat back to America for,' he clears his throat, 'Calley Yachts?'

'Uh, yes, sir.'

He asks a few more questions about my life in America. I have no idea where this is leading.

'Did you know a Mr Kranova? Mihai Kranova?'

A current of shock triggers a new caution. I think about Vlazo, and about Bainesfield and Alex.

'Yes. That is correct,' I answer warily.

'Could you tell me what your involvement with him was?'

I hesitate. 'I became friends with him while I was hitch-hiking,' I answer slowly. 'We got to know each other and then he offered me a job.'

'And what was that job? What were you going to do?' Lieutenant Naidoo appraises me.

'Mihai wanted to sail around the world with his wife. He wanted me to captain his boat for him, the boat he was going to buy.' Then I add helpfully, 'He had no experience with sailing, you see.' I'm not being asked about my association with the Priest, with the other Russians – questions that might lead to Vlazo and the murder. Does Naidoo know anything about this? Am I suspected of being an accomplice?

'Did you intend to use this boat for any other purposes? To transport stuff? Gold, maybe?'

I'm confused. I'm expecting an interrogation about drugs and murder. Why is he asking this?

'No. Never,' I reply, shaking my head.

'Did you ever do anything involving gold?'

I'm shaking my head again, phrasing a reply in my mind when there is a quick knock on the door and a policeman sticks his head into the room.

'You are wanted on the phone, sir. Urgent.'

'Excuse me for one moment,' the lieutenant says to me.

He leaves the room and I lean over and grab the piece of paper. I quickly scan it.

Federal Bureau of Investigation – United States of America
J Edgar Hoover Building, Washington DC

To the Chief of Intelligence – CID Suva division, Fiji.

Dear Sir,

It has come to our notice that you have apprehended one Robert Paul Fridjhon, AKA Robert Greene. This man is from Cape Town, South Africa, although he also purports to be from Portsmouth in England. There is currently a warrant of arrest and an application for his extradition being expedited in Washington, to bring him back to the United States of America where he is due to stand trial on charges of Grand Larceny and/or Piracy.

We suspect that his activities in the United States have reached

further than the theft of the yacht Recluse *for which he has been
arrested. His involvement with a certain Mihai Kranova, whom
we have been monitoring for some time now, and Robert Fridjhon's
South African origins, together with certain other activities of
theirs in America, have led us to believe that they are possibly
involved in a gold-smuggling operation in the United States
of America.*

*We would be grateful if you would present the questions below
to Fridjhon and try to elicit any information that might help us
with our investigations into this matter.*

Thank you very much for your cooperation.

Yours sincerely

Bureau Chief

Gold-smuggling operations? Shit. What is this? At the sound of
approaching footsteps, I shove the paper to the other side of the desk
and lean back in my seat. Lieutenant Naidoo re-enters the room.

He resumes his questions. It's a bit easier to answer, now that
I know the gist of what he is going to ask. But what the fuck's going
on here? Will I be extradited to America? And stand trial there on
grand-sounding charges? A gold smuggler – me?

The questions continue. Was I involved in a gold-smuggling operation into America with Mihai? Did we plan to smuggle gold? What
were we going to use the boat for? Who else was involved? I answer
some of the questions truthfully – denying any involvement with
gold – and hedging some, careful not to implicate Mihai in anything,
making no mention of the Priest or Vlazo.

The lieutenant thanks me and calls the warder, who has been
waiting outside. The jailer takes me back to my cell. I'm relieved that

the FBI don't seem to know about my involvement in Bainesfield's murder. But where will I go to jail? What will Vlazo's reaction be if he thinks I might try to strike a deal – information about Bainesfield's death, in return for a lesser sentence?

And what makes the FBI think I'm a gold smuggler? Okay, so they know I'm a criminal. I proved that by stealing *Recluse*. They probably know that Mihai and I were planning something nefarious in America, using a boat. That much they possibly got from my phone call to Joanne. They also know that Mihai was involved with MED, with its rather nebulous gold trading, and here I am, from South Africa, a country rich in gold. They added two and two together – and the answer came to ten.

I'm not really worried about the gold charge. I know at least that I am completely innocent here. The other charges are of course a different matter. And I'm worried not so much by the fact that the charges exist, but by the fact that I'll be facing them in America.

* * *

Mosquitoes. The night air in this hot cell is full of them, whining in my ear, drilling through my skin and feasting on my blood. My skin shudders and crawls at imaginary and real feathery landings, and I am in a torment of itching. I lash out futilely, with random slaps on my face and body. Or I lie huddled in sweaty discomfort under my urine-scented blanket until morning comes.

Clang, rattle and slam. Latches are thrown back, gates are opened, boots clonk on the stone floor and keys jangle. My stomach rumbles. The peephole opens and an eye stares at me. The peephole shuts again and a key turns in the lock.

The warder nods once at me as he deposits my breakfast just inside the door and takes away my tin dinner plate before pulling the heavy door shut behind him. It is always the same: tea and bread.

The bread is dry, but I am too hungry to care. Dipped in the tea it is edible. I eat as always, extremely slowly. This has become a habit, to prolong meal times as far as possible. In any case, the food is always cold by the time it reaches me.

By seven o'clock I have been awake for two hours already.

At eight o'clock, after breakfast, all twenty or so prisoners are lined up outside our cell doors, backs to the wall, with our buckets placed carefully to the right of our feet. When everybody is ready the warden gives an order and we pick up our buckets, marching in single file to a courtyard just outside the cell block. There we wait our turn at a trough with a large drain, emptying the contents of the buckets into it and then washing them out under a tap. We half-fill our buckets with water, and when everyone has finished, we carry them back to our cells.

At ten o'clock we are taken out to shower. It's the same procedure, minus the buckets, in the same courtyard, on the far side this time. There, we use the four outdoor showers, which have rusty pipes and no shower heads. The water is always cold, but in this warm climate that doesn't matter.

We all use the same piece of soap, passing it back and forth as we wash quickly, mindful of the limited time our guards allow us. Everyone is amused when I stamp on my towel as I shower, in an effort to rid it of the urine smell. But it doesn't work. Not once do I use the towel to dry myself.

Toothpaste is given to us only three times a week, and in minute quantities. I use soap on my toothbrush the other days.

Exercise is at around eleven in the morning, twice a week. We are led in single file into another courtyard, a slightly bigger one that is grassed in the middle. There, still in single file, we walk for about half an hour around and around the edge of the grass. After that, we are returned to our cells.

Lunch is tapioca or dalo – also a starchy root vegetable – and tea.

Occasionally we get a banana as well. I once tried eating the banana skin, but gave that up instantly as a gourmet failure. Most times I keep a bit of food for later – the banana, if there is one, or maybe some of the tapioca. This gives me something to look forward to in the afternoons, and also becomes a test of my self-restraint.

Almost nothing happens in the afternoons. These are the longest hours of the day, but I use the time to exercise. I have three forms of exercise: sit-ups, push-ups and walking.

When dinner comes, it's cassava or tapioca again, a lump of bread, the ubiquitous tea, and on some days a small piece of fish as well. Taking small bites and chewing each mouthful to a fine paste, I can make this meal last for a full hour. The only good thing about the food situation is that I only use the shit bucket every second day, which is fine with me as I don't have to endure the smell from its ill-fitting lid quite as much.

I am always hungry – not least because I've always had a big appetite. And now I'm in a dilemma over my need to exercise and the energy it consumes. The thought of escape remains in my mind, and if the opportunity presents itself I will need to be fit. I may have to run or climb, so I must exercise, even if it is only so that hope does not die within me.

Another thought, though one not quite at the forefront of my mind, is that I'll need to be fit and strong if I go to prison in America. I've seen plenty of movies about the rough treatment from other prisoners there.

The lights go off at ten o'clock, leaving me to my mosquitoes again.

* * *

About five weeks pass in this way. Then I receive a surprise letter from Mihai. I have no idea how he found out I was in prison. The letter is fairly short.

Dear Rob,

I was sorry to hear about your arrest. I hope that nothing too bad happens to you, and you don't spend too long in prison.

The reason I'm writing this is because of some information that I have. I've found out that it was Jack Nichols who gave the police the information that led to your arrest. I think he got a reward for the information. I want you to know that Mary and I never said anything to the police or had anything to do with you getting arrested. You are still my friend, and I didn't want you to get the wrong idea. There was a search for you for a while, but everybody thought that the yacht had been sunk in a big storm that came through a week after you left. You were declared lost at sea and then Jack Nichols turned you in.

All the best and I hope you come out of this okay.

Regards

Mihai

Okay. So it was Jack.

I was correct when I guessed that information was given to the FBI about my whereabouts. Jack, my friend and confidant, betraying me for some paltry percentage from the insurance company. I'd so nearly got away with it; the same storm that broke the self-steering was blamed for my death. But for Jack, I would probably never have been caught.

I can't believe it, the lousy fuck. He's a wealthy man. His parents left him hundreds of thousands of dollars, or so he told me. Why would he need another few thousand? Is that all our friendship meant? A deep rage fires inside me, even burning away at my concerns about my future. Bastard. His friendship was all a pretence, supporting my plan to steal *Recluse* and at the same time intending to sell me down the river.

Okay, maybe this wasn't his plan at the outset. Maybe it was the fact of the vast distance between us – this, together with an already shallow concern for my well-being. He probably just allowed some easy rationale to justify his making a few grand. Jack's probably not a bad person, he's just got easily corruptible principles.

*   *   *

Vamatu, a prisoner two cells down from me, tells me the date – I've been here three months now. He's a new arrival who speaks some English, so at last I can share in the conversations that take place through the narrow gaps under the cell doors. Up to now I've just lain flat on my side, not participating, listening with my ear pressed to the floor, forehead up against the door and peering at three other eyes staring out from under their doors on the other side of the corridor. But with Vamatu translating, I can now understand what the inmates are saying to each other.

They have always been friendly enough towards me during our brief periods together outside, showering, exercising, or emptying our shit buckets. But we've never been able to converse – though that is forbidden anyway during those times.

Before Vamatu's arrival, there was only one time when I'd managed to participate in the cell block's activities. It was the day a frog appeared in the middle of the corridor. Having jumped through the bars of the cell-block door, it just sat there, in the middle of the floor – a large olive frog, undecided about its surroundings. The prisoners all began to shout at it, and, as the frog became agitated and hopped closer to the cell doors, blankets and towels swished out from the gaps. I didn't know whether the others wanted to eat it, keep it, or just kill it – but I wanted the frog as a pet, a companion. I was even prepared to share my food with it. For about half an hour the frog teased us, hopping towards the cells and then away again as fingers grabbed at it from under the doors. In my eagerness to catch the creature, I scratched my wrist on the bottom of my door. But the frog eventually escaped, back to the outside world and freedom.

* * *

With Vamatu's help, I tell my story to the other prisoners. I'm not certain that they understand the circumstances of my crime, or why I took the yacht or why I want to sail on around the world. But the attention and the interest they show makes me feel that I have been welcomed back into human society. For a long time now, I have barely exchanged a word with either my captors or my fellow inmates. All communication has taken place by way of gestures, with only now and then a weird word or two of English.

I'm not treated badly. The guards are not mean or nasty, and neither are the prisoners. The only aggression I experience is when an older guy in the cell next to me takes to jostling me when we line up with our buckets, or pushes me on my back occasionally as we walk around the courtyard – something he does whenever he thinks the guards aren't looking. When I glare at him he gazes back with a strange look. The prisoners behind him wear inscrutable expressions, ready – or perhaps eager – for a fight to develop, or maybe they just can't be bothered about it all. I can't work it out. Is he testing me, maybe? Wanting a fight? Or having a go at me for no reason other than boredom?

One day, as we wait outside our cells to empty our shit buckets, he bumps me so hard that I almost overturn my bucket. I know that disobedience is quickly punished – I've already witnessed guards beating up two prisoners so badly that they landed up in the infirmary for a few days. But I must do something.

I wait for the guard to turn away, and then I shove my elbow backwards, hard, right into his midriff. I hear his breath whoosh out and wait for him to retaliate. I look back, but all he does is straighten up, clutching his side, and turn away. The guard is facing us now, and

I suspect the inmate might wait for another opportunity. I am tense the next day when we line up outside our cells, but when I glance at him, he half-smiles. He leaves me alone after that.

I am, in fact, left pretty much alone by everybody – disturbed only at meal times and for the daily excursions to empty my bucket, or to shower or exercise. I think sometimes that everybody here, guards and prisoners alike, regard me as a bit weird, some sort of alien curiosity perhaps. Often when I exercise I become aware of an eye at my peephole as a guard watches me doing my sit-ups or push-ups, watching sometimes for as long as twenty minutes or half an hour. Maybe they're as bored as I am. At sea, I was frustrated sitting and steering for interminable hours, or waiting for wind on an ocean where everything seemed to have been burnt to a standstill. But at least I was waiting. In prison it is different. There is no frustration here at time's slow passing, because there is no promise of an end. Just totally helpless endurance.

* * *

Vamatu tells me the story of George Ralu, who occupies the cell at the far end of the corridor, on the opposite side to me. He is a young man from Rotuma, an island some distance away. There, he lived with his wife on a small plot where he grew vegetables and dalo. He had never been in trouble with the law before – that is, until a new neighbour arrived, with a pig.

For a month or two they lived harmoniously together, but then the pig found a way through the fence surrounding the vegetables and uprooted half of them. George Ralu captured the pig and took it back to his neighbour, complaining about the damage to his garden. The owner of the pig was unrepentant, suggesting that George might consider putting up a stronger fence. Which he did, but unfortunately it wasn't strong enough. The pig, having acquired a taste for his vegetables, broke through again and devoured more of his crop.

George Ralu again returned the pig to its owner, but this time he told the still unrepentant man that he would kill the pig next time it happened. He warned his neighbour to keep the pig tethered or in a pen, or he would kill it.

George Ralu went back home and fixed the fence.

Two days later, he found the pig in his garden once more, happily finishing off the last of his vegetables. So he killed it.

The neighbour complained to the police and George Ralu was arrested for wilfully damaging his neighbour's property, and on a number of other charges too. He was remanded in Suva to await trial for an offence that could carry a nine-month or year-long prison term.

He has been on remand now for almost a year.

I am shocked. Not only for George Ralu, waiting to be sentenced to a prison term probably shorter than the time he has already served, but also because of the lax and ill-organised Fijian penal code and its inherent injustices.

I'm trapped in it too.

But George Ralu has asked for my help. All the court cases are conducted in English, a language that none of these prisoners, apart from Vamatu, understand. George Ralu had no idea what he was being asked when the court told him to speak in his defence. His interpreter asked him if he had anything to say, and he said no, not realising that he was being given a chance to plead his case. He did not even understand that he had, courtesy of his interpreter, pleaded guilty.

George Ralu has asked me to write a letter to the authorities, explaining his situation. A guard brings me a pen and paper, and I carefully compose a letter addressed to the governor-general of Fiji, Ratu George Cakobua, my one-time saviour. I explain the circumstances of George Ralu's 'crime' and his subsequent imprisonment, and I plead for his intervention. I make no mention to the governor of our meeting on Taveuni.

* * *

I have written only one other letter from prison. This was a letter to Jim Johnson, care of Calley Yachts, that I wrote less than a week after I was imprisoned. I explained that my intention was not actually to steal from him, because I figured that since *Recluse* was insured he'd still get the money he'd originally wanted from her sale. I apologised for any hurt he might have suffered as a result of my actions.

One and a half months later, I received a reply. Jim said he forgave me, and told me that he had tried to have the charges against me dropped – unfortunately to no avail. Whenever I think of him, I'm amazed at the kindness shown by a man I've never even met.

I intentionally haven't written a letter to my parents. I'm certain that I will be taken back to America to face a lengthy prison sentence there. And, in any case, I figure that my parents are used to my long gaps in communication now, so they won't worry too much about another lengthy silence. There's no need for them to endure the agony of my trial. I'll let them know of my circumstances as soon as the trial is over and I know my fate: whether I'll be serving my sentence in a US penitentiary or spending the next few years here in Fiji.

Other prisoners ask me to plead their case to the governor and I write three more letters, in each case outlining clear injustices to the men involved, and pleading with the governor for his intervention.

I still withhold any mention of our prior meeting, signing my name and hoping that he won't recognise who I am. Each time, I feel guilt and shame at what he must now know about my character.

* * *

Time drags on. It is excruciating. I remember Charrière's *Papillon*: the threat posed by years of solitary confinement to his sanity, and the methods he devised of mentally escaping his internment. By walking continually up and down his cell, for hours on end, he found he could transport his thoughts back to France, to country meadows and long walks with his fiancée, or childhood friends. He held conversations in his mind, and these, along with near-tangible sights and smells, became part of a mental 'reality'.

For long periods, Papillon was totally unaware of his actual surroundings, lost in a better place, as he counted twelve steps and then stopped, turned, and counted twelve steps and stopped and turned again, and so on. But I've found that I can't do this. The need to be aware of when to stop to avoid hitting the wall means that it doesn't work for me. The action of stopping and turning requires too much conscious attention, breaking my concentration and interrupting my meditation.

I've found another way, though. By placing my mattress in the middle of the floor I have a space of about one and a half feet on either side and two feet at each end. I carefully place my bucket in the middle of the mattress, along with my towel and shirt. Now there's a pathway around the edges of my cell, and as I walk, my turns eventually become automatic. Papillon's 'escape system' works.

I round the corners unconsciously, my mind far, far away. I am back in South Africa, surfing waves at sandy beaches, hiking over Table Mountain, or diving in the kelp at Cape Point, catching crayfish and abalone. I am with friends and family again, engaged in conversations that are as real as the faces and personalities that I remember.

Long hours I pass this way, unaware of where I am, of the eye watching through the peephole, and of what the rest of my life might be like.

* * *

I spot a nail lying in the grass. We are out exercising, and I see it off to one side of the path, almost hidden by the grass. I note its position as I walk past.

The next time I pass by the nail, I pretend to stumble and fall, tripping over my own feet. I get up, acting sheepish. The guards and the rest of the prisoners wait for me to resume my position in the line, and we continue walking.

I have the nail.

It is in my hand, caught between two fingers. I hold it until we have finished exercising and then slide it into my pocket when the guards are not looking. Back in my cell, I examine my new possession. It is three inches long and a little rusty, but it is mine, and I have a plan for it.

Holding the nail between my palms I rotate the point, rubbing it into the stone wall to make a depression. Then I angle the nail slightly downward, rubbing my palms together again and pressing the nail hard into the stone as it rotates. Three weeks later, the hole is deep enough to hold the nail. I have a peg to hang my towel on.

I use another trick to escape the oppressiveness of the dungeon. Placing a blanket over my shoulder, I press my back against the door and hurl myself forwards to the other end of the cell, where I leap up and grab hold of a window bar. The window is over eight feet from the floor and about two feet square, with four vertical steel bars across it, preventing any escape.

But the bars help me now. Hanging by one hand, I use the other to tie the blanket around the steel. It takes a while and a few more leaps, but eventually I have the corners of the blanket tied to the bars. I now have a small hammock-seat where I can sit and look out at a vista filled with light and openness.

I keep my gaze upward, away from the high wire-topped wall of the prison. I can even stretch my arms out over the stone, exposing my forearms to sunlight. The prison is close to the yacht club, and I think of *Recluse* sitting where I left her. Is she still there?

My view downwards is over the condemned cells, and a cell on the other side contains a condemned man. We spend long periods watching each other over the next few months, staring at each other impassively. Not once do we acknowledge the presence of the other with a wave or a nod. And then one day he is gone.

22

It's been over five months now. I still haven't heard any news about my trial, or about my extradition back to America. I'm one more lost soul in the excruciatingly slow legal system of Fiji. Christmas has come and gone, and I've had a birthday, but I was unaware when exactly these events happened. The days pass by in perfect uniformity; I spend endless hours doing almost nothing – exercising and thinking. I don't think there is a library in the prison, or maybe it's just not available to remand prisoners.

I've learnt to control my thoughts: I allow myself to dwell only on certain aspects of my past in South Africa, or times in the Caribbean and America – events or experiences that don't cause me any unhappiness. I construct fantasies, thinking of old friends and near-forgotten places. I avoid fantasising about any future. I've adapted to life in prison.

* * *

Clangs and rattles in the corridor. What's this? It is about two thirty in the afternoon, and supper is still another two and a half hours away. Boots reverberate, keys jangle. Maybe a new prisoner is arriving?

I jump over to have a look, pressing my head flat against the floor as I try to get my eye as close as possible to the crack under the door.

Just in time to see the boots stop at my cell.

I scoot back sharply as the peephole opens. My door is opened and a guard beckons to me. I've nicknamed him Tu-lips because a scar right across his face has divided his lips into separate segments. Also, he has a flowery disposition – he's one of my favourite jailers.

'You come,' he says with his cleft grin. I move towards him, but he points at the shirt that is hanging on the peg with my towel. I never wear it, but he indicates that I should put it on.

Wearing the shirt that is much too small for me, its buttons almost popping across my chest, and with the oversized shorts flapping about my knees, I follow Tu-lips out of the cell block. The eyes of the other prisoners swivel after us from under their doors as we move down the corridor.

He leads me through the courtyard of the remand block and into the main prison yard, where I again see prisoners working in the vegetable garden. This is very strange. I haven't been back here since the time I was first led to my cell. What's this all about? Once inside the administration block, I'm shown a door in a corridor. It is ajar, and Tu-lips waits next to the doorway. Hesitant, I look at him, and he motions me inside.

A man is staring out the window. He turns as I enter. My legs almost give way as I'm hit by a feeling of unreality, a kind of déjà vu that makes me feel dizzy.

It is my father.

I step towards him, my mouth gaping.

'Hello, Rob.' His emotions are playing with his features. His words I hear dimly, a faint drumming in my ears. My own emotions are constricting my throat so that I can hardly breathe. My first coherent thought is: how did he *find* me here?

'Hi, Dad.' My voice emerges at last, oddly flat. I clear my throat and try again. 'How are you? When did you get here?'

'I'm fine, Rob.' He steps forward, hesitates, then offers his hand. I have the feeling I should hug him, but I don't. I never have – we're not a demonstrative family. I shake his hand instead. There are two hard chairs in the room, and we sit down facing each other.

'But how are *you* doing?' He studies me intently, and I'm aware of the depth of his concern. I'm also aware of the indignity of my dress. 'Are you okay?'

'Yes, I'm all right. I'm good, thanks Dad.' I still sound wooden, but this is because I'm fighting the lump in my throat. 'How's Mom? And the others?' I have three brothers and a sister.

'Everybody's doing well,' he says. 'All just concerned about you. You seem to have landed yourself in a bit of a pickle, hey?' I catch the ghost of a smile as he tries to ease the gravity of the situation.

'Yes, well … but how did you know about me?' The question bursts out. 'I never told anyone.'

'I read about it in the paper, the *Argus*,' he says. 'I was having breakfast one Saturday. It made the front page.' His smile twists a little. 'The story was picked up by Reuters when the yacht – what was it called? – *Recluse*, when *Recluse* was returned to America.'

Wondering about my boat – the vessel that was mine, and so much a part of me – a question forms, but I'm unsure whether to ask it.

My father sees my hesitation, guesses the question I'm struggling to ask. '*Recluse* was taken back to America by ship. She's in Los Angeles now. She's fine, apparently. Had a bit of damage from the trip, I understand.'

I just nod.

'But it looks like you're not so fine,' he adds.

'I'm sorry, Dad. I'm really sorry about all this. I never intended for you to get involved.' My apology is a bit tardy, and totally insufficient.

'Yes, well, that's okay; it's done. What's done is done.' With a wave of his hand he dismisses the crime I've committed, even though I know him to be an extremely moral man. I'm wrenched by guilt and remorse. I want to apologise more, but the magnitude of what I'm apologising for makes it difficult to articulate what I'm feeling.

'What we have to do now is see if we can find a way to get you out of here.'

I feel a weight of a thousand tons being lifted off my shoulders. For the first time in over five months, genuine hope creeps into my heart. But I try to stem it. What can he do? How can he get me out of here? There's no possibility of evading prison for the crime I've committed, and I'm to be extradited to America anyway, to be charged with something even more serious. My emotions leapfrog each other, hope and despair, guilt and relief. What can my father do against the might of the FBI?

'I'm supposed to go back to America to stand trial,' I tell him, weary resignation creeping back into my voice. 'There's an extradition order for me to be taken back there, I think.'

'Yes, I know. I've already spoken to a lawyer – there's no actual extradition order. Well, not yet, anyway. I've brought a police report from South Africa that shows you've never been in trouble before.' He pulls his chair closer to mine. 'The only charge against you here is importing stolen property. Look, Rob, there's no getting away from it: this is a serious charge. But I'm hoping we can get some leniency because of your age and because it's your first offence.' I drop my chin and he puts a hand on my shoulder as he continues, 'The lawyer I've retained is supposed to be one of the best in Fiji.'

My heart lifts a little at this information, but then snags once more on the inevitable. 'But I'll still have to go to America to stand trial, even if my sentence here is reduced. How will you be able to stop the extradition process?' It seems hopeless. 'I mean, that isn't a matter for the courts; it's between the governments, isn't it?'

My words sound childish. I feel a sort of regression inside myself. I seem to have become a younger self again, but not in any good way, just more puerile.

'Well, there isn't a clear extradition agreement between Fiji and the United States, and I'm hoping to present an application to block this.' He gives me a faint smile. 'You're supposed to stand trial here within the next three months, and I'm trying to see if we can get the trial date brought forward.'

'Do you think it might be successful, blocking my extradition? That I might not have to go to America?'

'I don't know, Rob.' He says this slowly and looks at me with concern. 'We'll give it a try, but I can't promise anything. Don't get your hopes up too much, d'you understand?'

I nod, unable to answer. That treacherous lump has formed in my throat again. Even though there isn't really much hope that I won't spend time in prison, the knowledge that somebody has gone to this much effort for me is overwhelming. I change the subject.

'So, when did you arrive here?'

'Last night. I landed at Nadi airport, and I met with the lawyer this morning.'

My father's efficiency gives me heart. We chat about my case, about my mother and my siblings, about his flight. He doesn't ask me about my crime, doesn't remonstrate with me. I'm aware, though, that that might come later.

Eventually, Tu-lips sticks his head around the door and indicates that I must leave. I get up from my chair, and my father says, 'I'll see you again soon, Rob.'

Tu-lips leads me back to my cell.

* * *

The next day I have a second visit from my father, who tells me, 'The prosecutor has agreed to have the trial date brought forward. It'll be two weeks from now. But he's apparently going to be pressing for a minimum two-year sentence.'

'What about the time I've already been here?' I ask. 'Will they take that off?'

His shoulders slump as he shakes his head. 'No. That's in addition to the time you've already spent here.'

We're both silent for a while.

'And what about the extradition order?' I don't want any more bad news, but I feel compelled to ask. 'Have you heard anything?'

He shakes his head again, this time more vigorously. 'No. Nothing on that score. At least.'

We talk some more before he departs. This time we hug.

* * *

I experience time differently now. Before my father's arrival, I'd had a certain acceptance of the day's slow rhythm and routine. I guess I'd become sort of institutionalised. Living out my days without much thought of the future, concentrating only on matters within the prison walls: my exercise routine, my daily habit of sitting in my sling and tanning my arms, or lying against the door and watching the eyeballs of my fellow prisoners as they watch mine.

But I have been given notice of my future, and I have a sense of what my fate will be over the next few years. The faint hope brought by my father has eroded my ability to endure these dreary hours of waiting. I find it much more difficult to 'escape', to mentally transport myself out of my cell. My mind has become too active; the anticipation of serving a sentence here and then being put on trial in America mocks the 'realness' of my mental sojourns, reducing them to pallid insignificance.

Also, the realisation that my father will soon return to South Africa taunts me, making my life here nearly unbearable. His presence has become an enormous comfort to me, and I will miss his visits when he is gone.

I exercise more now; throwing myself into a routine of push-ups and sit-ups that tire me out, ensuring that I sleep at night. My cell walks are also more intense, as I try to escape the confines of my environment and to ignore thoughts of the impending trial.

* * *

My father arrives again. I am led past the now familiar vegetable garden and into the administration block, to the room that has begun to represent comfort and salvation. It is three weeks since I first saw my father here.

'Hello, Rob.' We shake hands. 'How're you doing?'

'Hi, Dad, I'm okay. Nervous, I guess. Kind of wound up, but ready.'

'You have to be strong. Whatever happens, whatever sentence you get, we can appeal. Remember that.'

An appeal will take months, I know, and I can't see how my father can stick around for much longer, or whether he'll manage to come back later. He has a life to go back to, a business to run, a family to see to. And all this takes money. I'm aware of how much this must be costing him, financially and emotionally. My father is a man of action, and this waiting has surely been torture for him. Everything works extremely slowly here, a hangover from colonial times that has been aggravated by the pace of island life.

But soon I'll know what my future holds. My trial is tomorrow.

23

The courtroom is sombre, with dark wooden panelling. It is an appropriate place for meting out punishment.

The judge is seated behind an enormous wooden desk with rolled edges, its ancient varnish scarred and the wood darkened with age. Middle-aged and bewigged, the judge is robed in black – a portentous figure who sits with sinister solemnity under a huge portrait of some eighteenth-century person, an earlier king of England possibly. Underneath it is a Latin inscription in faded gold on a varnished piece of wood, and I have no idea what the words mean.

My lawyer, Mr Supra, and the prosecutor are also wearing wigs and robes, although theirs are not quite as grand as those of the judge, who has his hands clasped as he listens to the prosecutor – staring at him all the while over the top of his reading glasses.

My father is seated in the public seating area directly behind Mr Supra, who is a large man, and rather rotund. Apart from my father, there are only three members of the public. And then there are three other people: a man who seems to be a clerk; near the door, a policeman wearing white puttees; and an elderly female court reporter – the first woman I've seen since going to prison.

Unsurprisingly, the trial has been quick. There were no witnesses to be called and I pleaded guilty, as instructed by my rather oily lawyer, whom I've met only once before, just two days before the trial. He has tried to persuade the court that there are mitigating circumstances that negate the seriousness of my crime: my blameless past record – he waved about the police report from South Africa – my youth, my remorse, and the fact that Jim Johnson has dropped all charges against me. Mr Supra almost made it sound like a eulogy, and as I listened to all this praise I could hardly believe he was actually referring to me. The prosecutor went on to point out the more obvious facts, the theft of the boat and my actual intention to steal it, and the fact that I deliberately falsified documents to sneak it into Fiji.

We're waiting for the judge. He's been writing the whole time, even when the prosecutor and lawyer were arguing, and he continues to do so now. Apart from a question or two, he's said nothing. The courtroom is deathly quiet, and I feel hollow.

Eventually, the judge lifts his head and stares directly at me. There's a look of cold disdain on his face, a look of harsh, judgmental authority. I fear this man as I have feared few people in my life.

'Robert Fridjhon. I hereby find you guilty of the crime of which you have been accused.' His eyes flick briefly down to his notes before engaging my own once more with malevolent intensity.

'This is a very serious crime, and you have shown total disregard for the moral integrity of our society.' The hostility in his tone is palpable.

'The prosecution has pushed for a lengthy and fitting sentence, and although Mr Supra has pleaded your youth and the fact that this is your first offence, I cannot and will not allow this crime to go unpunished.'

My heart dissolves into a puddle of despair around my feet.

'My judgment is to sentence you to two years' imprisonment,' he intones, 'to be served in the Suva prison until the time of your release.' He puts down his notes. I've expected this, of course, but still, the pronouncement shocks me.

'However.' He removes his glasses, polishing them on a corner of his robe. 'There has been an intervention in this case.'

Everything stops, like a freeze-frame picture in a film. And something seems to have softened in his face – which has less to do with the removal of his glasses and more to do with some sort of humanity asserting itself. I wait, unable to anticipate, too scared to hope.

'A very good friend of mine has spoken to me about this case, a man whose judgement I have the utmost respect for, and a man whose influence on these islands is unsurpassed.' The judge replaces his glasses and focuses intently on me once again. 'He has suggested leniency. He has put in some good words for you, and he is possibly the only man whose words I would heed in such a case. For that reason, and that reason alone, I am going to suspend this sentence for four years.'

I feel confused. And then it hits me: I'm free. I'm not going to a Fijian jail. I barely manage to suppress an involuntary whoop of joy. My heart is an expanding ball that threatens to explode from my chest. I struggle and struggle, but can't quite contain the grin that tries to wrap itself around my ears. Tears squeeze hotly, embarrassingly, from the corners of my eyes.

'Thank you, Your Worship,' I say to the judge. 'Thank you very, very much.' And silently I say, thank you Ratu George Cakobua – for it can only be the governor-general of Fiji of whom he is speaking.

I see my father behind the lawyer. He too has tears in his eyes, though he is smiling. Even smarmy Mr Supra is smiling and I think I love the man. I would rush out and shake his hand, hug the judge, kiss the prosecutor, if it weren't for the fact that I'm still enclosed in the accused box.

BUT I'M FREE!

This thought hits me with renewed astonishment. I can leave this box now. I can walk out of this building now, can't I? I'm not sure, so I carry on sitting.

As if reading my mind, Mr Supra motions me to come down. My father has walked over to him and is shaking his hand. Legs trembling, I join them.

'Thank you very much, sir,' I say to the lawyer, even though it wasn't he who secured my release. I turn to my father but find that I'm mute. He has done so much for me that I don't know how to put into words what I feel. He has shown me the truest love a father could have for his son. I don't know where to begin thanking him, so I just hug him instead.

'This is amazing,' he says. 'Totally unexpected. I can't believe it.'

I can't believe it either. I follow my father out of the courtroom, barely aware of where we are going. One emotion surfaces strongly, an emotion that is strangely inconsistent with my new freedom.

Remorse. People have been so kind to me, in spite of my actions. For the first time, maybe, I am truly cognisant of the consequences my actions have had on other people's lives. Those connected to me – my parents, Jim Johnson, and friends I've made along the way – and people I've never met, like the search teams that scoured the ocean for me when they thought *Recluse* had gone down in the storm.

I walk from the courtroom barely believing that I am no longer a prisoner. I have spent just six months in prison – which is almost nothing for such a serious crime.

* * *

Outside the courthouse, the sunlight seems exceptionally bright. We wait at the kerb for a taxi and I eagerly absorb the sights around me: a cyclist pedalling by with a cheery expression on his face, two women carrying baskets as they saunter along, a bus full of people – so much movement, everybody going about their daily lives with no restrictions. I am back in the world.

We get into a taxi and my father turns to me. 'Well, Rob. How do you feel?'

'Great! I still can't believe it, Dad. I can't believe this has happened.'

'Neither can I, and I don't understand.' He stares at me. 'Who was the judge referring to? Is it someone you met?' He shakes his head in puzzlement. 'I pretty much thought it was a forgone conclusion that you'd be given a prison sentence.'

I tell him about Ratu George Cakobua. How I met him and how he helped me free *Coracle*.

'He's the only person who could have done this,' I say. 'Unless the judge was talking about somebody from the States, or the Caribbean. And I don't see much chance of that having happened.'

'Well,' he says, still bemused. 'He must have taken quite a shine to you, the governor. What luck that he was at that island to help you, and now getting you free like this.'

'I know.' My answer sounds inadequate, but it's all I can say.

'But we're still not out of the woods yet,' my father cautions me. 'The FBI is still out there. We don't know how far along they are with the extradition order or if they'll try to stop us. We have to get out of here. We won't be safe until we're back in South Africa.'

Though his words introduce a small note of sobriety into the crazy drunk ecstasy I am experiencing, I can't stem my relief. 'I know. But I feel so great to be out here.' I fill my lungs with air, as though that too was restricted in prison. 'I just can't believe it's really happened. That I'm actually free.'

'Well, okay,' he says as we stop outside a hotel. 'Here's the plan now. We're stopping here to get my things and to book tickets, and then we have one more stop before we go to the airport. I promised your mom last night on the phone that I would bring her back some tropical fish.'

I can just hear her voice on the phone, giving my father a practical instruction, carefully keeping it free of emotional clutter, and not expressing what is uppermost in her mind: that he must do every-thing in his power to bring me back.

I yearn to see her again. If we are not stopped I will soon be back in South Africa with my family. I absolutely cannot believe that I'm going home, to a place where I can actually surf and dive and walk on a real mountain, rather than a tenuously conjured figment of my imagination. I'll be able to walk in the city, walk on the beaches, walk anywhere I choose to.

My father instructs the cabbie to wait while we go up to his room. He phones a travel agent and books tickets on a Qantas flight to Sydney, leaving that afternoon, with a connecting flight to South Africa. That done, we take his luggage to the taxi and drive to the travel agency.

I feel exhilarated as we emerge minutes later with the tickets.

'Last stop, please, driver – a tropical fish shop,' says my father.

* * *

I sit with a cardboard box next to me, glancing every now and then at its contents: six brightly coloured fish, each in a sealed plastic bag. At the small airport of Suva we have half an hour to wait before boarding a twin-engined aircraft that will take us to Nadi international airport on the other side of the island. My father frets and fidgets, but I've learnt to wait.

We land at Nadi airport and check in the bags and the fish. My father explains to the desk attendant that the fish need to be kept in a pressurised hold. She assures him that they will be okay.

It's two hours before the flight leaves. Our departure from Fiji is now imminent, but we both seem to have become anxious that we could still be stopped. We have no idea whether the FBI have been informed of my release, or whether there are moves afoot to stop us from leaving. Sitting in this small airport lounge with nothing to do but wait aggravates the tension we both feel. Small talk is an effort, and my father keeps checking his watch.

'WILL PASSENGER LIONEL FRIDJHON PLEASE REPORT TO THE QANTAS FLIGHT 276 CHECK-IN DESK? PASSENGER LIONEL FRIDJHON.'

The announcement freezes my blood. Aghast, I stare at my father. The FBI *have* caught up with us. I want to throw up.

His expression mirrors my feelings, and we both get up slowly. We are so close – another half an hour and we'd be boarding.

'Let's go see what they want.' My father tries to act unconcerned, but I see him swallowing nervously. I follow him to the Qantas counter.

'I'm Lionel Fridjhon,' my father announces to the attendant who just checked us in. 'You wanted to speak to me.' His voice is firm but I can detect the anxiety in it.

I look around and see no one apart from a scattering of waiting passengers. But maybe she's been told to detain us until somebody from the police force gets here.

'Oh yes, Mr Fridjhon.' Her Australian accent would be pleasing at any other time. 'We have a problem, I'm afraid.' She bends down behind the counter. My father and I exchange sickened glances. We watch as her head reappears. She is holding a box. It is the one containing the tropical fish.

'I'm sorry, but the pressure in the hold won't keep these fish alive, sir,' she says. 'You'll have to take them into the cabin with you, I'm afraid.'

My father takes the box and thanks her. We walk back to our seats, and on our faces there is just the hint of a grin – conveying more than a thousand words.

Epilogue

I'd been back in South Africa for a year when a man approached me while I was working on a yacht tied to a dock in Durban. He waved me over and I put down the screwdriver.

'Are you Rob Fridjhon? From the Mainstay Sailing Academy?'

'Yes, that's right.' I smiled at him as we shook hands.

'Can I ask you a few questions, about the school?'

'Yes, sure,' I replied. It was my job, after all.

The man questioned me about the boat, the horsepower of the engine and the range. He asked me a few other things as well, but not too many questions about the actual courses we taught at the academy. It seemed a little strange, but I didn't think too much of it.

The next day he appeared again, just as I was about to take off for lunch.

'Hi,' I returned his greeting, wiping my hands on a rag.

'Rob, could we go for coffee somewhere?' he asked. 'I'd like to talk to you some more.'

'Uh, yeah sure.' I figured he was going to ask me to instruct him on his own yacht – as I occasionally did with clients. We sauntered over the road to a café, where the man whose name I still did not know selected a corner table.

'Rob, I'm going to come straight to the point,' he said after we'd ordered our coffee. 'This isn't really about the sailing school. There's something else I want to talk to you about.'

This piqued my curiosity, and I waited with interest. The man hesitated, staring out at some distant object. Then his eyes swivelled back and he hitched his chair closer, leaning towards me.

'My partner and I have a … an operation.' He cleared his throat. 'We are involved in something that makes a lot of money. But it requires us to move about, changing the base of our activities period-ically.' He stopped, and I waited in silence, nodding once for him to continue. Encouraged, he leant even closer and spread his hands out on the table.

'We are involved in a gold-smuggling operation.' He'd lowered his voice, and flicked his eyes to the left and right. 'We smuggle gold out of South Africa onto ships that pass along the coast. The gold goes to America, where we sell it.'

Why was he telling me, I wondered. Why was he entrusting me, a stranger, with such incriminating information? I thought it better not to reply, and waited for more.

'The way we get the gold out to the ships is on small boats,' he continued. 'We've been operating off South West Africa, near Lüderitz, but things are getting a bit too hot there and we've decided to stop. We want to work from here now. From Durban.' He looked at me expectantly.

'So, what do you want from me?' I knew what the answer was.

'We need a new operative,' he said. 'We need someone to take the gold out on a small boat to meet the ship. We were wondering if you'd join us, and use your boat to take the gold out.'

I stared at him. He hardly knew me, and though he hadn't divulged his name, I already knew enough to make trouble for him.

'It's not my boat,' I told him. 'It belongs to somebody else who charters it to the sailing school. There is no way I'd use his boat like that.'

A thought occurred to me. 'Are you here because of the Fiji thing?' It was obvious. I'd be a ready accomplice. 'Because of what happened in the Pacific?'

'What? No. Not at all. What Fiji thing? I don't know what you're talking about.'

For a moment I was confused. Then everything became clear.

'Actually, I'm not really interested,' I said. 'I have a job, and I'm pretty happy with it. But thank you very much for asking. I don't know anything about smuggling gold and wouldn't be much good to you anyway.'

He was a police plant. A stool. I wasn't totally sure, but I figured that the FBI had probably asked the South African police to check up on me. I clearly remembered the document I'd read from the FBI to that CID guy in Fiji.

The man took my refusal with equanimity. He smiled and shook my hand, and I never saw him again.

His visit re-awoke memories and emotions I hadn't felt for a while. I took my lunch down to the beach and sat on the sea wall to eat and think. The curving span of ocean helped connect my thoughts across the world, to the Pacific and to the people I'd been involved with there: the islanders – Laisa and Penaia – and also the governor. And Mihai, who'd written just once in reply to a letter I'd sent him. He'd told me that Vlazo had been found not guilty on an unrelated charge of extortion – and he'd never been questioned about either Bainesfield or Alex. I felt bad about that. I wished he'd been caught and put away. Mihai himself had never had any problems with the law, and I was relieved to hear this.

I thought about Jim Johnson too. The insurance company had covered most of the costs I'd caused – the shipping and handling and repair of *Recluse* – but in the end Jim had to pay in $2 500. I was still paying that back to him, plus $3 000 to my father for his expenses. Neither Jim Johnson nor my father had ever hinted at any censure, and their forgiveness had a big impact on me.

Like the waves at my feet, the effects of my crime kept coming back to me, and to the others affected by it; it's not enough to think I can just go ahead and do what I like as long I don't hurt anybody. Life's a lot more complicated than that.

Do you have any comments, suggestions or
feedback about this book or any other Zebra Press titles?
Contact us at **talkback@zebrapress.co.za**